Liberation through Reconciliation

Liberation through Reconciliation

JON SOBRINO'S CHRISTOLOGICAL
SPIRITUALITY

O. Ernesto Valiente

FORDHAM UNIVERSITY PRESS
New York 2016

Visit us online at www.fordhampress.com.

Library of Congress Cataloging-in-Publication Data

Valiente, O. Ernesto (Orfilio Ernesto)
    Liberation through reconciliation : Jon Sobrino's Christological
spirituality / O. Ernesto Valiente. — First edition.
        pages cm
    Includes bibliographical references and index.
    ISBN 978-0-8232-6852-8 (cloth : alk. paper) —
    ISBN 978-0-8232-6887-0 (pbk. : alk. paper)
    1. Liberation theology.   2. Reconciliation—Religious aspects—
Catholic Church.   3. Sobrino, Jon.   4. Jesus Christ—Person and
offices.   I. Title.
    BT83.57.V36 2015
    230'.2092—dc23
                                                        2015019318

Printed and bound in Great Britain by
Marston Book Services Ltd, Oxfordshire

18 17 16   5 4 3 2 1

First edition

For Kari, Hannah, and Thaís,
and in loving memory of Orfilio, my father

Contents

Liberation through Reconciliation

Introduction

The origins of this book trace back to a pastoral experience some twenty years ago. In the winter of 1993, just shy of two months after the peace accords were signed between the Salvadoran popular insurrectional forces of the Farabundo Martí National Liberation Front (FMLN) and the government, I had the opportunity to work in the province of Chalatenango, in northern El Salvador. This was my first visit to the land of my childhood after the end of its twelve-year-long civil war; it was also my longest visit since leaving El Salvador as a teenager, when the war began. For four months, I engaged in pastoral work in the small town of Arcatao and its neighboring villages. This was a privileged time that allowed me to re-encounter the people whose cause I had briefly joined in my youth, and to begin to make some peace with my decision to leave this battered nation over a decade earlier.

The effects of the war were still acutely evident in the area. Throughout the war, the national military forces had repeatedly assaulted and bombed these villages because of their strategic location on the Honduran border and because of the high level of militancy among the well-organized civilian population. Many of the locals had only recently returned from faraway refugee camps and were now trying to resettle and restore some kind of normalcy to their lives. During these months of enjoying my compatriots' generous hospitality, I immersed myself in the numerous projects they undertook to ensure basic necessities and improve their communal life. While these tasks and the fraternal spirit that animated our shared efforts fueled my hope for the nation's future, the material and psychological scars of the war were impossible to ignore.

Some Salvadorans maintain that by the time the war began in the late 1970s, it had become the only unavoidable means for social and political transformation because all non-violent alternatives had been exhausted. Such voices remain convinced that armed struggle was the only way to stop the slow, but no less real, death that was being generated by decades of political tyranny, repression, and socioeconomic injustice. I cannot deny or minimize the extent of the crisis that preceded the war, and the historical judgment that violence was truly the only answer is difficult to counter. Yet the cost of that solution was horrific. The war-ravaged nation to which I returned was one that had witnessed the annihilation of more than 75,000 people and the creation of countless orphans, disabled veterans, displaced families, and other inconceivable measures of suffering: persistent poverty, chronic grief over dead loved ones, destroyed fields and houses, and the psychological and hidden scars of war.

This short season in post-war El Salvador confronted me again with the reality of poverty and injustice that had interrupted my late teenage years and exposed the privilege of my socioeconomic background. As a teenager, I had briefly joined my compatriots' movement for liberation, but I had also taken advantage of my middle-class resources to study overseas and become a distant observer of the gruesome conflict. My return to El Salvador was a way to begin a process of coming to terms with the past and more fully take up some of the issues that, in one way or other, have accompanied me from my youth.

Since that summer, I have closely followed the frustrated attempts toward reconciliation within the country. The failure of the post-war years to bring about a transformed society underscores how deeply entrenched the roots of the initial conflict remain. The persistence of injustice and social enmity has given rise to the questions that animate much of my academic work: What power allows a society comprised of victims, perpetrators, and observers to move forward together in some way? What difference can Christian life make in this process? What might allow the "victims" to heal and ultimately forgive? What will empower the "guilty" to repent and seek new ways of being? How can former enemies be reconciled in such a way that the causes of injustice and inhumanity that sparked the war might diminish and be replaced by increasingly just ways of being? In short, what resources does a society have to begin the process of reconciliation, and how are we to envision and participate in this project?

These questions are not unique to El Salvador, but are asked by people who live in similar circumstances across the globe. Indeed, such interrogators number in the millions. In the last one hundred years alone, more that 200 million people have been killed as a consequence of systematic repression, political revolutions, and ethnic or religious war.[1] As the Spanish-Salvadoran theologian Jon Sobrino, whose work provides the foundations for this book, wrote in 2001, while Auschwitz was humanity's shame half a century ago, Central America, Bosnia, Kosovo, East Timor, and Rwanda bear the shame of the human race today.[2] More than a decade later, we can sadly add the Sudan, Iraq, Afghanistan, Libya, and Syria to his list.

In some countries in which the immediate crisis or war has formally ended, including El Salvador, national processes have tried to uncover the truth of what took place in the hope that this will give way to lasting reconciliation. Indeed, in the last thirty years no less than forty national reconciliation commissions have been instituted in countries around the world to deal with past crimes and attempt to overcome the enmity that afflicts their divided societies.[3] But in all of these places, achieving a lasting and just reconciliation has proven to be a difficult and elusive task. Such commissions have been unable to fully address the roots of conflict, heal the wounds of the victims, or produce sociopolitical arrangements that foster peace and reconciliation in the midst of broken communities.

Any reconciliation process encounters myriad exigencies and difficulties. They include the inability to address all the individual cases of injustice, the different parties' conflicting interpretations of what constitutes justice, the absence of repentance among offenders and the desire for vengeance from victims, the perception that violence is the only instrument for seizing and wielding power, and the question of what constitutes proper reparation, particularly in light of the impossibility of restoring the life of the deceased. These tensions all point to the relationship between processes of reconciliation and the ultimate questions of human existence, including the finitude of the human person, the scandal of innocent suffering, and the desire for ultimate justice even though it means a renewed awareness of massive social evil. Consequently, every struggle to achieve reconciliation within a particular historical context has theological implications. This is so because it questions the intelligibility of our world and the promises of God's plan for humanity. Indeed, every reconciling struggle is, at its heart, a theological struggle that demands of any theology a clear articulation of how its claims about God and humanity impinge upon the lived reality of a given history.

While Christian communities have often failed to be reconciling forces in the world (and, in some cases, have been active participants in perpetuating situations of social enmity), their tradition and the lives of many followers of Christ continue to offer critical resources for the healing of conflict between peoples and the creation of just social environments and lasting cultures of peace. In fact, different processes of reconciliation have begun to stress the importance of identifying transcendent overarching values that can provide the common ground for dialogue and forgiveness.[4]

To be sure, the possibility for a just and enduring social reconciliation during and in the aftermath of conflicts such as the one in El Salvador does not lie squarely within the province of theology. It requires the contributions of all sectors of society and multiple disciplines, including the political, economic, and social sciences. But any Christian theology that maintains that the revelation of God in Jesus Christ matters for the world needs to take seriously the challenges that such entrenched injustice lays before it. Indeed, many Christian ministries and communities have made positive contributions toward reconciliation efforts in diverse places such as South Africa, Northern Ireland, and Latin America. These efforts have shown how the Christian understanding and praxis of reconciliation can positively influence public life and thus effectively contribute to processes that seek to overcome long-standing hostilities in order to create more just and peaceful social arrangements.

In keeping with this trajectory, this project finds its place among those that argue that Christian revelation offers an invaluable contribution to the mending of the nations and their processes of reconciliation. It maintains that hope for a reconciled world is at the center of Christian faith and insists that there is an inherent correspondence between God's gift of reconciliation through Christ and the pursuit of social and political reconciliation among human beings. In other words, though Christianity maintains that a full, harmonious, and just restoration of relationships among human beings and with God is an eschatological reality, one that will only be completed at the end of history, it also insists that human efforts that seek even partial and limited reconciliations are signs that anticipate this full restoration, ground the hope for the future, and are absolutely necessary to halt conflicts that generate widespread suffering and death.

This book examines the possibility and dynamics of social reconciliation from the perspective of Latin American liberation theology and in conversation with the work of Jon Sobrino. Its approach distinguishes it from previous book-length examinations on this topic. Although social reconciliation has recently gained much attention within the field of theology, the insights of Latin American liberation theology have yet to be fully utilized in a systematic study of reconciliation. This project benefits from a theological approach that prioritizes the viewpoint and contribution of the victims—the only ones who can offer forgiveness—in the process of overcoming enmity, while at the same time maintaining the significance of a transformative Christian praxis informed by eschatological values. The latter point is of particular importance because the manner in which Christians live in the here and now and confront the challenges that emerge from a conflicted world is critical for a theology that conceives as its ultimate purpose the transformation of reality according to the values that ensue from Jesus's proclamation of God's reconciling reign.

The project contends that liberation theology in general and Sobrino's work in particular offer the basis for a Christian spirituality and theology of reconciliation that effectively overcomes conflict by attending to the demands of truth, justice, and forgiveness. Building on Sobrino's Christology, it envisions a Christian discipleship inspired by Jesus's praxis and the eschatological values of God's Kingdom. This discipleship upholds both the need for personal forgiveness and the social restoration of justice without favoring one value at the expense of the other. The book argues that such discipleship must foster a ministry of reconciliation aimed at the eradication of structural sin, the corresponding humanization of its victims, and the rehabilitation of the oppressor.

Sobrino's theological reflection, which emerges from El Salvador, is particularly well suited to ground this project on reconciliation because it is shaped by and responds to an immediate reality of oppression, conflict, and widespread suffering. The deeply Salvadoran roots of Sobrino's contribution, however, do not preclude it from having wider application to places outside of this Latin American nation. It is the particularity of the Salvadoran experience, rather, that mediates and makes possible his universally valid insights.

Sobrino is one of the leading liberation theologians writing today and his essays and books are widely read in universities and seminaries around the world. Yet research on his theology is still rather limited and his work offers resources that have not been sufficiently plumbed. Few studies have systematically analyzed Sobrino's theological corpus and none have attempted to assess his contribution to the problem of reconciliation. By investigating his thoughts on this problem in light of his broader theological vision, this book contributes to the further understanding of Sobrino's work as it applies the insights of his theology to the area of social reconciliation.

Over the course of five chapters, this book argues that, while Sobrino has never explicitly developed a theology of reconciliation, the structure of his spirituality allows us to draw and configure from his Christology a Christian reconciling spirituality that, in turn, establishes the foundations for a theology of reconciliation.

The first chapter examines reconciliation from a Christian perspective in order to establish the necessary theoretical framework for a topic that is studied from the intersection of various academic disciplines. This analysis also enables us to identify the central theological questions and arguments in the field of reconciliation, as well as the main assumptions that ground them. The chapter goes on to offer an initial approach to reconciliation from a distinct liberationist perspective. It examines the relationship between reconciliation and liberation, addresses the main criticisms leveled against liberation theology, and describes how this theological perspective can be used to structure a reconciling Christian praxis that meets the demands of truth, justice, and forgiveness.

Because every theology emerges from a particular context, the second chapter explores the distinguishing features of Sobrino's life—his surrounding sociohistorical conditions, academic formation, personal experiences, and intellectual influences—in order to identify and examine the sources that have stimulated and shaped his theological thought. The chapter approaches Sobrino via the social reality that has dominated his life and the lives of most Salvadorans for the last thirty years: the entrenched oppression that led to the Salvadoran civil war and the ambiguous accomplishments of its recent peace process. The chapter then examines the intellectual influences that have shaped Sobrino's work, particularly the pastoral ministry of Archbishop Oscar Romero and the philosophical and methodological foundations laid by Ignacio Ellacuría. Special attention is given to Ellacuría's work because it provides the basic philosophical framework that undergirds Sobrino's spirituality.

The third chapter argues that Sobrino's life experiences, formation, and intellectual influences have converged to foster a particular spirituality that nurtures his imagination and integrates his theological work. This spirituality has both a general structure relevant to all human beings and a more specific Christian structure, namely the following of Jesus. Focusing on the general structure, this chapter examines the foundational anthropological elements that undergird Sobrino's spirituality—that is, the human dispositions that enable the proper relationship between any human person and reality. This examination is complemented with an analysis of the presuppositions that ground Sobrino's approach to the theological task. The analysis sheds light on how his spirituality enriches and organizes all of his theology and demonstrates how these same elements structure his understanding of the demands, concerns, and purpose of the theological enterprise. Such spirituality thus not only prescribes, for Sobrino, how the human person should relate to reality. It also exercises an integrative function in his theology that enables us to construct a discipleship and a theology of reconciliation that is coherent with the rest of his work.

The fourth chapter moves from Sobrino's fundamental spirituality to a spirituality explicitly rooted in Jesus Christ. Its purpose is to identify this Jesus whom we are to follow and what it means to follow him. To this end, the chapter shows how Sobrino's Christology can be understood most fruitfully in terms of its roots in spirituality. Hence, the general structure of Sobrino's spirituality is fleshed out with those elements of his Christology that are important for developing a Christian spirituality that is capable of fostering a renewed communal identity, a liberating praxis, and a theology of reconciliation. These elements are: Jesus's praxis and the spirit of his praxis as these unfold in his incarnation, mission, cross, and resurrection. In this task, preference is given to Sobrino's more mature work and thus to a close reading of his most recent Christological writings.

The fifth and final chapter offers a twofold constructive proposal. It first presents a Christian spirituality of reconciliation that responds to the Latin American situation. Such spirituality urges Christians to follow the structure of Jesus's life and engage reality with the same spirit of honesty, fidelity, and trust that empowered his life. In turn, this reconciling spirituality lays the foundations for a theology of reconciliation. Gathering the fruits of the Christian spirituality developed in the first part of the chapter, this theology engages the key themes relevant to reconciliation from a liberationist perspective: sin as the root cause of a conflicted reality; God as the transcendent principle of reconciliation and Christ through the Spirit as the mediator of this reconciliation; and the central role of truth, justice, and forgiveness in the historical appropriation of God's reconciling reign.

1   Liberation and Reconciliation

The good news that the gospel proclaims and that Christians are called to embody rests in the promise that in Christ God has reconciled the world. Yet an honest look at our personal lives and relationships, and at the world around us, will readily confront us with realities that contradict this vision of a reconciled world. The millions of victims of war, discrimination, and economic oppression attest to an empirical reality that is at excruciating odds with the good news of the gospel. This apprehension of negativity reveals that all is not well—that something is seriously wrong with the world in spite of God's promised commitment to it.

The gap between the world as promised and the world as it appears to us is even starker when one considers the ambiguous role played by Christians in events such as the Holocaust and the recent massacres in Rwanda. Some have acted with self-sacrificial love and courage, making efforts to address the consequences and roots of such conflicts. But many others have been passively or actively implicated in the violence. As the Croatian theologian Miroslav Volf notes, in some of these conflicts genuinely committed Christians not only failed to protect innocent victims but were willing participants in unspeakable genocides.[1]

The authority of such a history subverts any uncritical insistence upon God's or our own goodness. Rather, it calls for an articulation of the Christian message that is faithful to its sources and capable of empowering a Christian praxis that provides a hopeful and credible response to our social brokenness. Christianity thus must inform a new way of being and relating that has a transforming, reconciling effect on the world. This book contends that Latin America liberation theology's articulation of the Christian message offers indispensable resources to help mend our conflicted world. It approaches the pursuit of social reconciliation from this perspective and in dialogue with the theological work of Jon Sobrino.

Because "reconciliation" is a polyvalent term that is used in innumerable ways, I begin by outlining how this book understands reconciliation in three steps: by drawing the roots of its scriptural meaning; by determining the scope, agents, and context that it envisions for such reconciliation; and by identifying, at least at the theoretical level, the necessary conditions for its realization. In the second part of the chapter, I begin to examine reconciliation from a liberationist perspective in order to outline the distinctiveness of this approach and address some of the main criticisms leveled against it. This chapter establishes a theoretical framework for engaging reconciliation and helps us identify the most provocative arguments and questions of a complex subject that is studied from the intersection of different academic fields.

Sketching the Contours of Reconciliation

At its core, reconciliation involves the attempt to mend and renew broken or fragmented relationships, and to overcome enmity by transforming the parties involved. In the last thirty years, this basic concept has been studied from different fields, including psychology, the social sciences, law, politics, and theology. On the practical side, numerous international tribunals, truth and reconciliation commissions, and local civic and religious organizations have worked to achieve social and political reconciliation.[2]

The multiple efforts to confront the challenges posed by the pursuit of reconciliation have led to rapid growth and evolution in this area of study and have yielded many, often contradictory, approaches to reconciliation.[3] In turn, the rich output generated by this fecund subject has led to some imprecision surrounding its definition.[4] Authors enlist terms such as "peacebuilding," "restorative justice," "conflict transformation," and "transitional justice" to stress different aspects in the practice of reconciliation. While it is encouraging and fitting that reconciliation is an area of study that continues to attract a diversity of scholars, the unintended consequence is that "*reconciliation*—enjoys no tight consensual usage."[5] Indeed, the meaning of reconciliation continues to be somewhat elusive and remains to some extent an area of contention in current scholarship today.[6]

More serious than this lack of consensus, however, is how the meaning of reconciliation can be manipulated and distorted by social and political processes. Theologian Robert Schreiter, for instance, has detected three understandings of reconciliation that falsify its true sense: reconciliation as a shortcut to peace, as in the case of political amnesties that trivialize the demands of victims; reconciliation as an alternative to liberation that preserves the status quo; and reconciliation as a managerial and bargaining process of conflict mediation that demands no change in the perpetrator's practices.[7] Although it might not be possible to dispel all of the ambiguity in the use of the term, identifying such false understandings of reconciliation is crucial because, as Schreiter notes, violence and oppression seek to impose "the narrative of the lie" that threatens to destroy the narratives that sustain people's true purpose and identity.[8]

Thus, before interrogating Sobrino's work in search of a viable and credible account of how the Christian faith can be articulated and lived as a force for reconciliation, this study examines reconciliation's meaning within the development of the Christian tradition. Mindful of the inherent difficulties that ensue from the historical nature of the Hebrew and Christian scriptures and from the fact that they are written from a perspective that privileges a chosen people over "unchosen" ones, this project relies on contemporary biblical scholarship to address these limitations. By taking an examination of the scriptures as its point of departure, it recognizes the normative role of these writings in expressing the faith experience of the Christian community and its understanding of reconciliation.

The Scriptural Roots of Reconciliation

Central to the biblical narrative of redemption and reconciliation is the realization that something is profoundly wrong with human existence—that human beings live in a state of alienation from God, in enmity with one another, and in disharmony with their natural world. In the face of this reality, the Bible maintains that God is committed to healing humanity, mending our relationships, and living in communion with us. The book of Genesis traces this state of alienation back to the entrance of human beings into sin (Gen 3:1–21), which results in the rupture of the relationships between the first humans (Adam and Eve) and their immediate descendants (Cain and Abel), and a rupture in humans' relationship to the natural world.[9] Right after their act of disobedience, God confronts Adam and Eve and reveals the divine punishment for their actions, but not without simultaneously extending an offer of reconciliation, promising that the offspring of the woman will crush the head of the tempter (Gen 3:15) and thus eliminate the enmity it introduced. Although the Bible makes it clear that human beings are singularly responsible for their state of estrangement from God, it presents God as the one who takes the initiative to restore the relationship. The scriptures thus attest that God's grace and persistent desire to reconcile sinful humanity set the context for interpreting human history and the possibility of salvation offered therein.

The scriptures consistently convey that despite God's reconciling will, all relationships—God-to-human, human-to-human, and human-to-the-rest-of-creation—remain threatened and affected by the legacy of sin and humans' repeated rejection of God's way. God's desire to reconcile all aspects of human life is expressed biblically in terms of a covenant that provides a means for re-establishing and sustaining the relationship among human beings and between God and God's people.[10]

The compilers of the Pentateuch saw the foundation for the covenant emerge from both the promises God made to the patriarchs (Gen 12; 15; 17; 22; and so on), and the events of the Exodus.[11] In the Exodus account, God responds to Israel's sufferings and oppressive enslavement under the Egyptian pharaoh by leading the Israelites out of Egypt and subsequently entering into a covenant with them. Implicit in the description of the event is the insight that reconciliation demands the people's just liberation from oppression. As Gustavo Gutiérrez notes, "The covenant and the liberation from Egypt were different aspects of the same movement, a movement which led to encounter with God."[12] The covenant completes the liberation of the Exodus event by placing a seal on the reconciliation of the people with God: They are now constituted as the people of God.

From the earliest times, Israel's religion included the conviction not only that the people of Israel were a chosen people, but also that "as the covenant people of Yahweh, Israel was subject to [God's] comprehensive demands. They would encounter Yahweh's blessings or curse as they obeyed or disobeyed the law."[13] Indeed, the Torah dictates the prescribed way of life through which the Israelites expressed their fidelity to God and makes it clear that God perceives the people's manner of relating to each other and to outsiders as a direct reflection of their reverence (or irreverence) toward God.[14] This again reflects the biblical perception that reconciliation cannot be achieved without justice, and that the restoration of the relationship between God and humanity is always accompanied by the restoration of relationships among human beings. As Jason Ripley observes, "At the core, righteousness in the Hebrew Bible is inherently relational, involving the fulfillment of the demands of a relationship, both those among humans and those between humans and God."[15]

Even as it establishes the terms for living as God's people, the law anticipates the reality that the people will fail and thus includes provisions for reestablishing relationship when it is ruptured. Through ritual sacrifices performed by priests, the Israelites could seek to overcome their acts of infidelity and disobedience to God.[16] The purpose of these atoning rituals was to heal the breach in the covenant relationship with God that resulted from their sins.[17]

While the sacrificial system provided the Israelites with a means of reconciling themselves to God, this same system was opposed by the prophets when its rituals amounted to no more than empty signs that were not accompanied by sincere repentance and conversion. The biblical prophets decry the people's unfaithfulness toward God that is evident in their mistreatment of each other, especially the most vulnerable. As Hans Walter Wolff summarizes, such indictments are rooted ultimately in the fact that "the God of the history of salvation [has been] forgotten and rejected."[18]

Even as the prophets perceived God's punishing judgment in the destruction of Jerusalem (587 BCE) and the exile of the Israelites, they also saw God's purifying hand at play (Isa 1:21–26; Jer 27:6).[19] For them, these events were necessary to catalyze a turning point that would ultimately lead the Israelites to repentance.[20] As in the Genesis account of the expulsion from the garden, God's judgment is not the last word, but rather is administered with the goal of precipitating repentance and return, and the formation of a newly forgiven and reconciled community. This promise of a restored Israel is succinctly expressed in Jeremiah's prophecy of a renewed covenant:

> The days are surely coming, says the Lord, when I will make a new covenant with the house of Israel and the house of Judah. It will not be like the covenant that I made with their ancestors when I took them by the hand to bring them out of the land of Egypt—a covenant that they broke, though I was their husband, says the Lord. But this is the

covenant that I will make with the house of Israel after those days, says the Lord: I will put my law within them, and I will write it on their hearts; and I will be their God, and they shall be my people. No longer shall they teach one another, or say to each other, "Know the Lord," for they shall all know me, from the least of them to the greatest, says the Lord; for I will forgive their inequity, and remember their sin no more. (Jer 31:31–34)

Three elements in the renewal of Jeremiah's covenant are particularly important for our purpose. First is the centrality of divine forgiveness: While this forgiveness is preceded by God's judgment, it nevertheless anticipates the repentance of the people. Second, this covenant's novelty resides not in the promulgation of a new law, but in God's gratuitous transformation of human nature and the creation of a sinless and just community that will be eternally faithful to the covenant: God's will shall be written in the hearts of God's people, and all its members—from the least to the greatest—will live in covenant relationship.[21] Third, while the promise proclaimed through the renewed covenant points to an eschatological future, its hope and content directly impinge upon the concrete historical reality of the present.[22] The prophets were rarely concerned with God's abstract and otherworldly future, but rather with the tangible realities that confronted God's people. Indeed, the just and peaceful world that they announce as an eschatological promise also anticipates a new action of God in history that continues to be a source of inspiration and transformation for the people of God.

THE NEW TESTAMENT

New Testament commentators often use terms such as "reconciliation," "redemption," and "liberation" interchangeably. The problem associated with this practice is that the rich meaning that each one of these images conveys tends to be lost when we collapse them into concepts with analogous meanings. In fact, each term draws from different biblical traditions and metaphors and each stresses different aspects of the salvific work effected by God through Jesus Christ.[23] The words "reconcile" and "reconciliation," the English equivalents of the Greek *katallasso/katallage* and *diallasso*, appear only sparingly in the New Testament. With the exception of Matthew 5:24—a passage underscoring that reconciliation with

God first requires reconciliation with our brothers and sisters—the term only occurs in the Pauline and deutero-Pauline writings.[24] Although Paul uses "reconciliation" in different ways and contexts, our focus here is on his theological understanding of reconciliation and its implications for Christian discipleship.[25]

Paul's theological understanding of reconciliation is best captured in two of his letters: 2 Corinthians 5:18–21 and Romans 5:8–11. In the Epistle to the Romans, Paul reflects upon the reconciliation that emerges as a consequence of God's gratuitous justification.[26] He readily highlights God's merciful initiative, attesting that "God proves his love for us in that while we were still sinners Christ died for us" (5:8). The extravagant generosity of Christ, who does not wait for our contrition to offer us the prospect of a reconciled relationship, becomes especially clear when contrasted with the brokenness of the human condition. As sinners, human beings are not only "weak" (5:6), they are also "enemies" of God (5:10). Nevertheless, Christians have been reconciled because Christ, in his life and death, has borne the consequences of their sins (5:10),[27] and thus through his loving self-offering they have been granted a new "access" (5:2) to God's grace. For Paul then, reconciliation refers to "the restoration of the estranged and alienated sinner to friendship and intimacy with God."[28] As a result of this new relationship—this newfound peace with God—Christians may hope in their salvation (5:10) and boast in the merciful God they have experienced through Christ's actions (5:11).[29]

Though the initiative is always God's, the human person is not a thoroughly passive recipient of God's reconciliation. Christians now have access to a new relationship with God because they have been introduced into God's sphere of grace, but they can, and often do, reject God's mercy. Consequently the hope of our salvation also depends on our acceptance of God's reconciling act that is both "accomplished" and offered to us time and again. In this sense, reconciliation is best understood as a continuous process that must be appropriated and realized daily in the individual and social lives of men and women.

The need for our involvement in the process of reconciliation comes to the fore particularly in the Second Epistle to the Corinthians. This epistle addresses a short number of diverse themes each treated in relationship to the single purpose that governs the letter: "to orient the Corinthian Christians to the true nature of apostleship, and thus to establish them more firmly in the one true gospel."[30] It is within this larger discussion of the meaning of true discipleship that Paul addresses the subject of reconciliation and the Christian ministry of reconciliation:

> All this is from God, who reconciled us to himself through Christ, and has given us the ministry of reconciliation; that is, in Christ God was reconciling the world to himself, not counting their trespasses against them, and entrusting the message of reconciliation to us. So we are ambassadors for Christ, since God is making his appeal through us; we entreat you on behalf of Christ, be reconciled to God. (2 Cor 5:18–20)

In this passage, as in Romans, Paul categorically attests to the unique role of God as the initiator of reconciliation, and to Christ as God's sole agent, who exchanges the enmity between humanity and Godself for peace.[31] For Paul, Christ's whole life is geared toward the mediation of this reconciliation. This reconciling act points to both an objective change in the relationship of God vis-à-vis humanity and in particular to a change in humanity itself. For, once reconciled "in Christ," human beings die to their egotistical, death-dealing selves (2 Cor 5:14–15) and undergo a profound renewal to become a new creation: "everything old has passed away, everything is new" (2 Cor 5:17). As J. Christian Beker notes, this new creation—which no longer lives just for itself, but now for Christ and others—"must still wait for its future completion in the liberation of the whole creation (Rom 8:21), when 'we shall always be with the Lord.'"[32] Hence, in the temporal sense, reconciliation for Paul "refers to an event in the past and to an enduring relationship in the present, which is claimed to be eschatologically ultimate."[33]

In the meantime, Paul tells us, God has entrusted "the message of reconciliation to us" (2 Cor 5:19). Victor Furnish explains that in this passage reconciliation does not refer just to a message *about* reconciliation; it is a synonym for the gospel (*euangelion*), "which establishes itself with God's own power (Rom 1:16; 1 Thess 1:15)," and thus, in the way Paul uses it, "embraces the whole of God's coming and acting for his people, the whole of the salvation event."[34] In this sense, to bear the message of reconciliation entrusted to us means to make present the power and the reconciling reality of the Christ event to the world—that is, it means Christian discipleship. Hence, Christians are prompted to appropriate and prolong Jesus's mission (2 Cor 4:10) in such a way that God's grace sanctifies and transforms the world now also through the agency of re-created human beings and their ministry of reconciliation.

From this short scriptural reflection, I derive the following five claims that will prove to be central to our exploration of Christian reconciliation and our effort to construct a discipleship and a theology of reconciliation:

God's reconciliation with humanity takes place through God's acts in history, and it comes about as a response to, and in confrontation with, a historically sinful reality.

The scriptures stress God's initiative and gratuitousness in the process of reconciliation. God's judgment precedes God's forgiveness, but the offer of forgiveness precedes and is not dependent upon the sinner's repentance.

God's acts of liberation and reconciliation are different aspects of one and the same movement. They illustrate that the restoration of the relationship between God and humanity is accompanied by the restoration of the relationship among human beings.

The New Testament presents Christ's life as the decisive disclosure and effective presence of God's reconciling mercy. He restores the sinner to friendship and intimacy with God. If God's reconciliation is accepted and appropriated, Christians die to their egotistical self and become a new creation that now lives not only for itself, but for Christ and others.

Scripture claims that full reconciliation is eschatologically ultimate, meaning that we are destined to live in communion with God. While we await God's reconciliation, which will come with the full realization of God's kingdom, Christians, now a new creation, are called to prolong Jesus's reconciling mission by actively striving to make God's reconciling promise a tangible reality in the world.[35]

The claim that Christ has reconciled the world to himself not only refers to the promise that God's future will ultimately transform all of creation and bring about the fullness of God's kingdom, but also to the Christian call to collaborate, even imperfectly, in the realization of this promise. Hence, reconciliation is to be understood as both a process and a goal. Indeed, the promise of a restored communion with God is the conviction that prompts and guides Christians in their ministry of reconciliation as they seek to heal a broken world through personal and social actions. Although these two faith expressions—the eschatological promise of God's ultimate reconciliation and the ministry of reconciliation—are distinct, they are nonetheless interconnected and inseparable from one another. As the South African theologian John de Gruchy has argued, Christians should understand reconciliation in two discrete but interrelated modes: as "a human and social process that requires theological explanation, and [as] a theological concept seeking human embodiment."[36]

Although Christian efforts toward a reconciled society will always remain provisional, historical signposts that imperfectly anticipate God's ultimate reconciliation, the possibility of arriving at an imperfect but relatively stable state of reconciliation calls for a new *telos* and vision of humanity and society. Such a vision brings meaning and direction to the ministry of reconciliation and looks to the future with the hope that a new world dedicated to the common good is possible. In the Christian tradition, Jesus's proclamation of God's kingdom best articulates the ideal state of perfection towards which reconciliation moves.[37] As a reality that begins in history and points to an eschatological future, the kingdom establishes "that which humans are to reach for and by which all progress will be judged human or inhuman. . . . [It also] establishes the hope that humanness is possible."[38]

Reconciliation from a Contemporary Christian Perspective

While reconciliation has been a central theme of Christian faith since the apostolic era, Christian understanding of the meaning and scope of reconciliation has expanded over time. As German theologian Geiko Müller-Fahrenholz notes, traditional Protestant and Catholic teaching and spirituality related to reconciliation has "tended to address only the sinner and lost sight of the many who were 'sinned against.' "[39] This emphasis on the personal character of reconciliation—solely understood as the reconciliation between God and the individual soul—has been accompanied by Christianity's neglect of the social dimensions of reconciliation, and by extension, its political implications.

More recent theological research, however, has turned to the appropriation of God's reconciling work as a model for how human beings are called to relate to one another, overcome their conflicts, and seek reconciliation. In the last thirty years, and particularly after the achievements of the South African Truth and Reconciliation Commission in the late 1990s, Christian theologians have increasingly turned their attention to the interpersonal, social, and political aspects of reconciliation.[40]

Whether or not it is explicitly acknowledged, most research and reflection on the topic of reconciliation is shaped by the author's preconceptions and social context, as well as the specific questions that emerge from the conflicted historical circumstances (and legacy) that he or she is addressing. And this is as it should be. Christian teaching on reconciliation needs to be constantly reappropriated in light of critical thinking and the particular historical circumstances of a given conflict. This process of reappropriation explains the diversity of theological interpretations of the subject, each of which tends to emphasize particular aspects of reconciliation over others.

Although recent studies respond to different circumstances and types of conflicts, most Christian approaches to reconciliation focus on the resources that the Christian tradition and its church can offer to those seeking to overcome social violence, division, and enmity. Some of these theological projects draw from a variety of academic disciplines to propose broad Christian strategies to guide individuals in the process of reconciliation, while others identify the ethical principles, such as those derived from Catholic social teaching, that should inform the cultural climate and the social arrangements of a reconciled society.

With the exception of the work done by a few theologians who are also versed in the social sciences and have lent their expertise to specific processes of reconciliation,[41] theological projects tend to shy away from elaborating explicit political programs or advancing specific public policies to promote social reconciliation. Briefly stated, this is because "theology does not provide the specific knowledge necessary to comprehend the factors that structure our social and political world and must respect the autonomy of social-scientific knowledge."[42] This is not to say that theology should eschew the public sphere, but that to insist that theology must engage it in a way that acknowledges and honors its integrity. As Gustavo Gutiérrez warns, divorced from social-scientific reason, the direct imposition of faith claims on secular society can "result in dangerous politico-religious messianism which does not sufficiently respect either the autonomy of the political arena or that which belongs to an authentic faith."[43] Nonetheless a coherent adherence to Christian principles will implicitly support certain policies and question others. Most theological projects would reject, for instance, the implementation of blanket political amnesties that often disregard the claims of the victims and are, more often than not, established to protect human rights violators. Likewise, they would reject those policies that manipulate the value of justice in order to demonize the oppressor and justify transforming former victims into avenging victimizers.

Without denying the importance of social arrangements in the development of a more harmonious human community, some theologians focus on the spirituality of the human person and how Christian praxis might incarnate God's reconciling presence.[44] They draw on the Christian tradition to articulate a reconciling stance and way of being in the face of conflicted reality. This project falls within this framework, as it seeks to foster the development of persons capable of responding to God's reconciling initiative through their engagement with others in the world. It will stress how a person's capacity for self-transcendence enables her to heal and transform the different spheres of reality that she engages.

Thus, my approach to reconciliation can be thought of as comprising four distinct but overlapping levels of reality: the theological level, referring to the reconciliation between God and humanity and the impact that such reconciliation has on human relations; the interpersonal level, comprising the relationships between individuals; the social level, pertaining to the restoration of relations between ethnic, racial, and other social groups within a community; and the political level, which refers to state or national projects of reconciliation.[45] These dimensions of reality are deeply interrelated and continuously shape one another.

The Reconciling Agents and Their Task

Humans are beings in relation: Our lives are linked to others and are always inescapably embedded in the multilayered web of history. While the processes to overcome enmity within the various levels of reality outlined earlier are imbued with their own particular dynamics and demands, each involves the participation of both victims and perpetrators. Victims, those who have been harmed, and perpetrators, those who have been the agents of harm, are the main participants at the center of reconciling efforts.[46] Reconciliation occurs between these groups when they have repaired the damage done to their relationships and established relationships of mutual empathy and trust. They "do not see the past as defining the future, as simply a continuation of the past. It means that they come to see the humanity of one another, accept each other, and see the possibility of a constructive relationship."[47]

The categories of victims and perpetrators help denote the agency and moral responsibilities of those involved in a conflict. They aid in defining the reconciling task of the respective parties in the process of overcoming enmity. Nonetheless, when enlisted in a specific event, these categories need to be carefully contextualized. The distinctions between victim and perpetrator are not always clear cut, and some individuals may be both victim and perpetrator.[48] Moreover, these categories leave out those who had a more limited but nonetheless important role in the conflict—the bystanders and beneficiaries. To be sure, it is difficult to evaluate the responsibility of those who benefit, often without recognizing it, from the structural and systemic oppression endured by others. It is also hard to hold accountable those bystanders whose silent complicity enabled the action of the perpetrators.[49] Yet they, too, played a role in the conflict and must be somehow taken into account.

These designations thus should be used with care because they have the tendency to reduce the complexity of the participants' moral standing to a mere label. Their accuracy is often compromised not only because perpetrators rarely take responsibility for their offenses and use all means available to cover up their actions, but also because innocent victims can rapidly transform themselves into violent victimizers.[50]

Moreover, the designation of "victims" and "perpetrators" may foster a polarizing mindset in which the two groups are pitted against each other. In this context, it becomes all too easy to demonize one's enemy and ignore their inherent human dignity. This is why the *Final Report of the South African Truth and Reconciliation Commission* warns against the facile use of these designations, asserting that it is "essential to examine perpetrators as multi-dimensional and rounded individuals rather than simply characterizing them as purveyors of horrendous acts."[51] A less obvious but equally pernicious outcome of overstressing the victim/oppressor binary is that it may lead the participants in the reconciliation process to the incorrect assumption that reconciliation can be achieved from a position of self-righteous morality. Such a stance fails to account for our limitations and does not acknowledge the importance of modeling our praxis of reconciliation after the gracious manner in which God relates to us.

Our long human history—not to mention the Christian doctrine of original sin—shows us that it is virtually impossible to speak of blameless human beings. As Karl Rahner has argued, our actions always take place in a situation largely codetermined by the actions of those who precede us, and "our own freedom bears the stamp of the guilt of others in a way which cannot be eradicated."[52] We live in a deeply interrelated world in which the accumulated injustices of past and present generations are embedded in the same social and economic structures in which we participate. Hence, to different degrees, we are all accomplices in perpetuating situations of injustice and enmity in the world.

This is not to claim that all participants in a conflict share the same degree of responsibility, nor is it to deny that blame should be placed on the perpetrators. Rather, it is to stress what has been already suggested by other Christian theologians—namely, that the recognition of the universality of human sinfulness is an indispensable step in the process of reconciliation.[53] Indeed, the appreciation of this "universal noninnocence" has led Miroslav Volf to reject any reconciliatory project constructed around moral polarities that simply ascribe blame and innocence: the just against the unjust, the pure against the impure.[54] More importantly, it has led him to realize that any reconciliatory project must be "guided by the recognition that *the economy of undeserved grace has primacy over the economy of moral deserts.*"[55]

If, as was noted in the preceding scriptural examination, the initiative in any process of reconciliation ultimately comes from God, then our reconciling efforts can never solely depend on the uprightness of our moral character. Rather, they ought to be rooted in the acknowledgment of our received creaturehood—that is, in the recognition that our common humanity has been freely bestowed on us by God.

This recognition frees even victims to be open to repentance and transformation throughout the process of reconciliation. Hence, the immediate reconciling task for each group—victims, perpetrators, and bystanders—is delineated. On the one hand, the oppressors and those who benefited from the oppression or atrocity (even if they did not actively promote it) must become accountable and repent for their actions—or inaction—in the face of injustice, in order to be freed from guilt and begin a new and reconciling life. On the other hand, the victims are charged with the delicate task of striving to free themselves from anger and their desire for vengeance, not just for their own sake but also to forgive their oppressors and open the possibility for reconciliation. But although all parties have a role to play in the process of reconciliation, the victims must take the lead. This is not only because they are the only ones who can extend forgiveness, but also because their situation exposes the grave consequences of conflict and what needs to be corrected. It is the victims' needs and concerns that must guide the direction and efforts of any reconciliation process.

The Context of Reconciliation

The interpersonal relationships described in the previous section do not take place in a vacuum; rather, they arise as humans engage a material world through their physical bodies. These relationships are embedded and come to life within a network of social customs, cultural values, institutions, and complex economic and political arrangements. Just as the human person contributes to the shaping of society, this multifaceted social network impinges on the individual's well-being and the quality of his or her interpersonal relationships. Thus the efficacy of a reconciliation process demands that it be mindful of the context being addressed, including political and socioeconomic structures, cultural values, and all the forces that shape a particular society.

Approaching the problem of reconciliation from the perspective of the social sciences, Trudy Govier has built on the work of Australian political scientist Robert Manner to identify three broad historical contexts in which societies seek reconciliation: settler societies, societies convulsed by civil war, and post-totalitarian societies.[56] In settler societies—colonized nations, like the United States, Australia, and the Latin America countries—the harm occurred in the fairly distant past and was inflicted by one group, the colonizers, upon another, the indigenous peoples. In societies caught in civil war, on the other hand, harm flows in at least two directions. Govier notes that since political struggles often become more complex as they evolve, they frequently include more than two contending groups, as in the civil wars in Sierra Leone and the Balkan region.[57] The last and more recent category of post-totalitarian societies refers to those countries that have been wronged by politically oppressive systems and are usually led by police states. This category not only includes countries such as post-soviet Russia and Ukraine, but also nations that have endured harsh military dictatorships, such as Chile and Argentina. While systemic oppression is a central feature in these societies, assigning responsibility to those directly in power becomes a more difficult and complex task due to the high level of complicity and collusion among so many in the population.

Despite their generic character and other inherent limitations, these historical frameworks help us begin to appreciate the diversity and complexity of the challenges experienced by those directly or indirectly engaged in reconciling efforts. At a minimum, they highlight how essential it is that any discourse on reconciliation be rooted in concrete experiences and specific historical contexts.

Most of the countries of the Latin America continent—where large-scale conflicts have relatively recently erupted in countries such as Argentina, Brazil, Chile, Colombia, El Salvador, Guatemala, Haiti, Nicaragua, and Peru—seem to possess all of the features attributed by Govier to the three types of historical contexts noted. They are all settler societies whose indigenous populations endured the oppression of colonial powers from the sixteenth to the early nineteenth century. After their independence, most of them were ruled by either small, powerful oligarchies or by military dictatorships. And finally, during the last three decades of the twentieth century, the inequality inherent in most of these countries' socioeconomic structures, coupled with the illegitimacy of their political systems—often controlled by repressive regimes—gave rise to violent internal conflicts in a number of them.

Although Latin America has largely rid itself of political dictators, economic injustice and poverty continue to mark the lives of most of its inhabitants.[58] In the last twenty years, these seemingly perennial foes have been accompanied by the emergence of a new and equally destructive "idol of death": the widespread illegal drug trade propped up by crime and violence. In a continent where enmity and conflict still reverberate throughout most of the region, liberation theologians have rightly stressed the contextual character of theology and the need to attend to the signs of the times. These theologians have vigorously insisted on the continent's urgent need for an integral liberation.

This project builds on the work of Latin American liberation theologians, particularly that of Jon Sobrino, to propose a spirituality and a theology of reconciliation that engages the continent's conflicted reality from a liberationist perspective. In defining the context of this project, it is important first of all to note that Sobrino's work is written within and in response to the socioeconomic reality of El Salvador in the midst of a twelve-year civil war. While Sobrino has not developed a systematic theology of reconciliation, he critically observes that the term "reconciliation" is usually enlisted to describe armed struggles (such as wars or terroristic activity) and their solutions, but less so to describe how to overcome a more original and pervasive type of conflict: "socio-economic oppression . . . which generates the slow death of millions of human beings, their lives, and also their dignity and culture."[59] The discipleship and theology of reconciliation that I draw from Sobrino's work will be most relevant to situations characterized by socioeconomic injustice, though they could also be applied to other situations of overlapping and mutually reinforcing enmities (for example, racism, classism, sexism, and nationalism). Although this project develops a theology of reconciliation by first focusing on the stance and praxis that a Christian subject should develop in order to foster social reconciliation, its insights impinge on all of the levels of reality identified above—theological, interpersonal, social, and political.

A Liberationist Approach to Reconciliation

In spite of numerous social conflicts in Latin America that have given rise to the need for reconciliatory efforts, reconciliation has remained a thorny subject among Latin American liberation theologians and little has been written on it from a liberationist perspective.[60] This may stem in part from reluctance by liberationists to engage a theme that has often been misused on the continent.[61] The notion of reconciliation on many occasions has been enlisted by those in power to bolster political amnesties that protect human rights violators at the expense of justice. As one report documents, "Amnesty has been decreed to protect human rights violations in Chile (1978), Brazil (1979), Honduras (1981), Argentina (1983), Guatemala (1982), El Salvador (1987, 1992, 1993), Surinam (1989), and Peru (1995)."[62] This helps explain liberation theologians' reservations towards what has been passed off as reconciliation by political leaders. In this regard, Juan Pico writes, "Tranquility, stability, and reconciliation are suspect before the theology of liberation, because they conceal the 'open veins' of the majority of the least of Jesus' brothers (cf. Matt 25:45)."[63]

In addition to its misapplication in the political sphere, some Latin American bishops have proposed a theology of reconciliation as a less disruptive alternative to liberation theology. The late Cardinal Alfonso López Trujillo of Colombia, for instance, claimed that "a theology of reconciliation restores the Christian character to the notion of liberation, which has been denied by Marxist analysis or the ideological categories of antagonism and struggle."[64] Although these bishops rightly stress that all persons should be understood as sinners, they incorrectly presume a moral symmetry between the sins of the powerful perpetrators and those of the victims. Moreover, they endorse the perpetuation of the same social conditions that caused the conflicts while ignoring the need for structural change.[65]

Despite this, many of the major themes addressed in theologies of reconciliation have been central to Latin America liberation theology since its inception.[66] In the following pages, I consider the relationship between reconciliation and liberation along with two central features of liberation theology's methodology that highlight its distinctive approach to reconciliation: the preferential option for the oppressed and the centrality of praxis. Because the topics addressed here in a broad fashion will be revisited later in light of Sobrino's insights, in this section I draw from other liberation theologians, chiefly Gustavo Gutiérrez, who is arguably the most influential liberation theologian today.

Liberation: The Praxis Toward Reconciliation

Like "reconciliation," the term "liberation" carries a rich soteriological meaning that is both historical and transcendent. When speaking in transcendent terms, liberation theologians tend to equate the concept of liberation with that of reconciliation and other similar ideas such as redemption, salvation, or communion that convey the sense that God's promise for eschatological deliverance will be fulfilled. Brazilian theologian João Batista Libânio, for instance, refers to the "hope of total liberation, which begins in history but goes beyond it, sustained by God's grace."[67] While this eschatological dimension of God's salvation has never been questioned or ignored by liberation theology, its thinkers have stressed that "eschatology does not lessen the value of the present life" and that, at least in a partial manner, salvation is already available to us in the here and now.[68] It is in their articulation of how salvation takes place in history that one can detect a more nuanced language that distinguishes between the concept of liberation and that of reconciliation.

Liberation theologians consistently speak of historical salvation as the integral liberation of the human person: one that impinges on the different dimensions of his or her existence and establishes the necessary conditions for reconciliation. Gustavo Gutiérrez, who has profoundly shaped this theology's soteriological conversation, identifies three "reciprocally interpenetrating levels of meaning of the term liberation": liberation from social situations and structures of oppression and marginalization, liberation from that which prevents the personal realization of the human person and the transformation of his or her consciousness into one capable of envisioning and creating a utopian and fraternal society, and liberation from sin.[69] These oppressions are not understood as something natural, but as historical—the product of humans rejecting God's grace. While the last level explicitly refers to the rejection of grace and the presence of sin that prevents our communion with God and others, the first two indicate the manner in which sin manifests itself in the social and personal spheres of the human person. They embody the different expressions of sin that must be overcome in order to become reconciled with others and God.

Following a similar line of thought, Ignacio Ellacuría argues that "Liberation must extend to everyone who is oppressed by sin and by the roots of sin; it must extend both to unjust structures and to the people who do injustice; it must extend to the inner life of the people and to the things they do. The goal of liberation is full freedom, in which full and right relationships are possible, among people and between them and God."[70] Even as liberation theologians recognize that all liberating acts have a dimension of transformative self-realization, they also insist that historical liberation is always oriented toward love. It is done for the sake of entering into communion.[71] To this end, liberation theologians often rely on the widely held Christian tradition that distinguishes between liberation *from* and liberation *for*. As Gutiérrez explains in one of his lesser known works, *The Truth Shall Make You Free*, "The first refers to freedom from sin, selfishness, injustice, need, and situations calling for deliverance. The second refers to the purpose of the first freedom—namely, love and communion; this is the final phase of liberation."[72] A number of pages later, he adds, "Liberation . . . is a journey toward communion. Communion, however, is a gift of Christ who sets us free in order that we may be free, free to love; it is in this communion that full freedom resides."[73] Leonardo Boff puts forth an equivalent argument when he distinguishes between liberation from systems of oppression and liberation for the realization of the people.[74]

Each of these theologians suggests that the passage from enmity and conflict to social reconciliation can be understood as a process that entails liberation from all social, personal, or spiritual oppressions, as well as the cultivation of new ways of relating that foster communion with others and God. In this sense, historical liberation is none other than the praxis toward reconciliation; and as the title of this book intimates, we only reach full liberation through reconciliation.

A Preferential Option for the Oppressed, the Marginalized, and the Materially Poor

The development of Latin American liberation theology was profoundly influenced by the Second Vatican Council and its renewed attention to the historical dimension of the church. Vatican II's directive to scrutinize the signs of the times and interpret them in the light of the gospel has largely shaped both the method of liberation theology and the direction of the Latin American church. In heeding the call to discern these signs—that is, "the joy and the hope, the grief and anguish of the [people] of our time, especially of those who are poor or afflicted in any way"[75]—these theologians encountered the oppressed and assumed a stance of solidarity that informs and authenticates the liberative purpose of their theological work.

Thus, to speak about reconciliation from the perspective of liberation means to speak of God's redemptive work while facing the oppressed, the marginalized, and the materially poor. It is from within the reality of conflict and exclusion experienced by the oppressed that liberation theologians seek to offer both victims and oppressors an account of the hope embedded in the good news proclaimed by Christ. As Leonardo Boff puts the question, "What does it mean to be Christian in a world of the oppressed?"[76]

Choosing the situation of the oppressed as the point of departure for theological reflection, liberation theologians reject the notion that theology may remain neutral in light of the victims' fate. Instead they insist that the universal love of God has become concretely manifested in Christ's preferential love for the poor. In this they affirm that their partiality for the well-being and concern of the oppressed is not just an ethical option, but first and foremost a theocentric one.[77]

This preferential option is a central principle of liberation theology and, without doubt, one of its most important contributions to the universal church. As will become clear later on, the preference for the oppressed has significant epistemological, theological, and pastoral consequences. However, my concern at this preliminary stage is limited to addressing a criticism that is especially pertinent to constructing a liberationist theology of reconciliation, namely, that the preferential option contradicts the universal scope of Christian love, particularly the love towards one's oppressor.[78]

Criticism of the preferential option for the poor invariably emerges from a misunderstanding of the partiality that liberation theologians ascribe to God's love.[79] Liberation theologians often articulate God's partiality to the poor by drawing from scripture. They note that this preference is evident in Jesus's close identification with the poor (Matt 25) and the fact that his proclamation of God's reign is first directed to them (Luke 4:18). But, as noted previously, liberation theologians also stress that God's love is universal and never exclusive—never aimed at one group at the expense of another. In both the gospels of Luke and Matthew the resurrected Christ sends his disciples to all the nations of the world (Luke 24:47), and St. Paul tells us that God desires everyone to be saved (1 Tim 2:4).

Gutiérrez argues that to properly understand the divine preference, it must be considered from the context of God's universal and gratuitous love. He insists that there is no contradiction between preference and universality. Preference "simply points to who ought to be the first—not the only—object of our solidarity."[80] In fact, God's preference clearly exemplifies the gratuitous character of divine love. There is no indication in scripture that God's preferential concern for the oppressed is rooted in the assumption that they are more deserving than or morally superior to their oppressor or their enemies.[81] Rather, as Gutiérrez explains, "God loves the poor . . . simply because they are poor, because they are hungry, because they are persecuted."[82] In other words, the poor are favored because they are in greater need than the non-poor. This same sensitivity was expressed by the Latin American bishops in Puebla: "the poor merit preferential attention, whatever may be the moral or personal situation in which they find themselves."[83]

At the same time, liberation theologians are careful to reject paternalistic conceptions of the poor that further denigrate them by denying their responsibilities or ignoring their rightful agency in history. As Ellacuría insists, "The poor are to be not only the preferential passive subjects of those who have power, but the preferential active subjects of history, especially of the church's history."[84] In a similar vein, the bishops in Puebla noted that "the poor challenge the church at all times, summoning it to conversion."[85] As the oppressed become aware of their situation and the possibility of changing it, they assume their rightful role in the process of transforming and reconciling reality. The demands of this renewed agency call them to make an option for themselves and others who are oppressed. Such a reconciling mission summons them to abandon their desire for retaliation and extend to their enemies the offer of forgiveness. This is necessary if the pursuit of justice and reconciliation is to be located within the context of God's gratuitous love rather than the realm of just deserts. For, in the final analysis, it is the profound realization that God loves us unconditionally that generates the gratitude that enables us to love others the way that God loves them.[86] This love, in turn, is expressed in the praxis of reconciliation, which first attends to the needs of suffering victims but never excludes or gives up on the oppressor.

The Praxis of Reconciliation

The concept of praxis has a rich intellectual history that stretches back to Aristotle; liberation theologians have appropriated it as it is developed in the work of Hegel, Marx, and Paulo Freire.[87] While the term "praxis" takes on different meanings in various discourses, in liberation theology it is used to explain the relationship between theory and practice. Praxis indicates the type of action where theory and practice dialectically influence and shape one another. Thus, liberation theologians hold that praxis is action imbued with reflection and commitment that seeks the transformation of the social order. They reject the understanding of Christian living as the mechanical application of church teaching to their daily lives. Rather, Christian praxis is the informed and committed action that expresses the Christian faith as it is appropriated in a particular situation and context. It is not limited to the internal life of the church but is faith-filled action that places itself at the service of the world.

The importance that liberation theologians have assigned to praxis is largely a response to the profound disconnect that they perceived between the teachings of the church and its ministry throughout the Latin American continent. This chasm was most evident in the social sphere, where well into the twentieth century the church tacitly endorsed socioeconomic structures that relegated the majority of the population to substandard living conditions.[88] These theologians argue that it is useless to keep reiterating church teaching if it does not find concrete expression in the life of the people and their social arrangements. Thus, Leonardo Boff asserts that "it is not enough for faith to be true in terms in which it is expressed (orthodoxy); it is verified, made true, when it is informed by love, solidarity, hunger and thirst for justice. . . . Therefore, orthodoxy has to be accompanied by orthopraxis."[89]

By insisting on "right praxis," these theologians are underscoring the importance of a timely Christian praxis that adopts the modality best suited to meet current challenges. Above all, they are warning against the tendency to spiritualize and individualize the Christian message as a way to avoid the demands that ensue from a conflicted reality.[90] As David Tracy observes, for liberation theologians the proclamation of the Word demands the "recognition of the primacy of praxis, action in and for the church in a global society groaning to be set free from alienating events and oppressive structures in the contemporary situation."[91] Thus, inspired by God's eschatological promises of a reconciled world, Christian praxis departs from the reality of oppression to join in solidarity with those who are oppressed. It seeks the conversion of the culture and the social order that generates this marginalization and enmity, as well as the re-creation of both oppressed and oppressor so as to enable their reconciliation.

Even though Christian praxis takes different forms depending upon the circumstances and demands of a particular situation, it is important to note that this praxis does not pretend to impose faith claims onto the public sphere. While upholding the insights received from revelation, it recognizes the autonomy of the social order and understands itself as a rational enterprise that is open to public scrutiny and willing to engage in fruitful dialogue with the secular world. Indeed, Christian praxis also relies on reason and the social sciences to grasp the complexities of a particular situation and identify the best courses of action to overcome enmity.[92]

Hence, in what follows I draw from secular and religious sources to discuss three dimensions that most social scientists and theologians identify as critical for any process of reconciliation: the truthful uncovering of the events and sources of conflict, and the responsibility to attend to the memories and help restore the agency of those victimized by these events; an expression of justice that responds to the claims of the victims and seeks to construct a more harmonious socioeconomic order; and the forgiveness necessary to restore communal life and construct a different kind of future.[93] Analysis of these three distinct but interrelated moments of the reconciliation process—truth-seeking, justice, and forgiveness—will shed light on the complexities, opportunities, and limitations confronted by the Christian praxis that will be articulated as a discipleship of reconciliation in subsequent chapters. Exploring these three moments also offers the opportunity to identify some of the distinctive features that emerge when approaching the praxis of reconciliation from a liberationist perspective, and to engage some of the remaining criticisms leveled against this approach.

A HEALING AND RECONCILING TRUTH

Reconciliation requires that the causes and circumstances that led to a situation of conflict be uncovered. Without this, the parties involved and the society they share will continue to be shaped by impunity and unresolved grievances. This might seem obvious, but the reality of Latin American history testifies otherwise. The political leaders in most of the countries to emerge from authoritarian regimes and civil wars preferred general amnesties over the hard work of truth-finding. This approach, as Audrey Chapman observes, reflects two faulty assumptions: "that it is feasible to found a future on an unresolved past and that to remember is necessarily to nurse grievances and seek vengeance for the atrocities and violence experienced by individuals and communities."[94]

Scholars and practitioners of reconciliation have learned much from the South African Truth and Reconciliation Commission (TRC), whose truth-seeking process has become a reference point for subsequent commissions.[95] The TRC's final report identifies four dimensions of truth within this process, which are worth summarizing here:

> *The factual or forensic truth*, which seeks to establish the facts of what happened, when it occurred, and who was involved. This objective kind of truth requires the corroboration of claims about particular incidents and their agents.
>
> *Personal and narrative truth* attends to the victims' experiences and is gathered as victims are given the opportunity to narrate the past from their own perspective and in their own language.
>
> *Social or dialogical truth* emerges from interaction, discussion, and debate. It seeks to capture the social experience by unearthing the complex motives and perspectives of all those involved, including individuals from all walks of life, faith communities, nongovernmental organizations, and others.
>
> *Healing and restorative truth* goes beyond uncovering past abuses to incorporate the purpose for which truth is acquired. It stresses the public acknowledgment of the conflict through reports in order to restore the dignity of the victims and prevent the conflict from ever happening again.[96]

To be sure, uncovering what actually happened and arriving at a reconciling truth is always vastly more difficult than initially expected.[97] Theologians and social scientists alike acknowledge the human impossibility of grasping the entire truth behind a historical event, given the limited time and resources for investigation, and the ways in which our already imperfect memories are shaped by our social locations, preexisting perspectives, and vested interests.[98]

In recognition of these limitations, theologians such as Miroslav Volf and John de Gruchy, who have both written extensively on reconciliation, propose that our best hope for grasping the truth in conflicted situations is to enter into a dialogical process—a type of double vision—that calls each participant to move beyond her limited perspective in order to try to encompass the perspective of the other. Having enlarged one's understanding of the issue at hand, participants can seek a provisional common ground where conversation and empathy become possible.[99] Black liberation theologian James Cone similarly argues that sharing the narratives of our memories and experiences allows us to overcome the chasm between people, groups, and communities. He writes, "As I listen to other stories, I am invited to move out of the subjectivity of my own story into another realm of thinking and acting. The same is true for others when I tell my story . . . When people can no longer listen to other people's stories, they become enclosed within their own social context, treating their distorted vision of reality as the whole truth."[100]

Although Latin American liberation theologians would largely accept the importance of such deep listening, they would be swift to point out that not all social locations offer the same access to reality and thus are not all of equal epistemological value. Instead, they argue that the situation of the victims offers a privileged perspective from which one can best grasp the truth of a conflicted reality, since their status as the oppressed unmasks the complex ideological structures that conceal the multilayered mechanisms of oppression. While liberation theologians acknowledge that this perspective is not infallible and does not provide a universal viewpoint, they nonetheless insist that "it makes possible a *more* universal viewpoint from which to overcome bias and better appreciate other viewpoints."[101]

In any situation involving competing truth claims that are hampered by deficient memories and particular interests, getting at the truth will be an incomplete, dialogical process that imperfectly seeks to determine the relative merit of the partial accounts of others. Yet, despite the many difficulties involved in grasping the truth, the experience of numerous truth and reconciliation commissions demonstrates that it is possible to learn a great deal about the sources and the events that shaped a given conflict. Although incomplete, the recovered truth is often sufficient to bring about healing and drive a process of reconciliation. In the end, however, the critical issue is not just discerning how we can effectively get to the truth, as difficult as this process is, but also what we choose to do with the truth that has been exposed.

As the TRC's four dimensions of truth suggest, in the reconciliation process truth has much to do with past personal experiences, the recollection of facts, and historical events. In this sense, truth is intimately connected to the memories and the stories that emerge from those who participated in conflicted situations and particularly from the victims who have endured the ensuing suffering and loss. For the victims, the naming of this truth entails the recollection of painful memories, which can foster strong feelings of resentment as they relive the traumatic experiences of the past. As Robert Schreiter explains, these "traumatic experiences, especially those inscribed on the body, play themselves over and over again in our minds like a never-ending tape. They can eventually block out everything else and literally take over our lives."[102] These memories of suffering then pose a deep emotional threat to the victims and their immediate community. Moreover, insofar as they question the dignity and significance of human life, they implicitly represent a danger to all human beings. German theologian Johann Baptist Metz contends that confronted by meaningless suffering, one stands "in the face of the fear of losing one's name, one's identity, one's very self."[103]

These memories cannot simply be forgotten, and it is only by remembering and telling their stories that victims can begin to overcome the negative influence of their painful past and rebuild their lives. Such memories must also be dealt with at the social level in order to interrogate our present existence, prevent repeating the same mistakes in the future, and establish a shared sense of identity between the conflicted parties that can provide the basis for a reconciled future.[104] As Metz has noted, memory, along with the narratives that bear these memories, are "the fundamental categories for getting a firm grip on one's understanding of identity and for saving it in the midst of the historical struggles and dangers in which persons experience and constitute themselves as subjects."[105] It is largely because how we remember is so central to our personal well-being and the formation of our personal and social identities that reconciliation demands that we pay attention to the healing of painful and traumatic memories.

Robert Schreiter, in his examination of how memories and their narratives contribute to the process of reconciliation, identifies three moments through which the healing of memory often unfolds: acknowledging loss, making connections, and taking new action.[106] The first moment is characterized by the victims' confrontation and acknowledgement of their loss. It usually entails the expression of their anger, sense of betrayal, desertion, and violation. In this stage, victims appear overwhelmed by past events and bound by memories of those events and their lost ones. As Schreiter explains, to develop a new relationship with what has been lost, survivors must be provided with the support that may enable them to restore their capacity to trust as well as a safe space in which to share their story. The second moment takes place within this safe space in which the victims may begin to make new connections. Here, the victims' relationship to the past is no longer immediate but mediated, in a dialectical manner, by their new interactions with others. Aided by these new interactions, the victims begin to devise new ways of relating to the past and a renewed meaning for their stories emerges. In other words, they begin to remember differently—that is, the survivors begin to recover "the full extent of [their] relationships with [their lost ones], and come to place the moment of their deaths with that larger history. In this way, [their demise] is not forgotten, but it does not become a millstone that threatens to draw us too into the abyss."[107]

In a similar vein, John de Gruchy rejects the idea of suppressing or forgetting negative recollections and suggests that victims should learn to remember their painful past with a healed memory. Thus, he calls for a new type of remembering: one that "heals relationships, build[s] community, and anticipates[s] a new future."[108] A victim's capacity to remember in a new way makes it possible for her to overcome the painful memories of the past and re-direct her life without being consumed by her recollections of trauma. To be sure, though one can ameliorate some of the most damaging effects of past events, the consequences of certain deeds, such as torture or the loss of a loved one, can never be fully erased, but remains as part of the survivor's memory and identity.[109]

The third moment—taking new action—occurs when victims who are no longer paralyzed by their past are given the opportunity to mourn, remember anew, and reflect upon their stories. This explains in part the importance of providing the victims with a place, in the form of monuments and memorials, to honor and remember their lost ones. Schreiter notes that survivors also honor the fallen when they engage in actions that characterize the moral vision of the deceased. "This new vision may be an extrapolation of the vision of the dead, something that will allow the living to continue to participate in that heritage. It may, on the other hand, be something completely new."[110] The key point here is that the victim is finally free to construct a new future and that this future is no longer chained to the painful experiences of the past.

In examining the role that the narratives play in the restoration of a community's identity, Schreiter stresses their importance as "witnesses to the past" and as sources for a community's grasping of the truth.[111] As witnesses, the narratives that bear the memories of the victims "keep the past present to us" and expose how previous conflicts unfolded and continue to shape the current lives of individual members of society. These narratives also become a source for grasping the truth insofar as they gather the experiential accounts and voices of those previously silenced. Moreover, as different parties put forward their interpretation of past events and enter into dialogue with others who have a different version of past events, a social or dialogical truth begins to emerge. This dialogical truth may eventually lead the separated parties to a common understanding of the past and provide the foundations for a shared future.

In the last chapter, I will return to the issue of memory in the reconciliation process and examine how Sobrino's interpretation of Jesus's narrative shapes the identity of Christian disciples and guides their reconciling efforts. For now, it is important to insist that while the truth opens up the possibility for justice and forgiveness to be achieved in the process of reconciliation, neither justice nor forgiveness automatically emerges from truth-telling. As de Gruchy warns, "Truth serves the cause of reconciliation and justice only when it leads to a genuine *metanoia*, that is, a turning around, a breaking with an unjust past, and a moving toward a new future."[112]

A HISTORICAL AND ESCHATOLOGICAL JUSTICE

A second indispensable dimension in the process of reconciliation is the pursuit of justice, which leads us to attend to the enmity of the past by creating personal and social arrangements that foster new ways of relating. These arrangements can help to prevent the repetition of old harms and to anticipate, at least in some measure, the challenges that emerge from a dynamic and fast-moving world. Nonetheless, recent attempts at social reconciliation in countries like El Salvador have shown that even when enough political and social will is mustered to uncover the truth of what actually happened, these initial reconciling efforts are often derailed by a disregard for justice that trivializes the demands of the victims and ignores the roots of the conflict.

It was this concern to uphold justice that prompted a number of progressive South African theologians to write the *Kairos* document in 1985. The document confronted the South African apartheid regime and those churches that had supported it. Enlisting Bonhoeffer's language of "cheap grace," the drafters of the document talked of "cheap reconciliation" to argue against the idea of reconciliation without justice.[113] They wrote,

> In our situation in South Africa today it would be totally unChristian to plead for reconciliation and peace before the present injustices have been removed. Any such plea plays into the hands of the oppressor by trying to persuade those of us who are oppressed to accept our oppression and to become reconciled to the intolerable crimes that are committed against us. That is not Christian reconciliation, it is sin. It is asking us to become accomplices in our own oppression, to become servants of the devil. No reconciliation is possible in South Africa *without justice*.[114]

These theologians argue that one cannot demand that victims consent to reconciliation while injustices continue to occur. This position helpfully emphasizes that preferential attention should be given to the care and needs of the victims, particularly those under the threat of violence. But it can suggest that forgiveness and reconciliation ought to be pursued only after full justice has been achieved, when in fact justice is both part of the process of reconciliation and one of its goals.[115]

Justice, however, is neither a univocal nor unequivocal term. Like "liberation" or "reconciliation," the meaning of the term "justice" is rich and complex, largely depending upon the context in which it is employed and the interests of those enlisting it. In her book *Six Theories of Justice*, Christian ethicist Karen Lebackz likens the study of this subject to the proverbial examination of an elephant by blindfolded explorers. None of the theories reviewed by her encompass the definition of justice, but each contributes to its understanding.[116] In a similar vein, Volf argues that Christian conceptions of justice are always limited and shaped by particular cultures and traditions. Although he acknowledges that justice is indispensable for reconciliation, he dismisses the highly desirable but seemingly unattainable objective of developing a coherent and overarching conception of justice. Instead, Volf proposes what he describes as a piecemeal approach that looks for convergences and agreements among different traditions on justice issues.[117] For him, it is in the interaction—and embrace—of other cultures and perspectives that our conception may be corrected and enriched.[118]

Broadly speaking, processes of social reconciliation in the last thirty years have mainly stressed two distinct models of justice, which can be roughly described as *realist* and *teleological* in their approach to reconciliation.[119] I associate the realist approach with those scholars whom political scientist Daniel Philpott describes as "liberal skeptics" in his book *Just and Unjust Peace: An Ethic of Political Reconciliation*.[120] While there are clear distinctions among these "liberal skeptics," they share a practical political outlook that evinces three main features.[121] First, they recognize the central role that the distribution of power plays in both enabling and limiting the pursuit of justice. Power constraints among partisan parties require compromise and partially explain the historical incompleteness of any process of social transformation and reconciliation. Second, while the realist approach endorses the need for a rule of law, upholds human rights, and seeks the trial and punishment of human rights violators, it holds relatively modest expectations of the impact that the political order may have on the moral transformation of the participants, particularly regarding the issues of repentance and forgiveness. It sees the pursuit of these values and other desired virtues as beyond the purview of political processes that respect individual liberties. Third, the realist approach defends pluralism and fosters processes of open-ended deliberation among relatively autonomous individuals who question and discern the nature of justice and the good. Consequently, it rejects the notion that a society may embrace a single, comprehensive moral perspective.

Although this approach seems to ignore "the transformation of hearts and minds and the fostering of virtues among the citizenry,"[122] it has offered an important contribution to processes of reconciliation all over the world. Its commitment to protecting rights and punishing perpetrators has been implemented by institutions such as the United Nations, the International Criminal Court, and the human rights community. Mindful of the limitations inherent to the political enterprise, the realist approach sees social transformation and reconciliation as a complex process that is always partial, uncertain, and incomplete at best.

If the realist approach to reconciliation stresses its process, a teleological approach proceeds in anticipation toward reconciliation's goal. Emphasis is placed on justice and the ethical conditions necessary to arrive at a fully reconciled community. This teleological approach to reconciliation is evident in the proposals that often emerge from religious traditions as well as in restorative justice movements. Restorative justice represents, in a manner of speaking, a new reconciling tradition grounded in the way numerous ancient communities dealt with enmity.[123] It understands conflict as the rupture of relationships among offenders, victims, and the community, and it thus stresses the reconstruction of these relationships with the participation of all who are involved.[124] This does not mean that restorative justice necessarily excludes the offenders' obligation to take responsibility for their actions or even the need to provide compensation or make reparations. Its focus, however, is on the possibility of building a harmonious future.

In the area of social reconciliation, restorative justice began in earnest through the efforts of the South African TRC, and particularly through the work of Desmond Tutu. The Anglican archbishop captures the novel lens through which restorative justice sees the resolution to social enmity: "the central concern is not retribution or punishment but, in the spirit of *ubuntu*, the healing of breaches, the redressing of imbalances, the restoration of broken relationships. This kind of justice seeks to rehabilitate both the victim and the perpetrator, who should be given the opportunity to be reintegrated into the community he or she has injured by his or her offence."[125]

Thus, instead of offering a specific conception of justice, restorative justice provides an approach to thinking about it. Such an approach is not distant from the Christian tradition or, indeed, from liberation theology. In fact, Robert Schreiter explains that restorative justice includes two elements already incorporated within Catholic thinking about justice: a distributive form of justice concerned with the creation of social arrangements that assure the equitable distribution of economic goods, and a commutative form of justice that attends to needs of victims and the rehabilitation of oppressors.[126] Indeed, the ultimate purpose of both restorative justice and Catholic social thought is none other than the common good.[127]

The realist and teleological approaches to reconciliation are often pitted against each other as a result of their respective limitations and emphases. Proponents of the former often claim that the teleological approach is idealistic, utopic, and lacks "a method for building a principled consensus on the ethic in religiously plural societies."[128] Advocates of the latter, on the other hand, lament the realist approach's disregard for the development of moral virtues, its emphasis on retributive justice, and the implicit assumption that justice will be done "if wrongdoers are made to pay for their wrongdoing by being punished and suffering the castigation and hard treatment they deserve."[129]

These two approaches, however, are not mutually exclusive and proponents of one approach often draw valuable lessons from the other. While distinct, the realist and teleological approaches converge in their concern for human rights and the flourishing of the human person; they have indeed much to contribute to each other. The stress on the practical favored by the realist approach can offer an important corrective to the idealist tendencies inherent in the teleological approach. Because the realist approach insists that we engage the challenges of the conflicted present, even if in a gradual and piecemeal manner, it can help prevent the teleological goal of achieving comprehensive justice from becoming a paralyzing promise. Moreover, by drawing on the political expertise of realist and liberal scholars, the advocates of the teleological approach can better understand the social complexities that must be dealt with and identify the ethical mechanisms whereby they can effectively implement their insights within a pluralistic society.

In contrast, the teleological approach provides the realist with a more comprehensive understanding of justice and reconciliation to inform and guide the reconciling efforts. This holistic reconciling vision is rooted in the idea of restored relationship and the integral transformation of the human person and society. Hence, it promotes a more ambitious moral vision that includes virtues such as compassion, forgiveness, and fraternity, which extend well beyond the mere protection of human rights. Likewise, the teleological approach stresses the restoration of the victims while offering alternative ways to deal with the persecutors that extend beyond punishment to redress the wounds caused by the conflict.

In general, Latin American liberation theologians approach justice and reconciliation from a teleological rather than a realist perspective.

Distinctive to their approach among other Christian projects is their insistence on attending to the systems and structural causes that generate and perpetuate social conflict. They envision Christ's promise of God's kingdom as the ultimate reconciling reality that will overcome all conflict and shape the Christian pursuit of justice.

Some scholars argue that liberation theologians do not provide a clear definition of what they mean by justice, while others criticize their apparent juxtaposition of scripture and Marxist thought in order to construct a theory of justice.[130] Still other critics reduce the liberationist model of justice to an adoption of Catholic social teaching as seen through a modern liberal lens—a model that allegedly understands justice simply as the virtue of giving every person his or her due and not as "the principle of unity in a shared good."[131]

That liberation theologians often neglect to offer an explicit definition of justice can be largely explained by the fact that these theologians locate themselves within the rich Christian tradition and thus its broad conception of justice is already assumed in their writings. It is also true that they have drawn from the liberal tradition to defend the dignity and rights of the Latin American people, and that they have enlisted Marxist analysis and the theory of dependency to better comprehend the Latin America situation.[132] Yet, neither liberal political thought nor Marxism fully explains the liberationist approach to justice.

Liberation theology's understanding of justice is first and foremost biblical, and thus deeply relational.[133] Specifically, its understanding of justice is rooted in the Christian revelation of a loving God and God's aspirations of justice for humanity as communicated through the prophets and especially through Christ's promise of a reconciled kingdom: the last will be first (Matt 19:30); the poor will be blessed (Luke 6:21); enemies will be loved and forgiven (Matt 5:44b).

In line with Christian tradition, liberation theologians recognize these promises as unmerited gifts that, in turn, elicit in the believer a new commitment on behalf of other human beings. The promises themselves shed light on the conflicted human situation and guide a Christian praxis that seeks to anticipate and make present in history, even in a provisional and limited manner, the eschatological reality of God's kingdom.[134] As Gustavo Gutiérrez has noted, "The struggle for justice . . . is also the struggle for the Kingdom of God."[135] This struggle for justice expresses the manner in which Christian commitment and love become concrete and practical in a world of injustice and sin.

Because liberation theology's understanding of justice is located within the overarching vision of God's biblical revelation, the pursuit of personal and structural justice is never absolute. It is never allowed to become a reign of terror administered by avenging victimizers. Gutiérrez helpfully zeroes in on this point in his book *On Job*, where he notes that "justice alone does not have the final say about how we are to speak of God" and that only God's love and grace give justice its full meaning.[136] Indeed, he insists that "the gratuitousness of God's love is the framework within which the requirement of practicing justice is to be located."[137]

In response to the Latin American situation and following the teachings of the bishops who gathered in Medellin (1968) and Puebla (1979), liberation theologians have stressed that the pursuit of justice demands the confrontation of the structural dimension of sin.[138] This refers to the concretization, accumulation, and expression of personal sins (for example, greed, selfishness, indifference) in permanent social arrangements, and thus to the manner in which cultural and legal institutions as well as socioeconomic and political structures can generate conflict and perpetuate injustice.[139] Implicit in this structural emphasis is the theologians' recognition that human beings are "always inserted in a world of mediations and institutions" and that "the human community is always more than the sum of single human beings."[140]

Implicit also is the theologians' concern with upholding the human rights inherent to the dignity of every human person, and doing so with a special preference for the oppressed, whose rights are systematically violated. Hence Ellacuría argues that "Human rights must be primarily the rights of the oppressed. It is only by doing justice to the oppressed peoples and classes that an authentic common good and truly universal human rights will be fostered."[141] Our reflections so far should begin to dispel the notion that liberation theology assumes a model of justice that is simply a guarantee of rights, or that it understands justice after a liberal notion in which "human dignity consists largely in autonomy, that is, the ability of each person to determine for himself or herself a view of the good life."[142] Indeed, Ellacuría explicitly rejects this understanding of justice when he writes, "If one treats justice as a virtue that simply means giving each person what is her or his due, prescinding from the totality in which this call has its concretion, then it does not make sense to discuss priorities, much less relation. . . . Can one have justice if it is not the work of God? Is not justice the presence of Grace?"[143]

In the final analysis, it is not only moral conviction, but especially grace and the human grateful response to God's undeserved love that permeates the Christian struggle for a just society: one that fosters the dignity of the human person and honors the deeply interrelated character of human existence.

A GRATUITOUS FORGIVENESS

In 2002, under the shadow of the terrorist attacks of September 11, 2001, Pope John Paul II began his address celebrating the World Day of Peace by identifying justice and forgiveness as the two necessary pillars for reconciliation. These two values, he rightly claimed, are not themselves irreconcilable but rather converge in the process of reconciliation.[144] The pope's words respond to the widely held assumption that justice and forgiveness necessarily exclude one another and are opposing moral alternatives to human evil.[145]

Nonetheless, as events in Bosnia and Rwanda in the 1990s showed, our wounded memories and the value of justice can readily be used to rationalize an unwillingness to forgive and thus justify the former victims becoming the victimizers. In the Rwandan genocide of 1994, it is estimated that in about one hundred days nearly 800,000 people were killed by neighbors and even relatives, many of them in church buildings where the victims were seeking shelter.[146] Such horrors highlight the irreversible character of history—our inability to undo what has been done—and expose the limitations of justice. They raise the question of whether and how the survivors and all those involved in the event will be able to continue to live with one another. How are they to overcome the cycle of violence and revenge? In short, how are they going to let go of the past and make a commitment for a shared future?

Forgiveness is a demanding and delicate task. Although truth opens the possibility for justice and forgiveness, it also unveils acts of cruelty and injustice that are very difficult to accept. It is natural that the memories of these acts incite rage and a call for retribution. In spite of the dangers that such reactions entail, a victim's rage should not be dismissed as something primitive or unjustified, but rather understood as a legitimate anger directed against those who undermine the dignity of human life.[147] While vengeance is to be avoided, the victims' rightful call for just restoration must always be heard and understood as a "wakeup call to the pursuit of justice."[148] Indeed, as Volf reminds us, "at the heart of reconciliation lies the twin belief that evil must be named as evil and that the restoration of communion with the evil doer is not based . . . simply on justice done."[149]

Forgiveness is also a delicate task because the surviving victims often do not feel entitled to speak on behalf of other victims, particularly when they are no longer present. In fact, "forgiving can [often] be seen as a betrayal of the past, and especially a betrayal of the dead."[150] This quandary lies at the heart of Simon Wiesenthal's oft-cited book *The Sunflower*, where he narrates his inability to extend forgiveness to a repentant, dying Nazi soldier during their time at a concentration camp.[151] It is often no less difficult to extend forgiveness for crimes against oneself, especially in those cases where the perpetrators lack remorse or systematically deny any responsibility for their actions. It is thus not surprising that many victims are reluctant to extend forgiveness, not necessarily because they seek revenge, but simply out of respect for themselves and other victims. That forgiveness actually takes place is indeed a remarkable occurrence.

Although forgiveness carries with it a marked religious connotation, it is a subject engaged by different academic disciplines with a common interest in reconciliation. Psychologists and social scientists, for instance, often note that forgiveness is a personal decision—a victim's choice to see himself and his conflict with new eyes. They explain that forgiveness is not a one-time event, but a process of letting go that shapes a new attitude and marks a new way of life.[152] Two elements are essential in their understanding of forgiveness: the willingness to relinquish one's desire for vengeance against the perpetrator, and the nurturing of qualities of compassion and generosity toward the transgressor.[153] In a similar vein, psychologist Everett L. Worthington describes forgiveness as a "superposition of positive emotions over the cold emotions of unforgiveness in such a way that the unforgiveness is contaminated and overwhelmed by the more positive emotions."[154] Hence, for Worthington, reconciliation entails reducing the sources of unforgiveness at the social and interpersonal level, while at the same time fostering ways to promote forgiveness.[155] It should be evident, then, that forgiveness can be understood in secular terms and can be motivated by nonreligious concerns. In this sense, forgiveness is "a matter of changing feelings and attitudes away from bitterness in the direction of acceptance so that we can go forward in relationships with those who may have wronged us."[156]

In the Christian tradition, forgiveness begins with an awareness of being freely forgiven by God, who takes the initiative to bring us into communion. This realization is at the heart of the church's sacrament of reconciliation, whose central elements reflect much of what we have been exploring as part of the process of reconciliation. As noted at the beginning of this chapter, God's forgiveness reaches its climax in Jesus Christ, who was a victim himself and whose reconciling actions have the capacity to transform us into a new creation. Indeed, it is Jesus who first heals our wounds and enables us to forgive others. "By going before us," Schreiter writes, "Jesus teaches us how to carry the pain we do have to bear, the burdens of suffering that we do have to endure. Jesus teaches us how to move from victim to survivor, how to create spaces of safety where pain can be unfolded and memories healed."[157]

Although Hannah Arendt may have overstated her claim when she famously asserted that Jesus discovered "the role of forgiveness in the realm of human affairs," there is no doubt that Jesus placed forgiveness at the center of his praxis.[158] Arendt also touches on an insight that seems to inform Jesus's merciful ministry—namely, that given the irreversibility of our actions only forgiveness can release us "from the consequences of what we have done."[159] While revenge chains us to a never-ending spiral of vengeance, forgiveness opens up the possibility of beginning anew. This is clear in Jesus's teachings and deeds, which evince a praxis aimed at restoring the well-being of the sinner as well as his or her relationship with the community. Parables such as the prodigal son and the lost sheep depict an unbounded mercy that welcomes the sinner and enables his or her transformation. Similarly, the cross shows that bearing each other's offenses is indispensable to absorbing evil's power and putting an end to enmity's cycle of violence. Christian forgiveness, then, is modeled on Jesus's praxis and the recognition that the offer of reconciliation has already been bestowed upon each of us, since only one who has experienced forgiveness can begin to truly grasp what it means to forgive.

Nonetheless, the bestowal of forgiveness is always the prerogative of the victim. At the personal level, the victim's willingness to forgive is not dependent upon the transgressor's repentance but rather is a unilateral, gratuitous offer that may be accepted or rejected. This gratuity does not mean that forgiveness is simply "cheap grace" intended to replace justice. On the contrary, every act of forgiveness "draws attention to its violation precisely by offering to forego its claims" and clearly names "injustice as injustice and therefore demand[s] that its causes be removed."[160] As John Paul II explains, "Forgiveness is in no way opposed to justice, as if to forgive meant to overlook the need to right the wrong done. It is rather the fullness of justice . . . involving as it does the deepest healing of the wounds which fester in human hearts. Justice and forgiveness are both essential to such healing."[161]

The writings of most, if not all, liberation theologians echo John Paul II's understanding of justice and forgiveness as two values that converge in the process of reconciliation. Leonardo Boff, for instance, argues that "justice alone is not enough to maintain peace. There must be a gratuity and a self-giving that transcend the imperatives of duty. We need love and a capacity for forgiveness that go beyond the limits of justice."[162] In a similar vein, but explicitly arguing for the need of forgiveness in the process of reconciliation, Segundo Galilea writes, "Reconciliation also presupposes *pardon*. It is not enough to have achieved justice or to be on the way to achieving it." He adds that it is precisely because the pursuit of justice entails confrontations and conflicts from which attitudes of revenge arise that "Christian pardon is the only thing capable of overcoming this attitude and achieving a reconciliation that is not only formal and juridical but also fraternal."[163]

Some critics claim that liberation theology subordinates forgiveness to the primacy of justice. More specifically, as articulated by Daniel M. Bell, this argument proposes that "Justice remains [for liberation theologians] the fundamental demand of faith; only after it has been established does forgiveness becomes a possibility." This criticism reflects a misunderstanding of the church's preferential option for the oppressed. Liberation theologians do argue that Christian praxis must first focus its efforts on the eradication of structural sin and the humanization of the victim, and then attend to the personal rehabilitation of the oppressor.[164] The point of this emphasis, however, is not to establish some type of hierarchy between two moral principles, but instead to discern priorities in the pastoral response to a situation of conflict. The chronological priority given to redressing structural injustices does not assume that full social justice must be achieved before forgiveness can be extended, or that perpetrators should be excluded from the process of reconciliation. Rather, it insists that we must begin with what is most urgent: addressing the evil that is currently generating the suffering and death of millions of human beings. In fact, as you will see in more detail in subsequent chapters, this praxis presumes that the pursuit of justice is already informed by a profound compassion that is always willing to extend forgiveness.

The capacity to forgive is a gift to both victims and perpetrators. It liberates the former from the condition of victimhood and their desire for retaliation, and the latter from guilt; it restores and transforms their relationship from that of victim and victimizer to one in which each acknowledges the other's human dignity. It is difficult to underestimate the centrality of forgiveness and its indispensability in the process of reconciliation. However, it is important to clearly distinguish between forgiveness and reconciliation. While the perpetrator's apology is not indispensable to extending forgiveness, reconciliation demands both the victim's willingness to forgive and the perpetrator's repentance, and even the possibility of reparation for his or her past actions.

Praxis, Spirituality, and Theology

I have spent some time outlining the challenges and demands that frame a praxis of social reconciliation because of the essential relationship between and praxis and spirituality, and because of the central role that spirituality plays in the theology of Jon Sobrino. Indeed, this project proposes that while Sobrino never articulates an explicit theology of reconciliation, an analysis of the spirituality that undergirds his theology enables us to arrive at a theology of reconciliation that is faithful to and coherent with the rest of his work.

For Sobrino, a spiritual perspective has a direct impact on shaping the manner in which Christians live their faith. Theologians are no exception. While it may not offer specific theological content, a theologian's spirituality influences his or her imagination, priorities, and methodology. In line with theologians such as Karl Rahner and Marie-Dominique Chenu, Sobrino asserts that "Spirituality is . . . not just one dimension of theology, but rather an integrating dimension for the whole of theology."[165] In Chapter 3, you will see that Sobrino's theology of liberation is rooted in a particular spirituality, and it is this spirituality that will enable us to take the different elements of his Christology and put those elements in the proper configuration to articulate a theology of reconciliation.

In Sobrino's view, spirituality touches upon all aspects of human life and the manner in which the human person relates to reality. More specifically, for him, "Christian spirituality is no more and no less than a [way of] living . . . precisely in the concrete manner of Jesus and according to the spirit of Jesus. This is the following of Jesus."[166] In this sense, a Christian praxis of reconciliation is none other than the Christian expression of this following or discipleship in a situation of enmity and conflict. Understanding Sobrino's Christology in terms of its roots in spirituality—that is, in terms of the discipleship that ensues from it—is particularly fruitful for this project, since Sobrino's spiritual perspective provides us with a lens that illuminates and integrates his theological thought. In turn, further reflection upon this discipleship that seeks to follow Jesus in a conflicted reality will enable us to develop a theology of reconciliation.

The Christian discipleship of reconciliation, which lays the groundwork for a theology of reconciliation, will need to attend to the main demands of the reconciliation process that I have identified previously: the pursuit of truth, justice, and forgiveness. In addition, such discipleship will be structured around the essential moments of Jesus's life—incarnation, mission, cross, and resurrection—and empowered by the same spirit of compassion that animated his life. The work laid out ahead will demonstrate how this discipleship advances the theological conversation on reconciliation in at least four ways:

It rightly prioritizes the perspective, role, and contribution of the victims in the process of reconciliation.

It successfully holds in dynamic tension the need for a stance of personal forgiveness with the importance of a social restoration of justice.

It holds that a Christian praxis of reconciliation needs to be aimed first at the eradication of structural sin and the corresponding humanization of its victims, and then at the rehabilitation of the oppressor.

It puts forward the need to envision feasible historical projects as partial reconciling alternatives to the conflicted reality in which we live.

In the following chapter, I begin to elaborate on the preceding claims by turning to the examination of the context within which Sobrino has done his theology—his surrounding sociohistorical conditions, personal experiences, and intellectual influences—in order to identify and examine the sources that have stimulated and shaped the development of his spirituality and theological thought. The third chapter focuses on Sobrino's spirituality to show the integrative role that spirituality plays in his theology. Such spirituality has both a general structure relevant to all human beings and a specifically Christian structure that reflects the faithful following of Jesus. In the fourth chapter, this general structure is fleshed out with those elements in Sobrino's Christology that are important for developing a distinctly Christian discipleship of reconciliation. The fifth and concluding chapter reflects upon the fruits of the Christian discipleship of reconciliation developed in the previous chapters and outlines a theology of reconciliation from a liberationist perspective.

2   Confronting a Conflicted Reality

Nearly three decades ago, theologian Stephen Bevans noted that one of the most important recent insights about theology is the recognition of its contextual nature. Bevans insisted that contextualization is not a luxury, but rather is "at the heart of what it means to do theology, and the theologian who does not take the process seriously only contextualizes unconsciously."[1] Years before Bevans made this observation, however, liberation theologians were insisting that their theology flows from a conscious effort to reflect and articulate the Christian faith from and for a particular culture, place, and set of circumstances.[2] This insistence on the relationship between historical context and theological reflection indicates an appreciation of the historicity of human existence and of the impact that historical realities exercise on human consciousness. It also bespeaks a mindful awareness of the plurality of ways in which people from different cultures, societies, and historical situations interpret their religious experiences.[3] Beyond these general epistemological insights, Latin American liberation theologians stress the importance of theological context in order to highlight the relevance that God's Word and theology should have for their particular situation of poverty and oppression, and, conversely, the impact that a particular situation has on our understanding of revelation and the theological task.[4]

In line with this contextual approach, this chapter explores the milieu within which Jon Sobrino's theology has taken shape—his sociohistorical environment, academic formation, personal experiences, and intellectual influences—in order to identify and examine the sources that have stimulated and shaped his spirituality and theological thought. My point of departure is the social reality that has dominated Sobrino's life and the lives of most Salvadorans for the last thirty years: the Salvadoran civil war. I begin with a brief presentation of the historical and social forces that led to the war and to this day continue to shape the country. I complement this historical overview with a synopsis of the peace process and an assessment of what it has accomplished since its inception in 1992. The second section of this chapter briefly traces Sobrino's intellectual biography. Here I examine the changes that the study of philosophy and theology, first in the United States and then in Germany, wrought in his life, and the key influence that theologians such as Karl Rahner exercised on his theological formation. This section also recounts Sobrino's permanent return to San Salvador and locates him within the specific social and ecclesial context of El Salvador. It underscores how his experiences in El Salvador prompted the critical transformation of his consciousness, turning a young, European-born Jesuit full of missionary zeal for converting the poor and uneducated into a theologian infused with the realization that he was the one who had been awakened and converted through his encounters with the dispossessed. This section concludes by singling out the influence that Oscar Romero and Ignacio Ellacuría each had on Sobrino's personal life and theological development.

No other theologian has influenced Sobrino's work more directly than Ignacio Ellacuría. Thus the third section of this chapter explores Ellacuría's philosophical and methodological foundations. There I identify Ellacuría's most important contribution to Sobrino's work: a threefold model of how the human person confronts and engages reality. Because Sobrino has appropriated many of Ellacuría's epistemological, anthropological, and metaphysical theses, this final section provides the essential foundation for a comprehensive approach to Sobrino's theology and spirituality, as well as an opportunity to delineate the main features that will shape this project's discipleship of reconciliation.

El Salvador in Continued Crisis

In January 2012, the people of El Salvador marked the twentieth anniversary of the peace accords that ended their twelve-year civil war. While the accords brought an end to a violent conflict and were initially seen as a successful enterprise, recent appraisals of the Salvadoran peace process suggest a more ambiguous reality. In 1997, fifteen years after the accords were signed, Gregorio Rosa Chávez, the Roman Catholic auxiliary bishop of San Salvador, noted that "The [Salvadoran] people are disenchanted and do not feel that peace has arrived, because every day their anguish in-creases due to the poverty, lack of security, unemployment, and the high cost of living."[5] The bishop's comments reflect a persistent complaint against the Salvadoran peace process: that the deep-seated causes that gave rise to the gruesome war remain unresolved. As Christine Wade has pointed out, "Much of this re-evaluation of El Salvador's 'success' has been motivated by the failure of the Salvadoran peace process to redress pov-erty and inequality, which threaten to reignite conflict."[6] This reality has prompted some human-rights advocates to wonder whether there is enough political will "to solve the problems of injustice and marginaliza-tion which caused the conflict in the first place."[7]

The roots of the Salvadoran civil war lie in two interrelated factors: the historical inequality of the country's socioeconomic system and the illegiti-mate character of the political system that preserved it. Broadly speaking, the disparity of the Salvadoran social order and economy are a product of the unequal distribution of land and wealth that emerged, first, from the Spanish colonial systems of the *encomienda* and *repartimiento*, and later—and more directly—from an economic model based on the production and exportation of agricultural products that, since the nineteenth century, has centered on coffee.

Coffee production linked El Salvador with international markets and shaped the local economic structure through the financing and develop-ment of a national oligarchy that came to dominate the nation's destiny for most of the twentieth century. The oligarchy's exploitation of this crop demanded the expropriation of Indian communal lands (*ejidos*) and the creation of new laws to guarantee the availability of cheap labor. In time, the production of coffee fostered the economic expansion of the nation in other areas and became the axis of domestic political power.[8]

For the greater part of the last century, following a large popular in-surrection in 1931, military dictators governed the nation with the oligar-chy's blessing and charted the course of the country's development.[9] The acute inequality inherent in the country's socioeconomic system histori-cally benefited and supported a wealthy minority that enjoyed a lifestyle similar to that of developed countries, while most other Salvadorans expe-rienced chronic unemployment, wretched housing, deficient nutrition, in-adequate medical and educational services, and generally subhuman living conditions.

In the 1970s, after decades of fraudulent elections and increasing political repression, the absence of peaceful, transparent, and democratic
methods to attain and preserve political power further polarized an
already conflicted society and generated widespread insurrectional violence. Frustrated with the electoral system, people began to affiliate with
different types of revolutionary organizations. As political tensions deep-
ened, the level of violence increased and by the middle of 1980 a full-
scale civil war had erupted between the government and the leftist guerrilla
groups of the Farabundo Martí Front for National Liberation (FMLN).[10]
After twelve years of violent conflict, war-related casualties have been estimated at more than 75,000 dead, 8,000 disappeared, and 18,000 people
left with physical disabilities.[11]

On January 16, 1992, the FMLN and the government both reached the
conclusion that a military victory on either side was not possible, and they
jointly agreed to seek a political resolution.[12] The peace accords ended the
hostilities and called for the demobilization of military and guerrilla forces,
as well as the integration of their combatants into society.[13] These agreements mandated the formation of a truth commission to investigate the
most serious acts of violence that had occurred during the war, and to recommend methods to promote national reconciliation. In 1993, a year after
the accords were signed, the Salvadoran Truth Commission issued the
document "From Madness to Hope: The 12-Year War in El Salvador," which
noted that 85 percent of those who testified about violent crimes attributed
them to agents of the state and associated paramilitary organizations.[14]
The report was welcomed by human rights organizations within the country and was aptly described by Jon Sobrino as "the most important official
document in the country's recent history . . . a symbol of subversion and
liberation . . . [that] must be a foundational document for a new El Salvador."[15] Yet just five days after the commission published its findings, the
National Assembly passed a sweeping amnesty law for all those involved in
political crimes during the civil war, at the request of President Alfredo
Cristiani. The law prevented any legal action against the perpetrators named
by the commission.[16]

As a crude political solution aimed at the immediate pacification of the
country, the amnesty provided an expedient way to avoid dealing with
the abuses committed on both sides of the conflict. Today it continues to
be supported by some who prefer to "forgive and forget" rather than risk

the stability of the nation's still nascent democracy. The amnesty ignored the rights of the victims and rendered the findings of the Salvadoran Truth Commission largely nugatory. As theologian Juan Hernández Pico recently observed, the amnesty not only impeded the widespread and honest recognition of the crimes that transpired during the conflict, it also prevented the nation from taking responsibility for them.[17] In the end, the amnesty reinforced a social atmosphere of impunity and effectively pitted the hope for national justice against the wish for forgiveness and reconciliation.

Although the political amnesty and resulting impunity continue to haunt El Salvador, the problems that stem from the persisting inequality of the country's socioeconomic structures are even more serious. The transformation of these structures was one of the main objectives of the insurrectional forces, but the direct and strong influence exercised by the private sector on the peace talks guaranteed that these unjust structures were barely mentioned.[18] It should be noted that in the years since the war, neoliberal economic policies have been credited with stimulating moderate economic growth.[19] This growth, however, has chiefly benefited transnational corporations and the most affluent sectors of the population. Indeed, these policies have left the unjust socioeconomic structures essentially unchanged.[20]

In the meantime, El Salvador has become one of the most violent countries in the world, partially due to a surge of gang activity generated by the repatriation of thousands of young Salvadorans who were deported from the United States.[21] Although this violence is a complex problem, many social scientists agree that gang formation and criminal violence are tragic manifestations of the social exclusion, inequality, and poverty in which many Salvadorans still live.[22] Commenting on the situation of the country, political scientist Roland Paris has observed that "the current combination of endemic poverty, widening income inequalities, and pervasive criminal violence, suggests that liberal economic policies have, in several important ways, impeded rather than facilitated the consolidation of peace in El Salvador."[23] As a national poll conducted by the Jesuit-run University of Central America (UCA) in 2011 showed, all of this has led to a general dissatisfaction with the peace process.[24] Today, with its persistent economic inequality, widespread corruption and criminal violence, and fragile democracy, the situation of El Salvador can only be described as one of extended crisis. The deep ideological divisions evident in the war have

remained largely entrenched and the relatively frail civil society continues to be deeply polarized between the well-funded organizations that
represent the interests of the dominant class and those with very limited
resources that represent the concerns of the population at large.[25]

This is not to say that the peace accords contributed nothing toward the
reconciliation of the Salvadoran people. To the contrary, they led to the
purging of the armed forces, the reform of the national judicial and electoral systems, and the establishment of the FMLN as a legal political
party. In other words, the accords helped bring about a democratic transformation of the country's political life, opened the possibility for the further development of civil society, and planted the seeds of hope for a new
nation. Nevertheless, the prospect of a lasting reconciliation in El Salvador demands that past crimes be acknowledged and enduring sources of
conflict addressed. It also hinges on the renewal of the nation's culture
by a spirit of forgiveness that neither trivializes the experience of the victims nor excludes the former oppressors, but instead provides the stage
for a reconciled future.

This rehearsal of El Salvador's recent history has allowed us to locate
some of the key problems outlined in the previous chapter within the specific set of circumstances that unfold from the particularity of Jon Sobrino's adopted country. It is within and in response to this situation of
persistent conflict that Sobrino's theology was formed and developed. He
alludes to the contextual character of his theology when he notes that "I
never understood the [theological] task as a way to enter into an already
self-constituted reality called 'theology,' but as a way of thinking, reflecting, pondering if you want, on reality as this has been present and affected
me."[26] Indeed, it would be impossible to extract Sobrino's spirituality and
theology from the Salvadoran reality, where social contradictions and
persistent injustices are juxtaposed with an unrelenting hope for a better
future. This reality both challenges and kindles Sobrino's religious imagination just as it offers him the raw materials with which to engage, critically
appropriate, and make relevant the Christian tradition. At the same time,
the Salvadoran context offers us some initial insights into what we may ex-
pect from his theology: why certain themes, like liberation and the promise
of God's kingdom, are so central to it; why he approaches his theological
reflection from the perspective of the victims; and why the transformation of reality in light of God's Word is the central purpose behind his

theology.[27] The following section examines in more detail the intersection between the Salvadoran reality and Sobrino's life, and the impact that this encounter has had on the development of a theology and a spirituality that seek the healing, transformation, and reconciliation of the Salvadoran community and beyond.

The Transformation of a First-World Consciousness

In 1958, soon after joining the Society of Jesus, an eighteen-year-old Jon Sobrino was sent to El Salvador to continue his religious formation and begin his work as a missionary. Like many other young Jesuit missionaries before him, Sobrino arrived in Central America less intent on encountering and engaging a new world than on expanding his own.[28] He recalls that at the time he understood his mission as one to "help the Salvadorans replace their popular 'superstitious' religiosity with a more sophisticated kind, and . . . help the Latin American branches of the church (the European church) to grow."[29] With his heart still in Europe, and like many who initially witness Latin American poverty as something alien, distant, and entrenched within an unfamiliar landscape, Sobrino recounts that the poverty of the Salvadoran people did not move him. He did not believe it had anything to teach him. Although it was in front of him, he did not truly see it—"aun viendola . . . no la veía."[30] In time, however, this poverty would reshape his entire understanding of his missionary vocation, his work, and, indeed, his whole life.

Awakening from Dogmatic Slumber

Sobrino described his journey of personal transformation in a few autobiographical articles, noting that his personal and theological development was largely shaped by two turning points or awakening events that led him to a fuller and more honest engagement with the reality that surrounded him.[31] The first awakening was wrought by his formative studies in philosophy and theology—what he, alluding to Kant, calls his awakening from "dogmatic slumber."[32] In 1960, having finished his novitiate formation, Sobrino was sent to Saint Louis University, in Missouri, where he spent five years studying toward degrees in philosophy and civil engineering. After a brief period in San Salvador teaching math and philosophy as a Jesuit regent, Sobrino returned to the first world in 1968 for theological studies at the Hochschule Sankt Georgen in Frankfurt, Germany, which he completed in 1974, earning a doctorate in theology.

During this latter period of study, Sobrino was exposed to the rich philosophical heritage of the Enlightenment as well as to the unsettling thinking of the "masters of suspicion." His studies of Kant, Hegel, Marx, Unamuno, and Sartre were complemented by theological studies that not only reflected the legacy of modernity and the impact of historicity on scriptural criticism, but were also fueled by the new insights and enthusiasm with which Vatican II had infused the Catholic Church. As a result of these innovative currents of thought, Sobrino's theological understanding began to move away from a positivist study of dogmatic formulas toward one more contextualized by historical reality. Sobrino recounts that while working on his doctoral thesis on the Christologies of Jürgen Moltmann and Wolfhart Pannenberg, he disposed of abstract christological formulations and instead began to concentrate on the historical dimensions captured by the narratives about Jesus of Nazareth. "I discovered," Sobrino explains, "that Christ is none other than Jesus and that he conceived a utopia on which all too few have focused: the idea of the kingdom of God."[33]

Sobrino credits Karl Rahner with leaving him with "the most lasting and beneficial impression" during these years of theological formation.[34] Rahner articulated a topic that, at that time, was beginning to take center stage in Sobrino's theological development: the ultimate mystery of God, humanity, and all of reality. Even as a young theologian Sobrino came to realize, with the help of Rahner and others, that "this mystery bears within itself, at once, an excess of darkness as well as an excess of luminosity . . . little by little I began to see this mystery from the perspective of its luminosity."[35]

Writing years later on the twentieth anniversary of Rahner's death, Sobrino gratefully noted the significance of Rahner's theology to his understanding of God as ultimate mystery, and of the human person as a hearer and doer of God's Word who confronts this mystery in his or her daily life. Sobrino explained that Rahner reveals a God who, although remaining a holy mystery, is ultimately a God who encounters us in history in order to act on our behalf. In other words, this God is chiefly a saving God.[36] Rahner refers to God as the inescapable holy mystery that grounds the human person and all of reality, and thus notes that God will always remain the primordial and permanent mystery for humanity. At the same time, he insists that God has also offered Godself in radical proximity to his creation, thereby becoming present in the depths of human existence, summoning all human beings (and all of reality) into wholeness, and orienting them toward an encounter with mystery itself.[37] This orientation toward God, however, "cannot be understood as a capacity which is given and lived, and experienced and reflected upon independently of history."[38] Rather, for Rahner, any human experience of God is tied to the world and mediated through the concrete and particular human histories in the world.

If the young Sobrino stressed the content of Rahner's theology, a more mature Sobrino highlights the importance of Rahner's approach to the theological task—that is, "his way of approaching God through reflection on human reality, and of approaching human reality through reflection on God."[39] Reflecting on Rahner's influence upon liberation theology, Sobrino praises Rahner for underscoring the critical role that historical reality can play as a source and guide for theological thought. He notes that Rahner was a theologian who rejected dogmatic or idealized affirmations of what history or God might be, and instead took as his point of departure reality itself and reality's symbolic capacity to mediate the presence of God. "What struck me in Rahner's theology," Sobrino writes, "was how *reality itself* was its foundation. . . . [He] was outstanding in his fidelity to the real."[40]

In a similar vein, Sobrino thanks the German theologian for emphasizing the sacramental character of reality and the discernment of God's presence therein. He draws on Rahner's theological reflections on the Ignatian Spiritual Exercises, particularly his examination of the experience of "consolation without cause" in the rules for the discernment of spirits, to argue that just as Godself and God's will can be detected in those personal experiences of consolation that are not deducible from any other previous knowledge or universal principles, God's will and presence can also be grasped in history through the discernment of the signs of the times, which manifest a similar type of undeducibility (*indeducibilidad*).[41] As examples of such signs, Sobrino points to "the events, the needs and the longings" of the people, which "may be genuine signs of the presence or of the purpose of God"[42] as indicated by Vatican II and concretized in liberation theology's recognition of the irruption of the poor as the true sign of the times.

We will return to the discernment of the signs of the times and its central place in Sobrino's theological reflection in the following chapter. For now, it is sufficient to underline Rahner's impact on Sobrino's theology in at least three aspects: first, the understanding of God as salvific mystery; second, the sacramental understanding of reality, insofar as reality bears within itself the manifestation of God that can be discerned in the signs of the times; and third, the conception of the human person as a being freely endowed with the constitutive capacity to discern and grasp God's presence and will in history. This capacity to receive God's word—what Rahner would call openness to the transcendent—is what enables human beings to properly engage reality. It is this openness that grounds Sobrino's understanding of spirituality.

Although Sobrino credits his academic formation with helping him break away from the shackles of dogmatism, he also notes that this same training fostered in him a theology that was exclusively European in character. Moreover, he would come to recognize that he needed to undergo a more profound personal transformation, since this new knowledge had not given him the eyes or heart to respond to suffering in the world. Thus, as Sobrino expressly acknowledges, he "continued to sleep in the much deeper sleep of inhumanity."[43]

Awakening from the Sleep of Inhumanity:
Faces of the Poor, Faces of Christ

Sobrino's second, and perhaps more important, awakening began when he returned to El Salvador permanently in 1974 to work as a theologian at the Jesuit-run Central American University (Universidad Centroamericana "José Simeón Cañas"). This time the destitution and oppression in his adopted homeland would force him to reassess what he had learned in the universities of the First World and would shape his thought for years to come. Summarizing these events, Sobrino writes:

> In 1974, already in El Salvador and already with teaching responsibilities and taking my first steps in doing theology, there emerged another summons to awake. This was no longer the call elicited by Kant, but

prompted by Antonio Montesinos when he said: Why are you sleeping
in such a profound and lethargic slumber? It was the awakening to a
new reality: the reality of the poor and the victims, product of human
sin and oppression, including mine.[44]

Sobrino's awakening to the realities of a suffering world took place
within the larger transformative process already underway within Latin
American Christian churches as they struggled to recognize and come to
terms with "the irruption of the poor" in their midst. Since the 1950s,
when the continent experienced a demographic explosion that accelerated
internal migration among the rural poor as they sought better living conditions in urban areas, the poor had become increasingly visible to the non-
poor. The rapid shift of population from the countryside to the urban
slums made it hard for the non-poor to overlook the acute economic inequality and poverty that afflicted most of the population. Alarmed by these
injustices, many Latin Americans struggled to respond to the situation of
the whole continent.[45]

In countries throughout the continent, including El Salvador, lay movements that had begun to stress the active role of lay people in the world,
such as Catholic Action, *Cursillos de Cristiandad*, and the Legionaries of
Mary, started to expand at an exponential rate.[46] Catholic Action, arguably the largest and most influential among these groups, stimulated the
formation of labor unions as well as professional and student organizations, and eventually inspired the formation of Christian Democratic
parties. Even more decisive was the formation of *comunidades eclesiales
de base*, the base ecclesial communities (CEBs) that grew from a successful catechetical experiment initiated in 1956 at Barra do Pirai, Brazil.
These lay-led Christian communities anticipated the important responsibilities that Vatican II and Medellín would later ascribe to the laity. They
also played a crucial role in the development of a more autochthonous
Latin American church.[47]

Thus when Sobrino returned to El Salvador, he encountered a Christian community already engaged in the struggle to liberate themselves
from a world of poverty and injustice. As he recounts, "[I] found that some
of my fellow Jesuits had already begun to speak of the poor and of injustice and of liberation . . . [and] also found that some Jesuits, priests, religious, farmers, and students, even bishops, were acting on behalf of the

poor and getting into serious difficulties as a consequence."[48] Compelled by their faith to concretize their Christian hope through their actions, some Christians had joined not only explicitly religious movements, but also secular political organizations that were committed to the liberation of the oppressed and the eradication of injustice in the nation. The participation of countless Christians in social movements of liberation gave rise to a call for a new expression of the Christian church—one better attuned to the realities and difficulties of the vast and subjugated majorities.

Until this era, Latin American theologians had largely borrowed and applied to their situation insights from European theologies that had little or no bearing on their own social and historical context. Now they began to shift the focus of their reflection toward Christians' commitment to the cause of liberation, and to the conditions that inspired their actions. From this approach, new interpretations and language began to emerge as these theologians attempted to articulate the meaning of contemporary events for the Christian faith.[49] The theologians' horizon had been interrupted by the poor and the poor's efforts toward emancipation, and from this irruption a new soteriological question emerged: "What relationship is there between salvation and the historical process of human liberation?"[50]

Latin American theologians including Sobrino and Ellacuría built upon the insights of European theologians who had already rejected the radical neo-scholastic division between the "sacred" and the "profane," conceived of as two realities in which grace and nature coexist as absolutely separate layers on top of one another. In that view the experience of salvation was confined to the "sacred" order. As Ellacuría explains,

> On the one hand there was the *supernatural*: the Trinitarian God revealed to us by divine favor and grace. On the other hand there was the *natural*: [the human person] as he [or she] appeared to be *in se* [i.e., in him- or herself] and once and for all. This problematic has had incalculable impact on theology, preaching, asceticism, and the Church's encounter with the world, so that by our own day it has deformed Christian praxis and undermined the relevance of our theology.[51]

In place of the neo-scholastic scheme, liberation theologians emphasized a theology of grace that maintains a distinction, but not a separation, between the natural and the supernatural orders and that stresses the intrinsic orientation of the human person toward God.[52] Hence, Latin

American liberation theologians insisted that there are not two histories—one profane and one sacred—but only one wherein God and human beings interact and salvation takes place.[53] They further emphasized that it is within history and through the mediations provided by our world that the human person accepts or rejects God's grace. As such, salvation encompasses all of humanity and calls for the integral liberation of the human person in his or her interrelated material, spiritual, personal, and social-political dimensions.[54] The foregrounding of these concerns, and the choice of the poor as the main interlocutor, marked the birth of Latin American liberation theology.[55] These same concerns and options would largely shape both the agenda of the Second Conference of Latin American bishops, held in 1968, as well as Sobrino's theology in the years to come.

Medellín and the Salvadoran Church

The Latin American church of the mid-twentieth century was in many ways still a European transplant whose identity was rooted in its historic and institutional ties to the Spanish and Portuguese colonial powers. These connections informed the church's tendency during the nineteenth century to oppose independence movements while strengthening its ties with groups representing the traditional alliance of "conservative parties, landowners, and the old aristocracy."[56] Indeed, until the mid-twentieth century the church maintained this alliance and, at least institutionally, it tacitly sanctioned the socioeconomic structures that relegated most Latin Americans to oppressive living conditions.

Thus, the 1968 General Conference of Latin American Bishops in Medellín, Colombia, which sought to interpret the teachings of Vatican II in light of the Latin American reality, stands as a historical turning point in the life of the local and global Catholic Church.[57] If Vatican II left unaddressed the economic challenges facing the Latin American church, it nonetheless provided the methodological framework to confront them through its renewed attention to the historical dimension of the church and its corresponding change in attitude toward the modern world.

This attention to history was expressed by a scriptural image that would become a guiding principle in the Latin American reception of the council: discerning the signs of the times (Matt 16:3). The call to heed the signs of the times was already present in John XXIII's convocation of Vatican II, and it was further articulated in the council's documents (*Gaudium et Spes*, 4, 11).[58] These texts "call for the positive acknowledgement of history as an authentic 'place' wherein the imminent presence of the kingdom may be perceived."[59] It is only by attending to the situation in which people live and their experiences that the church can ground itself in its particular reality and discern from everyday facts the signs of consistency between the Christian tradition and the desires of human beings.

The bishops' analysis of the signs of the times—Latin American realities and the experience of the poor—marked Medellín's point of departure in formulating the church's renewed vision and mission. The conference took an honest view of the people's situation, describing it as "dismal poverty, which in many cases becomes inhuman wretchedness."[60] Indeed, the bishops fiercely denounced the extreme inequality between social classes, the forms of oppression exercised by the dominant groups, and the unjust actions of world powers. In a similar vein, the bishops called their own church to conversion, asserting that "the Church in Latin America should be manifested, in an increasingly clear manner, as truly poor, missionary, and paschal, separate from all temporal power and courageously committed to the liberation of each and every [human being]."[61] Hence, the conference clearly understood that the church's solidarity with the poor is at the center of its vocation to follow Christ and serve as he did.[62]

Giving voice to the experiences of the poor throughout the continent, Medellín described the situation of the Latin American nations as one racked with "institutionalized violence" stemming from structural injustice. Anticipating the widespread violence that would erupt in the following decade in countries like El Salvador, Nicaragua, Chile, and Peru, the bishops urgently insisted that peace must be rooted in the work of justice. As one of the most important final documents that came forth from the conference put it:

> Peace is, above all, a work of justice. It presupposes and requires the establishment of a just order in which persons can fulfill themselves as human beings, where their dignity is respected, their legitimate aspirations satisfied, their access to truth recognized, their personal freedom guaranteed; an order where persons are not objects but agents of their own history.[63]

Both the Medellín conference and the subsequent conference of the Latin American bishops at Puebla (1979) echoed and reinforced the efforts of the progressive movements within the Salvadoran church to mobilize their communities in response to the growing social and political crisis. As discussed previously, the El Salvador that Sobrino returned to in 1974 was rife with appalling poverty and inequality, as well as increasing violence. The vast majority of Salvadorans had steadily become aware of the country's socioeconomic trends and inequality, and many had begun to organize in popular movements to express their aspirations and demand justice. In response, the government had transformed the country into a militarized state in which oppression, repression, and widespread violence ruled.

Within this context, the bishops' call for the church to become a "church of the poor" became a rallying cry for those Salvadoran church leaders who began to speak out against the inequalities of the country. For these leaders, "the problem came down to fidelity to the pastoral approach outlined by the Second Vatican Council, and already applied to Latin America by the Latin American Episcopal Conference in Medellín. . . . [T]his approach implied . . . an identification with the sufferings and with the hopes of the people, especially with those of the poor and the oppressed."[64]

Not all within the church, however, embraced this new ecclesial vision. Old alliances and interests, combined with ignorance and fear of change, persisted within much of the Salvadoran church, and many of its leaders remained deaf to the pleas of the poor. Nonetheless, the Society of Jesus, of which Sobrino is a member, along with other religious orders, a significant and active part of the laity, and the more progressive members of the Salvadoran clergy, adopted the teaching of the Latin American bishops and began to forge theological and pastoral answers to the demands of the Salvadoran reality. Significant parts of the church, under the leadership of Archbishop Luis Chávez y González (archbishop of San Salvador from 1939 to 1977), sought wider participation from the laity by developing new centers for training lay leaders who in turn assumed important responsibilities within the church's life. New organizations of Christian workers and peasants were founded, and base ecclesial communities, which met regularly to discuss how to live the Christian faith within the Salvadoran reality, spread rapidly.

By the late 1970s, these initial ecclesial efforts were flourishing under the unconditional support and courageous leadership of Archbishop Oscar Romero, who succeeded Chávez y González in 1977. With this shift in pastoral approach, the church began to undermine the prevailing social order that was founded on injustice and oppression. Soon, the consequences of such a stance would become clear as members of the Salvadoran church became increasingly persecuted.[65]

The Influence of Two Martyrs

Throughout this time in El Salvador, two church figures with distinct charisms emerged in Salvadoran public life to appeal for the rights of the disenfranchised and to advocate a peaceful solution to the national crisis: Monsignor Oscar Arnulfo Romero and the prominent Jesuit philosopher and theologian Ignacio Ellacuría. These two men, whose exemplary lives were cut short by politically motivated violence, greatly influenced Sobrino's personal and theological development at this stage in his life.

Monsignor Oscar A. Romero

Sobrino met Monsignor Romero soon after the former's return to El Salvador, but the beginning of their relationship was by no means auspicious. Sobrino distrusted Romero, at that time the auxiliary bishop of San Salvador, because he had developed a conservative reputation when he initially resisted those who sought to implement the Medellín directives. It did not help that Monsignor Romero had been instrumental in removing the Jesuits from teaching at the seminary of San Salvador in 1972—a formation task they had performed since 1915—nor that in the following year, Romero, as auxiliary bishop and editor of the diocesan weekly *Orientación*, had published an editorial that indirectly accused the teachers of the Jesuit high school, Externado San José, of indoctrinating the students with Marxist political ideas that perverted the principles of Medellín.[66]

Likewise, Romero was not initially impressed with Sobrino's way of thinking. In 1974, Romero attended a talk that Sobrino gave to Salvadoran seminarians on the "historical Jesus"; Sobrino recounts that this was the first time he actually saw Romero and that he was daunted by the way the future archbishop had subtly but clearly shown his displeasure with the topic of the presentation. Such displeasure was concretely expressed two years later when Romero, preaching from the pulpit of the Metropolitan cathedral on the occasion of the national festivities of the Divine Savior, implicitly criticized Sobrino's historical Christology as being "rationalistic, revolutionary and hate-filled."[67]

Romero's initial misgivings toward Sobrino's christological approach and, more generally, toward most of the emerging liberation theology, were gradually complicated by his experience ministering directly with the poor. This encounter began a profound personal transformation that would forever alter his relationship not only with Sobrino, but also with the Society of Jesus and the nation as a whole. This transformation began with Romero's experiences of his rural and impoverished constituency as bishop of Santiago de Maria (1974–1977), and intensified after the murder of his close friend Father Rutilio Grande.[68]

Grande's death, in particular, marked a turning point in Romero and Sobrino's relationship, and over the next three years Sobrino became a close friend and collaborator of the archbishop. In his capacity as archbishop, Romero often asked Sobrino to shed theological light on some of the gravest challenges experienced by the Salvadoran church at that moment. The collaboration was decidedly mutual, and Romero proved a strong influence on the development of certain themes in Sobrino's theological work. Notably, Sobrino credits Romero with leading him to reflect on the issues of martyrdom, violence, and the church and its mission of evangelization.[69]

Even beyond their professional relationship, Romero's friendship, leadership, and example were immensely significant for Sobrino's life and work. As Sobrino's writings reflect, he regarded Romero not only as a true prophet, teacher, and witness of God, but above all as someone who, like Jesus, was *good news* for the poor.[70] Sobrino writes that Romero was good news in his manner of being toward the poor and the victims, in his commitment to bringing the kingdom of God, and in the solidarity and love that his faith expressed.[71] When Sobrino assesses the influence that Romero exercised on his life and work, he attests that Romero has been his "theological light and inspiration." In Sobrino's own words:

[W]ithout Archbishop Romero, I could never have achieved a satisfactory theological formulation of things as basic as the mystery of God,

the church of the poor, hope, martyrdom, Christian fellowship, the essence of the gospel as good news, or even Jesus Christ, whose three years
of life and mission, cross and resurrection, have now been illuminated
for me by Archbishop Romero's three years as archbishop. Archbishop
Romero also made me realize that one must also use reality as a theological argument.[72]

This apprehension of reality as a theological argument would prove
central to Sobrino's theological contribution. That being said, Romero's
influence on Sobrino cannot be grasped solely in terms of theological
themes, insights, or method. Perhaps a better way to describe the monsignor's influence is to say that through the concreteness of his life and example and amidst an oppressive and conflicted reality, Romero embodied for
Sobrino what it means to be a follower of Christ. As such, Romero illuminated for Sobrino like no one else the "what" (content), the "how" (method),
and the "for whom" (purpose) of a theology incarnated in the Salvadoran
reality.[73]

Ignacio Ellacuría, the Friend

If Sobrino learned the importance of right Christian praxis from Romero,
from Ignacio Ellacuría he learned that there is nothing more practical than
a good theory.[74] By the time that Sobrino returned to San Salvador for
good and went to live in the same community as Ellacuría, the latter was
already widely known as an accomplished philosopher and theologian who
had become a highly respected and somewhat controversial leader among
the members of the Central American Jesuit Vice-Province.[75] After com-
pleting his doctoral studies in philosophy at the Complutense University
in Madrid, Ellacuría returned to El Salvador in 1967 to work at the recently
founded University of Central America "José Simeon Cañas" (UCA), and
the following year was appointed to the university's steering board.

Two years after Ellacuría's return and a year after the Medellín conference, the Jesuits of the vice-province of Central America gathered for a
week-long Ignatian retreat that began to transform their missionary self-
understanding and redirect their apostolic efforts in accordance with the
guidelines set by the Latin American Bishops' Conference. As a co-director
of the retreat, the young Ellacuría caused a great stir and some division

among the members of the vice-province with his confrontational style and his demand that the Central American Jesuits forego the values of the First World and instead engage in apostolic work that more effectively addressed the Latin American reality.[76]

Ellacuría's initial request for a shift in the direction of the mission of the Central American Jesuits was eventually confirmed by the Society of Jesus's Thirty-Second General Congregation (1975), which called Jesuits to the service of faith and the promotion of justice. This call for social justice emerged from the Society's legacy of incarnational Ignatian spirituality and framed the mission and ministry of both Ignacio Ellacuría and Jon Sobrino.[77]

The sixteen-year collaboration between Sobrino and Ellacuría revolved around their work at the UCA but was never distant from the reality of the nation. Ellacuría, who in 1979 became the UCA's rector, firmly believed that the university had the responsibility to become an effective tool in serving the poor majorities through uncovering and studying the causes of their country's unjust reality.[78] As the UCA used its full institutional power to promote the democratic transformation of the nation, Ellacuría dedicated his life to forging a philosophy and theology of liberation. In the last years of his life, the conflicted situation of the country prompted him to become a public intellectual and an active participant in the Salvadoran political process until his murder on November 16, 1989—along with five other Jesuits with whom he lived at the UCA, their housekeeper, and her daughter—at the hands of an elite U.S.-trained battalion of the Salvadoran army. Sobrino was out of the country at the time, and thus became the community's sole survivor.[79]

Sobrino has written candidly and frequently about the exceptional impact that Ellacuría had upon him as both of their lives and projects were moved and shaped by the heart-wrenching reality of the Salvadoran people. At the personal level, Sobrino has noted that as important as Ellacuría's prodigious intellectual capacity and creativity were, it was Ellacuría's passion for service that ultimately defined his close friend—a service dedicated to the ones Ellacuría defined as the "crucified."[80] This service had one objective in mind—"to take the people down from the cross"—and was concretized in three areas in which, for Sobrino, Ellacuría was exemplary: "his hunger and thirst for justice for the crucified people, his tireless condemnation and analysis of the truth about their crucifixion, and the steadiness and fidelity of his praxis toward seeing them taken down from the cross."[81]

In Sobrino's first "Letter to Ignacio Ellacuría," which was read in 1990 at the liturgical celebration that commemorated the anniversary of the massacre at the UCA, Sobrino synthesized the fundamental legacy that Ellacuría bestowed upon him: "nothing is more essential than the practice of compassion for a crucified people, and . . . nothing is more human and humanizing than faith."[82] This insight captures the concerns at the heart of Sobrino's spirituality and theology. Thus, to better understand the development of these two thinkers we must further examine the intellectual influence that Ellacuría had on Sobrino's work, particularly as it pertains to the development of his approach to encountering reality and pursuing the theological task.

Ellacuría's Legacy: A Philosophical Framework for Sobrino's Spirituality

Most students of Sobrino's theology are initially startled by the ubiquitous influence of Ellacuría's philosophical and theological thought on his work. That influence, however, is not really surprising since, as I have discussed, Ellacuría was for many years both one of Sobrino's closest friends and his main intellectual interlocutor. Indeed, as one moves through Sobrino's theology, it becomes apparent that he depends upon Ellacuría's work to engage some of the most important theological themes. The following sections thus examine specific aspects of Ellacuría's thought to ascertain his contribution to the development of Sobrino's spirituality.[83] This spirituality grounds Sobrino's approach to the theological task and provides the foundation for the Christian discipleship of reconciliation that I will advance in the following chapters. As we will see, Sobrino defines spirituality as *the spirit with which a human person engages reality*. Attending to Ellacuría's intellectual legacy, then, is essential for this project given that no other theologian, perhaps not even Karl Rahner, has informed Sobrino's understanding of the human person and his or her relationship to reality more deeply than Ignacio Ellacuría.

Ellacuría's philosophical and theological approach is itself influenced by the work of the Spanish philosopher Xavier Zubiri (1898–1983). Ellacuría relies heavily on Zubiri's metaphysics and epistemology to explain how human existence is dynamically and deeply interwoven with reality. While a comprehensive treatment of Zubiri's or Ellacuría's work is beyond the limits of this project, I start with a brief summary of Zubiri's appreciation of human intelligence since it is so vital for understanding Ellacuría's—and by extension Sobrino's—interpretation of how the human person can and should engage reality. After that, I examine the anthropological and theological elements in Ellacuría's work that will prepare us to approach Sobrino's spirituality in the next chapter. Thus the rest of this chapter is divided into four parts: Zubiri's understanding of sentient intelligence (sensory intelligence) as a means to overcome the distortions of idealistic thinking, and as the cognitive function that enables the human person's engagement of reality; Zubiri's *theologal* understanding of reality, which offers an account of God's presence in the world; Ellacuría's concept of *historical reality* as the highest manifestation of reality in which the human person encounters God; and Ellacuría's formulation of how the human person through his or her intelligence confronts and apprehends reality. The first three philosophical and theological presuppositions in turn shore up the last.

Sentient Intelligence: Encountering Reality Within Its Midst

The Salvadoran philosopher and former student of Ellacuría, Héctor Samour, has argued that his teacher found in the thought of Xavier Zubiri the basis to deploy a novel type of realist philosophy. This philosophy is characterized by a distinct explanation of reality and a new understanding of human intelligence that converge to overcome the pitfalls of idealistic thinking.[84] Ellacuría's point of departure resides in Zubiri's claim that from the times of the classic Greek philosophers, beginning with Parmenides (early fifth century BCE) up to modernity, most of Western philosophical thought has been afflicted by an idealism that has had a reductionist and thus distorting effect on our understanding of both human intelligence and reality.[85] For Zubiri, and later Ellacuría, the roots of this distortion can be traced to the epistemological error that arises when the functions of human sensation (seeing, touching, hearing) are artificially separated from those of human intellection (explaining, interpreting, judging) in the process of cognition. This separation has led to largely disregarding the contribution that our senses make to the process of understanding. It has also reduced our concept of understanding to solely what our intelligence can logically predicate, conceive, or judge about reality. Simultaneously, the separation of the functions of the senses from those of the intellect has led us to equate our conceptualization of reality with reality itself, rather than perceiving it in its interrelated and open-ended dynamism.[86]

Such an idealized understanding of reality has serious repercussions for the way human persons engage and relate to the world. It precludes us from what Sobrino calls "being honest with reality," since it largely prevents us from properly grasping reality as this truly is and thus from attending to the demands that reality places upon us.[87]

To correct this distortion, Zubiri "attempts to forge a middle road between a realism that prioritizes reality over reason, and an idealism that prioritizes knowledge over reality."[88] He argues that there is a convergence between the overall nature and structure of reality (metaphysics) and human beings' epistemological power. Zubiri explains that "it is impossible to assert an intrinsic priority of knowing over reality or of reality over knowing. Knowing and reality are, in their very roots, strictly and rigorously codetermining."[89] Thus, the Spanish philosopher locates the human person as firmly embedded within the reality of the world (intramundane reality) and insists that human sensation and intellection, though distinct, constitute a single and unitary act of apprehension in the process of gaining knowledge.[90] In a similar vein, Ellacuría argues that "[r]eality is sensed, is apprehended as reality by the senses, and only if reality is in some way sensed can it really be conceived and thought, that is, as reality."[91] Thus, in the moment of apprehension, human sensation not only provides us with content but it also actively recognizes that the objects sensed are both interrelated and have their own independent constitution—that they are something in themselves apart from us.[92] Essential to Zubiri's and Ellacuría's structure of human cognition is the recognition that "[t]he human being's total physical reality is the primary reality from which the human apprehends intelligently (intelige), knows (conoce), and understands (entiende)," and thus that it is through their sentient intelligence that human beings are immersed in and have direct access to reality.[93] By making reality formally present to the human person, sentient intelligence enables us to honestly respond to what reality requires from us.

Reality, however, goes beyond what we can directly grasp. As Diego Gracia notes, "the word 'reality' has two meanings in Zubiri: reality as formality (reality *qua* given in apprehension), and 'reality as fundamentality' (reality *qua* the actualization in a sensible apprehension of the thing beyond apprehension)."[94] Proposing an understanding of reality that can be described as open material realism, Ellacuría explains that reality as fundamentality refers to the transcendental function of reality "through which, by being installed in real things and without abandoning or annihilating them, we physically extend and expand ourselves by means of our modest intellective sensibility toward the real as real, toward reality that is always open."[95] In other words, reality understood as fundamentality points to the transcendental dimension of reality that humans encounter through their sentient intelligence, and ultimately to the relationship between God—the absolute reality that grounds all other realities—and the world.

The Human Person and the Theologal Dimension of Reality

In order to speak of the relationship between God and humanity, Zubiri first turns to the human person's experience in the world, noting that human beings find themselves already existing; they are not the cause of their existence but are "implanted into existence . . . implanted in being."[96] Existence, for Zubiri, is something freely bestowed on all human beings that prompts them to realize their selves, and this process of actualization takes place within a reality that shapes, supports, and fosters their existence.

This interdependent relationship with reality is why the Spanish philosopher describes the human person as a "relative absolute."[97] While the human person is an "absolute" insofar as she possesses her own features that distinguish her from other things in reality, such absoluteness is relative since her existence is always structured by interactions with other things in reality. Indeed, it is through these interactions that she confronts herself, shapes her identity, chooses certain possibilities over others, and realizes her existence. In a similar fashion, Sobrino avers that "being a person is being able to enter into relationship with another" and argues that it is only through its engagement with reality that human life achieves its full meaning.[98] As you will see, he also intimates that reality itself is constituted by a "more" that supports and gives direction to our engagement of reality.[99]

In more precise philosophical terms, Zubiri defines this "more" present within reality as the *power of the real* and describes it as a force that while not a proper feature of things or beings themselves is present in and empowers all of reality.[100] For Zubiri, that the presence of the power of the real is something *in* but *distinct from* the things and beings of reality suggests an internal structure that, although distinct from reality, roots and supports this same reality. As noted previously, Zubiri describes this structure as the *fundament* of reality. Thus, Zubiri asserts, the "power of the real in things is none other than the occurrence of the fundament in them."[101] It is because of the presence of this power—this "more" in reality—that reality imposes itself on the human person as something ultimate that functions as a ground of possibilities from which she is impelled to choose how to act and configure her own reality.[102] In the end, it is only because of and through the power of the real that humans can realize themselves as human beings.

Zubiri enlists the term "religation" to describe the human person's constitutive dimension through which she is tied back (religated) to the fundament of reality and the empowerment that this fundament bestows upon her through the power of the real.[103] Indeed, for Zubiri, that which religates and thus empowers the human person is none other than God. He writes,

> The human being finds God as she realizes herself as a person in a religated manner, encountering God in the dimension of the power of the real. As such, she finds God in all the real things and in her own person (which also mediates the power of the real). Thus, the power of the real precisely consists in that real things without being God or a moment of God are nonetheless real "in" God, that is, their reality is God *ad extra*. Therefore, to say that God is transcendent does not indicate that God is transcendent "to" things but that God is transcendent "in" things.[104]

Clearly, for Zubiri, God is not a reality we encounter as an entity, a concrete being, or a thing among other objects of reality. God is not something opposed to or separate from human beings and things, nor is God proper to or coextensive with them. In fact, it is precisely because God is transcendent *in* humans and things and not *away* from them that "in some mode they are a configuration of God *ad extra*."[105] As Zubiri notes, "What of God there may be in [the human person] is only the religation through which we are open to Him, and in this religation God becomes patent to us."[106] Hence, while religation does not place human beings before the precise reality of God *in se*, it opens up for them the sphere of the divine (the power of the real) and places them constitutively within it (that is, within the fundament).[107]

Religation then confronts the human person with what Zubiri, Ellacuría, and later Sobrino call the theologal dimension of reality—that dimension of reality that is ultimate because it is both imbued with God's presence and rooted in God. "There is," Ellacuría tells us, "a theologal dimension of things and based on this dimension a religious encounter with God is possible."[108] Because God grounds all of reality the human person must turn to and confront reality in order to reach God. Through her religation to the power of the real, the human person is, in a manner of speaking, seized by what is absolute and ultimate in her and in reality— God. God empowers the human person to freely accept and respond to the demands and possibilities that reality in its ultimate dimension places upon her, and to configure her life according to God.

Through concepts like the "power of the real," "fundament," and particularly "religation," Zubiri articulates the theologal dimension of reality and thus outlines the relationship between God and the world. As Michael Lee has rightly noted, Zubiri provides Ellacuría (and later Sobrino) with a way of speaking of God's radical transcendence without this transcendence ever opposing God's involvement in the world or this involvement implying that there is an identification between the divine and the human realm.[109] In other words, while a deist posits a self-sustaining world from which God removes God's involvement after creation, and a pantheist claims an immanent God who is synonymous and coextensive with the creation, religation describes a God who grounds and energizes reality even as God transcends the world. The world is rooted and subsists in God, and it is *in* the world's reality—and not away from it—that God transcends the world.

By way of comparison, Zubiri's notion of religation functions in the relationship between humanity and God in a manner somewhat analogous to Karl Rahner's supernatural existential—the God-given existential capacity of every person to receive God's gratuitous self-communication as a constitutive element of human existence that is nonetheless not part of the person's original nature. Rahner's formulation of the supernatural existential captures his important contribution to last century's theological debate on the relationship between nature and grace, and represents one of the most important insights from which Ellacuría and Sobrino also develop their understanding of human salvation as one taking place in history.[110]

Like Zubiri, Rahner holds that human experience can give us privileged access to the mystery of God. Such access is possible because from the moment of creation God has transformed human existence, radicalizing it with the capacity to receive God's own self-communication. Even if only in the form of an offer, God's self-communication orients the human person toward God.[111] While Rahner understands human persons as free beings responsible for their self-realization, the supernatural existential preconditions the way their freedom is exercised and how their realization is attained. Because human beings are in their constitution always oriented to God, their acceptance of who they are as beings and their efforts toward self-realization necessarily coincide with their acceptance of God's self-communication. This means that a human person's genuine development and self-realization are inexorably tied to actualizing her capacity for God. Since, for Rahner, "all beings are by their nature symbolic, because they necessarily 'express' themselves in order to attain their own nature,"[112] when the human person positively corresponds to God's self-communication she becomes symbolic reality—a personal embodiment of divine love that expresses her ontological reality—and thus she becomes a living manifestation of the mystery of God in time and space.

Both Zubiri's religation and Rahner's supernatural existential constitute the human person as having the capacity to encounter and be empowered and aided by God's grace, in order to be configured according to the divine. Both define God's relationship to humanity as an integral part of the historical condition of human existence without identifying this existence with God *in se*. In other words, they argue for a unity of nature and grace that fully acknowledges the distinction between them. While the notion of the supernatural existential allows Rahner to speak of salvation as taking place within the history of the world,[113] his theology stresses the individual and the subjective relationship of the human person with God. As the next section demonstrates, Ellacuría builds on Zubiri's notion of the reality of the world (intramundane reality) to expand Rahner's understanding of the supernatural existential by placing the latter in the context of history, and more specifically, within what he calls *historical reality.*

Historical Reality and the Ethical Principle of Reality

Ellacuría's notion of historical reality has a specific metaphysical meaning. It does not primarily refer to particular historical events. Rather, for him, reality is best understood as an intrinsically dynamic and diverse unity in which "ever higher forms of reality emerge from, retain, and elevate those forms which preceded them."[114] Sobrino shares a similar intuition when he notes, "Life is a reality that is by its very nature always open to more; it is something dynamic that points to a development of itself to fulfill itself on various levels, with new possibility and new demands."[115] For both Ellacuría and Sobrino, within this dynamic and complex unity that encompasses all of human life, the dimension of the historical represents the highest qualitative form of reality in that it assumes all other types of reality—material, biological, personal, and social. Historical reality "is the whole of reality assumed into the social reign of freedom; it is reality exhibiting its richest manifestations and possibilities."[116] As such, it is where the possibilities for new ways of reality are more clearly disclosed. History is where human beings work out their personal self-realization, where the members of the human species seek their social reconciliation, and where finite reality, through the human person, opens itself to the absolute and seeks its transcendent realization.

Martin Maier has rightly argued that Ellacuría rearticulates Rahner's notion of the supernatural existential within historical reality, and consequently that "Ellacuría supplants a naturalistic conception of reality with a historical conception of reality, and an individualistic conception of the human person with a sociohistorical conception."[117] Hence, for Ellacuría, history, and not the natural world or the human person in his or her individual capacity, is the most proper locus of revelation because it is in history that human freedom interrupts and transforms nature by positively responding (or not) to God's communication and thus making (or not) God present in the world. As such, history is the most appropriate hermeneutical vantage point for any interpretation of reality, particularly in contrast to the cosmological starting point of the Greeks or the anthropocentric one of modernity.[118]

While Rahner stresses the distinction, but never separation, between the natural and the supernatural orders within the human person, Ellacuría emphasizes the distinction between "salvation in history" (human history) and "salvation history" (history of God),[119] even as he insists that in actuality there are not two separate histories but only one history in which both God and humans intervene.[120] Similarly, if for Rahner the notion of pure "human nature" (humanity devoid of grace) is not a historical fact but a concept signifying the remainder of what would be left if we were to subtract the supernatural existential from a person, for Ellacuría history is never ungraced nor without the possibility of giving more of itself—that is, of transcending itself. Following Zubiri, Ellacuría argues that history itself is always constituted with and elevated by a theologal dimension—a transcendental openness to God—that grounds, infuses, and directs history toward its self-realization in God, which gives history the capacity to become a saving history.

Speaking from a theological perspective, Ellacuría notes that, while God is manifested analogically in all of reality (because in every act of creation there is a manifestation *ad extra* of God's Trinitarian life), personal and social history represent the only dimensions of reality that incorporate both the metaphysical density and the openness to transcendence that allows humans to participate in God's Trinitarian life.[121] In other words, only in social and personal history can the double gratuitousness of God's creation and salvation come about.

"Salvation in history," then, refers to the potential character of history as a structure of possibilities that generate the capacity to mediate salvation or, conversely, the rejection of salvation. Hence, whereas "salvation in history" is the privileged and inescapable medium for salvation, "salvation history" underscores the actualization of this capacity through the historical praxis of the human person that becomes evident in concrete historical events. Salvation history does not happen mechanically and thus is not assured. Rather, human history presents itself as a single but deeply ambiguous reality that bears a history of both grace and sin, which confronts us with the question of whether it will become a history of salvation or one of perdition.[122]

As you have seen so far, the conditions of possibility for history's realization are given by the convergence between the structure of reality and the structure of the human intellect, which allows the human person to open herself to reality and its transcendent dimension.[123] It is sentient intelligence's capacity to be open to reality that makes it possible for the human person to apprehend things in their own right and beyond the stimuli they offer, to confront herself in the midst of other realities, and to choose among different possibilities available to her. While the human person's freedom is not absolute, because she is bound to reality and supported by the power of the real, she is called to self-determination through the choices she makes.[124]

Nevertheless, Ellacuría is mindful of the possibility that the human person may ignore the demands of reality and thus implicitly the demands for the realization of human history. This may occur when a person does not move beyond her biological nature and the sensible, stimulatory capacity that gives her access to reality.[125] To be sure, this biological or "animal" nature is necessary for human realization. But it can also be a source of alienation since it may ultimately dominate the human person by confining her, for instance, to pursue only the more functional, biological human concerns and thus to neglect the possibilities that her openness to reality affords her.[126]

In this regard, Ellacuría insists that it is in fact the human person's openness to reality that gives her the capacity to take an ethical stance vis-à-vis reality. As a being capable of transcending some of her natural determinations, the human person has the responsibility to abide by what Ellacuría calls the "ethical principle of reality," and thus to exercise her openness to reality in order to foster her own realization and to respond with her actions to the demands of what is ultimate in reality.[127] Here, Ellacuría is asserting in philosophical terms that which is central to Christian praxis: personal conversion and transformation of reality according to God's will. For Ellacuría, such praxis of collaboration is vital to the world because "reality will not come to be what it should be with respect to the human, if the [human person] does not positively take charge of it."[128] This taking charge of reality has a well-defined structure that unfolds according to the manner in which human intelligence relates to reality.[129]

Engaging Reality

In his 1975 article "Toward a Philosophical Foundation for Latin American Theological Method," Ellacuría explains the philosophical presuppositions that support his theological method. These presuppositions proceed from Zubiri's understanding of sentient intelligence, reflect Ellacuría's historical interpretation of reality, and assert the ethical role of human intelligence. They indicate that, for Ellacuría, the end purpose of human intelligence is not only to capture the meaning of reality and advance knowledge, but first and foremost to apprehend reality itself and to confront its demands in order to transform it toward its greatest possible realization.

Sobrino has been quick to recognize the profound soteriological implications that this way of understanding human intelligence has, both for defining the theological task and for the manner in which the human person should engage reality. In fact, he acknowledges that "this way of envisaging the functioning of understanding is one of the aspects of Ellacuría's thought that has made the greatest impact on me."[130] Indeed, Ellacuría's text on the subject is often referenced in Sobrino's work and it has become a classic for many Latin American theologians.[131] For our purpose, it is worth citing at length:

> This act of confronting ourselves with real things in their reality has a threefold dimension: realizing the weight of reality, which implies being in the reality of things (and not merely being before the idea of things or being in touch with their meaning), being "real" in the reality of things, which in its active character of being is exactly the opposite of being thing-like and inert, and implies being among them through their material and active mediations; shouldering the weight of reality, an expression which points to the fundamentally ethical character of intelligence, which has not been given to us so that we could evade our real commitments, but rather to take upon ourselves what things really are and what they really demand; taking charge of the weight of reality, an expression which points to the praxis-oriented character of intelligence which only fulfills its function, including its

CONFRONTING A CONFLICTED REALITY   81

character of knowing reality and comprehending its meaning when it assumes as its burden doing something real.[132]

Thus, human apprehension and confrontation with reality has three interrelated dimensions: realizing the weight of reality (*el hacerse cargo de la realidad*); shouldering the weight of reality (*el cargar con la realidad*); and taking charge of the weight of reality (*el encargarse de la realidad*).[133] As Sobrino and other Ellacuría scholars have noted, these three dimensions correspond respectively to the noetic, ethical, and praxical ways or levels through which the structure of human intelligence encounters reality.[134] In this regard, it is important to keep in mind that, for Ellacuría, the exercise of intelligence always includes all three dimensions and that each of them includes the other two: "each reflects the operation of intelligence, each engages the person as a moral being, and each is geared to action."[135]

Realizing the weight of reality stresses the noetic aspect of our confrontation with reality. It is the act of knowing that seeks to grasp reality as it fully presents itself to us in all of its dynamism. In theological terms, it entails the human person recognizing the ambiguous character of reality as both sinful and graced. This knowing, however, is not simply the gathering of data, nor the passive observation of an event from a distance, nor even standing before the meaning or the concept of things as if reality were something extrinsic to the human person. Rather, the knower is himself fully embedded in reality.

Thus, to properly grasp reality the human person must take a stance before reality and actively situate—incarnate—himself in those situations of reality from which he can best be "in touch with the reality of things" and discern the demands that reality places upon him. To this end, Ellacuría insists that not all locations offer the same epistemological access to reality, but rather in certain places or situations the theologal character of reality is more clearly manifest. Hence, as a facet of the theological exercise of intelligence, this noetic dimension also incorporates an ethical and praxical aspect of engaging reality. For it calls us not only to scrutinize the reality that confronts us but also to locate ourselves in those places of reality that manifest a greater density and dynamism—that is, in those places or situations where the fullness of reality as a historical bearer of sin and grace is most apparent.

It should be noted, then, that while historical reality has its own dynamism and seeks its own realization, because it reveals itself to us as something ambiguous—as something bearing both grace and sin—such reality presents itself not only as a ground of possibilities but also as a burden of negativity that must be grasped, shouldered, and transformed.

Shouldering the weight of reality stresses the ethical dimension of intelligence. While realizing the weight of reality leads to discerning the ambiguous character of reality as both sinful and graced, shouldering reality's weight demands that the subject be willing to assume the responsibility that reality places upon him. In other words, the reality we apprehend also confronts us, questions us, and makes demands upon us. As self-reflecting and religated beings who are both intimately interwoven with all of reality and yet capable of transcending their natural determinations, humans can partake in the responsibility of moving history toward its own realization (and reconciliation) and thus must be willing to shoulder its weight. In a world weighted by the negativity of sin, opting to engage this ethical dimension of intelligence will often lead the human person into direct conflict with those forces that foster the negativity of the world and cause us to experience and bear, in our own existence, the negativity we initially opted to confront.

As noted previously, for Ellacuría, how well we honor our commitment to reality depends on the location from which we choose to engage and be affected by reality. More specifically, he argues that the world of the oppressed is the place from which God's revelation and reality are best grasped. Hence, from a theological perspective, recognizing the irruption of the poor in history and opting to incarnate oneself therein stresses the noetic dimension of engaging reality, while a commitment to the poor and willingness to accept responsibility for the demands that this option ensues evinces the ethical dimension of engaging reality.

Taking charge of the weight of reality points to the praxical dimension of intelligence. If realizing the weight of reality leads to discerning the sinful and graced character of reality, and if shouldering the weight of reality unfolds in making an option vis-à-vis reality, taking charge of its weight means participating in actions that seek the transformation of reality into what reality should be. As Ellacuría explains, the duty to engage in the project of transforming reality points to the "essentially praxis oriented character of the human person and of human life, which is manifested ethically as the necessity of taking charge of the weight of reality, his own and that of others, which has to be realized gradually and whose realization is his responsibility."[136] Thus the praxis that emerges when the human person properly exercises her openness to reality has both an ethical as well as a metaphysical character because upon this praxis depends not only the "ultimate realization of humanity and the distinct human groups, but also and even more radically, the realization of reality as reality, that is, in its transcendent constitution."[137]

Speaking from an epistemological perspective, for Ellacuría, praxis is constitutive of human knowledge in that it is necessary to verify one's knowledge and also because it connects human knowing back to its referent in reality, which remains the principle and foundation of all realistic activity and the source of much of its content.[138] Because the human person is deeply immersed within a reality that is infused with its own dynamisms, his knowing cannot be limited to a passive receptivity or a detached conceptualizing of what reality may be. To properly know, he must actively engage reality by partaking of and collaborating with those dynamisms that move the history of reality—and the person— forward. In this process the human person transforms reality as he himself is also transformed. Thus, speaking now from a theological perspective, this means that through his active engagement of reality, the human person encounters God, makes God more present in history, and becomes transformed as he makes himself present to God.

Ellacuría's interpretation of the human encounter with reality serves as the foundation for his theological method, which stresses the responsibility that theology must assume in truly knowing, ethically assessing, and continuously transforming reality toward higher levels of realization. Theology must seek to discern, accept, and respond to the demands of reality in a practical and concrete manner. Indeed, Ellacuría envisions theology as the "ideological moment of ecclesial and historical praxis . . . the conscious and reflective element of praxis."[139] Thus, he insists on the priority of reality over the interpretation of its meaning and notes that "no real change of meaning occurs without a real change of reality; to attempt the first without intending the second is to falsify the intelligence and its primary function, even in the purely cognitive order."[140]

The preceding exercise of synthesizing some foundational aspects of Zubiri's and Ellacuría's thought—sentient intelligence, the theologal dimension of reality, historical reality, and the threefold manner in which human intelligence apprehends and confronts reality—provides us with the basic epistemological and philosophical framework to better grasp Sobrino's spirituality. Sobrino appears to endorse these philosophical presuppositions, although they often remain implicit in his work. Like Ellacuría, Sobrino proceeds from a sacramental understanding of reality, insists on the relational character of the human person, conceives creation as being grounded in God, and understands human salvation as taking place in history. Sobrino explicitly draws from Ellacuría's threefold structure of human intelligence to approach and expound important christological themes, but I suggest that its influence is particularly significant in two areas that are essential to the development of his overall theological vision: the foundations of his spirituality and his theological method.[141] To these we will turn in the following chapter.

Conclusion

This chapter argues that Sobrino's spirituality and theology arise as a Christian response to a sociohistorical situation of oppression, enmity, and violence. The main sources that inform and shape his work include the Salvadoran political and ecclesial context, Sobrino's own intellectual biography, and the influence of Karl Rahner, Monsignor Oscar Romero, and particularly Ignacio Ellacuría. Although special attention has been given to Ellacuría's thought because this provides the basic philosophical framework that undergirds Sobrino's spirituality, all these sources converge in Sobrino's work to foster a theology imbued with a commitment to the integral liberation of the human person that leads to social reconciliation.

As the following chapter discusses, Sobrino largely relies on Ellacuría's epistemological and theological interpretation of reality to articulate his own interpretation of the proper relationship between the human person and reality. Indeed, while Ellacuría establishes the necessary structure that conditions the human person's proper engagement of reality, Sobrino will identify the spirit—or disposition—that actualizes this engagement. In his interpretation one can also detect the influence of Karl Rahner's theology of grace and its attendant understanding that human experience gives us access to the mystery of God.

Sobrino's own reflections have led him to add an additional dimension to Ellacuría's threefold structure of confronting reality—that of "letting ourselves be carried by reality," which stresses the active presence of God's grace in reality. This additional dimension will be explained more fully in the next chapter, but for now I suggest that each of these four dimensions of engaging reality—realizing the weight of reality, shouldering the weight of reality, taking charge of the weight of reality, and letting ourselves be carried by reality—may be correlated with one of the presuppositions that ground both Sobrino's spirituality and his theological method.

3 Theology as a Task Guided by the Spirit

Jon Sobrino's sociohistorical milieu, personal experiences, religious formation, and intellectual influences coalesce in a theological intuition that nurtures his imagination and guides his theological work. These forces have helped develop the spiritual disposition that informs and integrates the whole of Sobrino's theological endeavor. This chapter advances the investigation of Sobrino's foundational framework by underscoring the central role that spirituality has in enhancing and organizing his theology. This spirituality will later provide the basis on which to develop a Christian discipleship and theology of reconciliation that effectively responds to a world riddled by the effects of injustice and conflict.

Before exploring Sobrino's spirituality, it will be helpful to clarify the meaning of the word. The term "spirituality," broadly understood, refers to both the lived faith experience and the discipline that studies such experience.[1] As the theologian Sandra Schneiders defines it, spirituality is "the experience of conscious involvement in the project of life-integration through self-transcendence toward the ultimate value one perceives."[2] By way of contrast, theology is most commonly described in terms of the Anselmian conception of faith seeking understanding—"the effort to understand our faith in God's revelation through the historically and culturally conditioned articulation of our beliefs and praxis."[3] Though they are distinct in the Christian tradition, the two disciplines are closely interrelated and mutually inform one another. One's spirituality—that is, one's lived faith experience—already assumes certain theological premises, and the theological task critically reflects upon one's faith experience in light of Christian revelation.[4] In this sense, spirituality can be understood as both the fruit and the source of theology.[5]

The reality that one's spirituality implicitly or explicitly influences and shapes one's theology has been duly acknowledged by some of the theological giants of the last century. Karl Rahner, Hans Urs von Balthasar, and the French theologian Marie-Dominique Chenu have all stressed the relationship between theology and spirituality and the central and constitutive role that spirituality plays in the development of any theological system.[6] Writing in the late 1930s, Chenu asserted:

> The fact is that in the final analysis theological systems are simply the expression of a spirituality. It is this that gives them their interest and their grandeur. . . . One does not get to the heart of a system via the logical coherence of its structure or the plausibility of its conclusions. One gets to the heart by grasping it in its origins via that fundamental intuition that serves to guide a spiritual life and provides the intellectual regimen proper to that life.[7]

Pursuing this insight further, the present chapter examines the foundational anthropological elements of Sobrino's spiritual perspective in order to better grasp how his vision of the human person, God, and all of reality enriches and organizes his theology. It then demonstrates how these same elements structure his understanding of the demands, concerns, and purpose of the theological task. Because Sobrino has not developed a systematic theology of reconciliation, this examination is essential to the underlying methodology of this project. As noted in Chapter 1, I propose that because Sobrino's spirituality integrates all of his theology, we can construct a discipleship and a theology of reconciliation that coherently build upon the rest of his work. This spiritual foundation will be fleshed out in the next chapter when we turn to explore those elements in Sobrino's Christology that are important for developing a Christian discipleship of reconciliation.

The present chapter proceeds as follows: It first examines, in broad terms, the impact of spirituality on Christian praxis and theology and the prominent role that liberation theologians have ascribed to spirituality in developing their theology. The chapter then considers the foundational structure for what Sobrino defines as *theologal spirituality* and its relationship with Christian spirituality. The chapter concludes with a synthesis that demonstrates how Sobrino's spirituality offers both a privileged perspective from which to understand the roots, method, and purpose of his theological endeavor, and the basis for a reconciling way of living the Christian faith today.

The Impact of Spirituality on Christian Praxis and Theology

The recognition of spirituality as an academic discipline that articulates a distinct aspect of theology and not simply a derivative of it is relatively recent.[8] While the study of spirituality benefited from the revival in patristic theology during the early part of the last century, Christian spirituality has emerged as a subject of formal study only within the past few decades. Bernard McGinn, for instance, noting a dramatic increase in published research on the subject over the last forty years, regards it as "a major new factor on the map of American religion."[9]

McGinn's assessment is confirmed by the attention that church organizations, universities, and the academy have devoted to the study of spirituality in recent years. In general terms, this newfound attention responds to an increasing interest in the subject among laity, ministers, and theologians. Within the academy, as Sandra Schneiders indicates, the turn toward spirituality is due in no small measure to the recognition by an increasing number of well-known theologians that constructive theological work is ultimately rooted in the experience of faith and thus must bear fruit not only in the church's teaching but also in its praxis of faith.[10]

That Latin American liberation theologians have drawn similar conclusions is no great surprise, for they have consistently insisted on the logical priority of the faith experience and praxis to systematic reflection, and they have long understood theology as a second step that is dependent upon critical reflection on Christian praxis.[11] From the inception of liberation theology, Latin American theologians realized the limitations that purely theoretical categories have in fostering a Christian praxis of liberation, and correspondingly they stressed the central role of spirituality in shaping both praxis and theology. In his groundbreaking work *A Theology of Liberation*, first published in 1971, Gustavo Gutiérrez already insisted on the need for a spirituality of liberation, noting that "We need a vital attitude, all-embracing and synthesizing, informing the totality as well as every detail of our lives; we need a spirituality."[12]

Fifteen years later, reflecting upon liberation theology's accumulated experiences, Sobrino noted that liberation theology has "been very attentive to spirituality . . . because this theology wishes to take account of, and constitute a response to, concrete, historical church reality, with its real cries and hopes."[13] He adds, "The very fact that liberation theology is an account of something concrete, formulated for the purpose of turning that concrete reality into something really new, demonstrates that a particular spirit has been present in the very execution of its task." In a similar vein, Sobrino explains that among liberation theologians, "spirituality is a dimension as original and necessary as liberation, and these two demand each other. . . . [Liberation theologians] believe, moreover, that spirituality is best understood not only as a dimension of theology, but as the integrating dimension of theology itself."[14]

Even though a particular spiritual perspective might not directly offer specific theological content, it nonetheless informs an overall attitude—a disposition or spirit—toward reality that informs the theological task. A spiritual perspective not only influences a theologian's imagination, priorities, and methodology, but first and foremost has a direct impact on shaping the manner in which Christians—theologians and others—live their faith.[15]

The essential role that Sobrino ascribes to spirituality in forming Christian praxis is evident in the contribution that an authentic Christian spirituality can offer to the practice of liberation. While Sobrino consistently advocates for a praxis aimed at fostering the integral liberation of the individual and society, he is nonetheless mindful that, for all its precious possibilities, such practice is vulnerable to human limitations, temptations, and sinfulness. Thus, "the practice of liberation runs the risk of generating negative by-products . . . [which] are not remediable from within liberation practice itself."[16] These by-products include the presence of conflict among those involved in efforts toward liberation, the improper use of power, and the lack of representation of the people's concerns and interests in the organizations leading the liberation process.[17] Spirituality, Sobrino insists, is necessary to avoid these negative by-products in that it enables those engaged in the practice of liberation to remain open to the transcendent, and to a utopian vision capable of integrating "the disparate elements of historical liberation: the personal and the structural; a genuine struggle and the longing for peace; justice and forgiveness; triumph and reconciliation."[18]

The centrality that Sobrino ascribes to spirituality in Christian praxis and in his own theological vision is indisputable. But what does Sobrino mean by "spirituality," and what is his particular spiritual perspective? In the following section, I explore Sobrino's foundational approach to spirituality and to the particular "spirit" that he insists should guide both human life and one's theological reflection upon it. This initial treatment of Sobrino's understanding of spirituality stresses the fundamental anthropological constants and theological dimensions that, he argues, structure all spiritualities—including Christian spirituality—and lays the foundations for the work that will be taken up in the following chapters, namely, the development of a Christian discipleship of reconciliation that is explicitly informed, as we will see, by its christological and pneumatological elements. Because the way that I use the terms "spirit" and "Spirit" may not become fully clear until later in the chapter, it is important to note here that Sobrino's spirituality consistently emphasizes the Trinitarian role of the Spirit in her historical instantiations—that is, the manner in which the Spirit of God becomes manifested in the lives of Jesus and his followers. Although the distinctions that Sobrino makes between the transcendent and historical expression of the Spirit are not always precise, following his general practice, I will use the capitalized form *Spirit* to refer to the third person of the Trinity and the lowercase form *spirit* to refer to the manifestations of the Holy Spirit in history.[19]

Foundations for a Theologal Spirituality

In mapping current research in the field of Christian spirituality, scholars such as Schneiders and McGinn have identified three distinct but often interrelated methodological approaches: theological, historical, and anthropological.[20] The theological approach stresses the distinctly Christian character of spirituality and the central role that theological discourse and methodologies play in the study of the subject. The historical approach enlists hermeneutical and critical methods to locate and consider spiritualities within their proper sociohistorical contexts. The anthropological approach recognizes spirituality as a human constant and so focuses on the human person's existential capacity for self-transcendence through his or her engagement of the world and envisions Christian spirituality as the actualization of this capacity. This approach typically stresses how the Christian interpretation of religious experiences can best respond to pressing contemporary questions.[21]

Although those studying spirituality often combine different methods, Sobrino's initial approach most closely fits within the anthropological category. He insists that "every human being has a spiritual life. Like it or not, know it or not, each of us is confronted with reality and endowed with the ability to react to that reality with ultimacy."[22] Hence, even before he begins to address Christian spirituality, Sobrino seeks to identify the fundamental transcendental and anthropological dimensions that actualize our capacity to encounter and mediate God's presence through our engagement of reality. It is only after these fundamental dimensions have been established that Sobrino turns to develop an explicitly Christian spirituality that deepens and actualizes how the human person should engage reality in light of Jesus's revelation.

Challenged by a conflicted reality fraught with injustice and oppression, encouraged by the liberative praxis of the Latin American poor, and building on the theological insights of Rahner, Ellacuría, Medellín, and Vatican II—all of which stress the single integral vocation of the human person—Sobrino insists that a subject's spiritual life and his or her historical activity do not belong to separate planes of existence (i.e., the transcendental and the material) but rather converge in historical reality.[23] While our historical life cannot be reduced to the material or to the purely historical, our spiritual lives are always mediated through history, and it is there that they unfold and flourish. Our historical existence contains both distinct material and transcendental elements, but the latter are only accessible through the former. This means, as Sobrino notes, that "there is no *spiritual* life without actual, historical *life*. It is impossible to live *with spirit* unless that spirit *becomes flesh*."[24]

Sobrino acknowledges that the relationship between our spiritual and our historical lives may take different forms, but he forcefully rejects those "spiritualities" that "leave reality to itself" and thus welcome "an alienating parallelism in which the spiritual life and historical activity never meet."[25] For him an authentic spirituality involves all the different aspects of our existence and can never be understood as a constellation of attitudes or practices that separate us from and make us unaccountable for the demands of our surrounding reality. In a similar vein, Sobrino discards the idea of an individualistic spirituality that only promotes the actualization of the individual person and does not "include an expression of the collective subject, and especially the people as subject."[26]

Sobrino also rejects the notion that spirituality may be first developed in the solitude of one's interiority and only later applied to the situation in which a person lives. Rather, for Sobrino, contemplation and action are two distinct but deeply interrelated moments that continuously illumine each other and converge in the manner in which we encounter God in the world. He writes,

> Contemplation and action are not moments having distinct objects, as if contemplation were directed toward God and action were directed toward the world. It is God who must be contemplated and practiced; and it is by virtue of the unicity of this divine object that both moments find their profound unification. At the same time, the world, too, becomes the object both of action and contemplation. The contemplation of God is simultaneously a contemplation of the world with God's eyes; and the practice of God is the implementation of God's word according to God's will.[27]

Hence, Sobrino will insist on a profoundly relational spirituality that seeks to engage the different dimensions and dynamisms that mediate God's presence in historical reality. For him, the duality that makes spirituality possible is not one rooted in the distinction between contemplation and action, but is rather implied in the human being's relationship with God. This relationship comprises, first, a moment of initiative and gratuity on the part of God and, second, the moment of response on the part of the human person also enabled by God. Indeed, Sobrino argues for a model of contemplation *in* action that "recognizes the difference in its two constitutive terms, but . . . subsumes this difference in a more primordial one, that between gratuity and response."[28]

As noted previously, Sobrino argues that all persons have some form of spirituality because "Spirituality is simply the spirit of a subject—an individual or a group—in its relationship with the whole of reality."[29] Thus he distinguishes an authentic spirituality as the spirit or disposition with which we most fully engage reality and most honestly confront the concrete history in which we live. In other words, because every human being has the capacity for a spiritual life, the question is what spiritual perspective and spirit best inform the manner in which the person engages reality.

To illuminate the proper relationship between the human person and reality, Sobrino largely relies on Ellacuría's epistemological and theological interpretation of historical reality as being open to the transcendent. As discussed in the previous chapter, Ellacuría examines the anthropological and metaphysical conditions that make possible our encounter with God in our daily existence. He explicates how the function of human intelligence is to confront reality through the three interrelated dimensions (noetic, ethical, and praxical) that configure the human person's apprehension of reality. Building on this metaphysical, anthropological, and epistemological foundation, Sobrino advances the need for a spirit that affirms the individual's transcendent character and seeks to actualize this transcendence within history through his or her comprehensive and transformative engagement of historical reality. Sobrino further identifies this spirit with the historical appropriation and mediation of the Holy Spirit. It is the Spirit who enables the human person to remain open to the transcendent in history, and to fully and effectively engage reality in such a way that both the human person and historical reality are transformed by the pursuit of an increasing degree of flourishing and actualization. Such actualization can be understood, in theological terms, as a process of reconciliation: the increasing communion among human beings and God.

Consequently, Sobrino tells us that an authentic spirituality entails "being-human-with-spirit—which responds to the elements of crisis and promise residing in reality, unifying the various elements of a response to that reality in such a way that the latter may be definitely a reality more of promise than of crisis."[30] As Matthew Ashley rightly notes:

> For Sobrino . . . "being human with spirit," and [Ellacuría's] "confronting reality" are tantamount to the same thing once one understands what "spirit," "human," and "reality" mean. To "have spirit" or to live in terms of a transcendent horizon is precisely to engage reality as a multi-dimensional field of elements and dynamisms, most fully instantiated and actualized at the level of human history (in other words, as *historical* reality).[31]

To ensure a fruitful engagement with reality, Sobrino distinguishes three basic and interrelated dispositions that actualize the spirit that every human person should manifest: honesty with the real, fidelity to the real, and a willingness to be carried by what he calls "the 'more' of reality." Although deeply interrelated and impossible to isolate from one another, these dispositions primarily stress distinct dimensions of the human person's encounter with reality as explained by Ellacuría and include an explicit transcendental dimension added by Sobrino. Hence, I suggest that *honesty with the real* stresses the noetic dimension (i.e., Ellacuría's realizing the weight of reality); *fidelity to the real* emphasizes both the ethical and praxical dimensions (i.e., Ellacuría's shouldering the weight of reality and taking charge of the weight of reality); and *willingness to be carried by the "more" of reality* underscores the transcendent or graced dimension of encountering reality.[32] It is to these dispositions, which provide the foundations upon which an explicitly Christian spirituality may be built, that we now turn.

Honesty with Reality

Being honest with the real refers to the act of spirit that seeks to grasp the truth of historical reality in order to respond to the demands that this reality places upon us. It involves discerning the presence of sin and grace therein. An honest engagement with a suffering world that is weighted down by sin, Sobrino argues, will elicit a reaction of compassion, which constitutes the most appropriate response to such a world.

From the perspective of the knowing subject, properly grasping reality is not just a matter of overcoming ignorance by moving from a state of non-knowing to one of knowing, but especially entails overcoming our inherent tendency to avoid, conceal, and distort the truth according to our own interests.[33] In describing this disposition, Sobrino often enlists the language of Paul's letter to the Romans and its account of God's wrathful condemnation of "the irreligious and perverse spirit of [those] who . . . hinder the truth" (Rom 1:18) to vividly convey the sinful stance that corrupts or obscures a truthful engagement with reality. It is indeed when we do not engage reality honestly that our perception of reality becomes distorted and things lose their proper meaning, and thus their capacity to mediate God's transcendence. The subject is thus precluded from adequately knowing reality and from establishing a proper relationship with it.[34]

Expressed in theological terms, honesty with reality demands that we accept historical reality for what it is—both as grounded in God and thus enjoying a sacramental capacity, and as vitiated by the sinful choices of human persons and therefore "weighted" by sin and conflict. Because historical reality is open to the transcendent, a truthful and honest encounter with it summons us to engage in reality's inherent and dynamic bent toward restoring itself and bestowing life. In Sobrino's eloquent words,

> Unless it is "hindered in perversity," as Paul puts it, reality itself utters an unconditional no and an unconditional yes. The no of reality is no to its own negation, absence, lack, annihilation. . . . [T]he yes demanded by reality is yes to life. And inasmuch as the greater portion of human creation lies prostrate in the death of subjugation, this yes to life becomes a yes to the restoration of life: a yes then, not only to life, but to the bestowal of life.[35]

From an ethical and practical perspective, our honest confrontation with a sinful and conflicted reality demands that we acknowledge and prioritize the value of life, which in turn elicits from us a compassionate response that first and foremost seeks to alleviate the suffering of millions of human beings living under the weight of oppression. From an ontological perspective, this response also replies to the demands of the theologal dimension of reality—a graced creation that in its inherent dynamism and orientation also groans, to use Paul's language again, for its liberation from bondage and decay. By virtue of its theologal character, we may affirm that God is also present in the midst of sinful reality, but God's presence here is one of condemnation; and it is the human person—when he or she acts like a prophet—who recognizes what God rejects and thus calls for reality's conversion.

As noted previously, Sobrino tells us that the proper human response to our broken reality and a crucial component of an honest engagement with reality is compassion. Compassion, which assumes both the interiorization of the suffering of another and the willingness to overcome this suffering, becomes practical and takes different forms depending on the nature of the suffering one beholds and the context in which the victim is embedded. Compassion, Sobrino further tells us, is the primordial act of spirit through which the human being is perfected and becomes whole: "It is that in terms of which all dimensions of the human being acquire meaning and without which nothing else attains to human status."[36] Thus, compassion is the fundamental invitation and demand that reality places upon us, and it is in responding mercifully that we both become more human and encounter God. Honesty with reality leads the subject to engage and persevere in a process that Sobrino calls the "forgiveness of sinful reality"; that is, the liberation of reality from the sinfulness that permeates its historical structures and denies God's reconciling will for humanity.

Fidelity to the Real

Fidelity to the real requires a spirit of perseverance—of continuous adherence to our service of reality despite the difficulties that we may encounter in the process. The decision to be honest with the real prompts the subject to embark on a long journey of struggling against what is negative and fostering what is positive. Time and again, our honesty with reality awakens us to our own limitations and to the fact that our efforts—even when they are the manifestation of love—are not always rewarded with the expected results. More significantly, this honesty also confronts us, at the personal level, with our own shortcomings and sinfulness and, socially, with the enormous power of structural sin. Hence, the initial commitments and hopes that compassion gives rise to are soon challenged by the lack of progress we see, by self-doubt, and, more often than not, by the opposition of those whose privileges are questioned by our actions. In some cases, this opposition will demand that we bear at great personal cost—possibly including the cost of our lives—the consequences of struggling against sin.

In these situations, the temptation arises to abandon our initial honest response to reality and yield instead to the paralyzing forces of despair, and it is particularly here, in the midst of darkness, that a spirit of fidelity is needed. Fidelity, Sobrino tells us, "is simply and solely perseverance in our original honesty, however we may be burdened with, yes, engulfed in, the negative element in history. . . . [W]e shall know only that we must stay faithful, keep moving ahead in history, striving ever to transform that history from negative to positive."[37] Thus, the fulfilling of such faithfulness is also an act of spirit that is always difficult and costly, and that in some cases brings with it the demands that Christians associate with the cross.

As the following section details, a spirit of fidelity to the real is manifested in holding to the hope that is offered by reality and whose limited
realization in acts of love helps reality come into its fullness.

Allowing Ourselves to Be Carried by the Real

As human persons engage reality with a spirit of honesty and faithfulness,
they discover that reality not only offers difficult demands but also contains
a promise—the good news—that carries them and lightens their burden.
Thus, "just as there is an original sin that becomes a structural dimension
of reality, so also there is an original grace, which becomes a graced structure of reality."[38] Sobrino does not diminish the seriousness of the demands
that reality makes of us, but he reminds us that "reality itself, in spite of its
long history of failure and misery, posits ever and again the hope of fullness."[39] In other words, we need to recognize that history is not only sheer
negativity but also contains a liberating promise—a hope—that leads us to
a reconciled future that today we cannot fully comprehend.

This hope, Sobrino tells us, runs unsilenced throughout the history of
humanity and is nourished by and manifested through partial victories
of love—limited events of fellowship, liberation, and reconciliation, as well
as through the heroic lives of people like Moses, St. Paul, and Romero who,
with their words, proclaimed the ushering in of the new reality, and with
their actions, showed us that a better world is possible.[40] Hence, when
Sobrino insists that we are to let ourselves be "carried by the real," he
is prompting us to rely on the hope and the love already present though
not wholly fulfilled in reality.

While Sobrino insists that for all its brokenness reality calls us to have
hope, "the hope it calls for is an active impulse. . . . [I]t is a hope bent upon
helping reality become what it seeks to be. This is love. Hope and love are
but two sides of the same coin: the conviction put into practice, of the possibilities of reality."[41] Hence, according to Sobrino, there is, in reality, "a
hope-filled, honest, loving current . . . which becomes a powerful invitation to us, and once we have entered it, we allow ourselves to be carried
along by it."[42]

Expressed in more explicit theological language, this hope and love can
also be understood as grace, and thus as the mediation of God's self-
communicating presence in the world. While Sobrino does not himself

offer a detailed philosophical treatment of the nature of reality, he compares it to the human nature of Christ and argues that "reality too can be understood as the presence of transcendence in history."[43] Thus he insists on the primordial and ultimate goodness of a graced creation. "To accept [this] grace," says Sobrino, "is to plunge headlong into reality and allow ourselves to be borne up on the 'more' with which reality is pregnant and which is offered to us freely, again and again, despite all."[44]

Sobrino explains that this freely offered grace infuses us with the necessary strength to confront the undeniable presence of sin in the world and provides us with an initial sense of direction to move history forward in the long search for its and our own fulfillment. Hence, reality not only demands our honesty and our faithfulness, but also grants us the opportunity to be swept forward by its goodness. This goodness promises and enables a future that in its fulfillment will always remain beyond both our merit and control. In this sense, the acceptance of such a grace is also the act of a subject who lives with a spirit of utter trust and who stands in proper relationship with his or her surrounding reality.

Allowing ourselves to be carried by reality means letting those in whom God is most clearly present—the poor, the victims of history—help transform our lives. It also means allowing ourselves to be assisted by "those who have generated the best of human and Christian traditions, who invite us to graft ourselves onto these traditions and build on them."[45]

Fundamental Theologal Spirituality and the Following of Jesus

As the previous section showed, for Sobrino, the proper relationship between the human person and reality demands, first, that the subject engage reality with a spirit of honesty necessary to truthfully discern and compassionately respond to the demands of a sinful and conflicted reality. Second, the subject is called to nurture a spirit that remains faithful to this first honesty in spite of the obstacles and negativity that he or she encounters in reality. Finally, this faithfulness is nurtured by an expectant and active hope that enables the subject to bear the taxing cost of such perseverance. The honest and faithful subject is called to embrace a spirit of trust that allows her to recognize and utterly rely on the ultimate goodness of reality, and thus be moved and guided by this goodness.

Taken together, these three dimensions constitute what Sobrino defines as a fundamental theologal spirituality that actualizes the human relationship with reality and God. He calls it *fundamental* because each one of these attitudes, whether actualized or not, concerns all human beings' inherent capacity to engage reality in the most fruitful manner. In words that echo Rahner's theology of grace, Sobrino contends that "anyone who enters into a correct relationship with this reality is corresponding to God objectively, and . . . God will bestow self-communication to this person, although this communication may not be in a thematic reflexive form."[46] Hence, honesty with reality, fidelity to reality, and allowing ourselves to be carried by the real form a spirituality that Sobrino calls *theologal*, because in his view they capture the correct mode in which human beings should relate to reality and the person's positive response to God's revelation in this same historical reality. Although these dispositions are not the only ones that actualize God's spirit in the world, Sobrino notes that it is especially through them that the "mystery of God . . . becomes present *in* reality. Transcendence becomes present *in* history."[47]

While this fundamental theologal spirituality is relevant to all human beings and encapsulates the basic requirements for any authentic spirituality, Sobrino acknowledges that it already assumes the Christian view of God that emerges from the historical revelation of Jesus Christ. For Christians this spirituality becomes explicitly historicized in the following of Jesus Christ because it is in Jesus that the true human being and the true spirit with which we should engage reality have been revealed. As Sobrino explains, "Christian spirituality is no more and no less than a living of the fundamental spirituality that we have described, precisely in the concrete manner of Jesus and according to the spirit of Jesus. This is the following of Jesus."[48] In other words, it is in Jesus's life that we can best witness how a human person should engage reality honestly, faithfully, and trustingly.

Jesus's proper engagement with reality enabled him to discern God's will and to correspond to a God whose love says "no" to that which dehumanizes human life or annuls human solidarity, and says "yes" to a world that has to be reconciled and to the task of working toward such a utopia. In other words, "Jesus' discernment was directed primarily to corresponding to the objectivity *in* history of God's 'yes' and 'no' *to* history."[49] As I will develop in more detail in the following chapter, Jesus's life provides us with *a posteriori* criteria for how to engage reality and a basic path or channel—incarnation, mission, death, and resurrection—by which we may, in spite of our limitations, follow him.[50] Nevertheless, one "cannot speak *a priori* and in the abstract of what [the] discernment [of God's will] should be today, since this would be setting limits to the Spirit and denying the greater being of God for our own history."[51] While Christians arrive at a discernment of God's will in the process of following of Jesus, from Jesus's history "we learn not so much the replies to our discernments as, more basically, how to learn to discern . . . on the basis of the choices and historical commitments that Jesus made."[52]

Just as exemplary Christians throughout history have understood the need to live and engage reality as Jesus did, they have also realized that following Christ and discerning God's will do not occur in a historical vacuum, nor are they matters of simply mimicking him. When reality is engaged with a spirit of honesty, fidelity, and trust, each historical context generates particular challenges and insights that must be discerned and incorporated into our life of discipleship. In this regard, Sobrino further argues that it is the Holy Spirit who guides the Christian follower to properly actualize Jesus in each new context through the discernment of an objective historical reality in which the activity of the Spirit can be seen anew.[53] Recalling how the bishops at Medellín discerned the people's longing for liberation as a sign of the Spirit in light of the irruption of the poor, Sobrino claims that in Latin America, where the effects of injustice and large-scale social conflicts still reverberate, one can discern that "the fundamental act of the Spirit today . . . is the option for the poor."[54] This option is nothing other than liberation theology's contextual articulation of the Spirit's, Jesus's, and indeed, the Trinity's compassionate response to a conflicted and suffering world.[55]

Compassion or mercy—properly defined as the interiorized reaction to someone else's suffering—occupies a central and comprehensive place in Sobrino's spirituality and theology because it captures the fundamental manner in which God engages the world.[56] He enlists the term "principle" to describe how mercy originates, guides, and remains present in all of God's and Jesus's salvific activity.[57] "By the principle of mercy," writes Sobrino, "we understand a specific love, which while standing at the origins of a process, also remains present and active throughout the process, endowing it with a particular direction and shaping the various elements that compose it."[58] Sobrino equally stresses how this principle must inform all aspects of a human life that wants to engage reality as God does. He writes, "The fundamental exigency for the human being, and specifically for the people of God, is that they reiterate this mercy of God's, exercising it toward others and thus rendering themselves like unto God."[59] In similar terms, but now addressing contemporary Christians, Sobrino writes, "The authentic following of Jesus today occurs by reproducing the whole of that life in terms of the option for the poor. . . . It is an option involving the totality of the human being in his or her confrontation with reality."[60]

Sobrino's spirituality, therefore, calls Christians to follow Jesus not only with his same dispositions and according to the path that his life has laid out for us, but also hand-in-hand with the poor. This following should seek to incarnate Jesus's values, praxis, and mission anew in each particular historical context and thus should be guided by a Christic imagination and empowered by a spirit of hope that responds with honesty and fidelity to the situation that such reality demands.

In the next chapter, I will more carefully examine Sobrino's interpretation of Jesus's identity, life, and mission in order to identify the christological and pneumatological dimensions that should be taken into account in articulating a Christian discipleship of reconciliation from the perspective of the victims. Then, in the final chapter I propose a discipleship and theology of reconciliation rooted in Sobrino's Christology. For now, it is important to return to the examination of Sobrino's theologal spirituality in order to demonstrate how this spiritual perspective shapes his approach to the theological task and informs his theological vision.

In Sobrino, this task assumes three novel features. First, it ascribes a central role to the option for the poor as theology's compassionate response to a suffering world and as theology's primary perspective from which to interpret all of reality in an honest manner. Second, it defines as theology's final goal the transformation of historical reality in order to eradicate suffering and make God's reconciling will faithfully present in the world. And thirdly, it explicates why theology must allow itself to be carried and informed by the grace in reality. Hence, just as Sobrino's fundamental theologal spirituality identifies the dispositions that actualize the human person's proper relationship with reality, his methodological presuppositions emphasize what the proper relationship between theology and reality should be so that the former may accurately interpret and effectively respond to the demands of the latter.

Sobrino's Methodological Presuppositions

In very general terms, Sobrino's methodology may be described as one of mutual critical correlation in which his interpretation of the Christian faith (*fides quae*) enters into a mutually enriching dialogue with his interpretation of Christian praxis (*fides qua*) in the Latin American historical situation. This description, which presupposes God's initiative—that "God has made a self-bestowal on us by grace"—begins to capture the importance that Sobrino's theological approach ascribes to correctly engaging historical reality.[61]

Without neglecting the central role that scripture and Christian tradition have in the theological enterprise, Sobrino has stressed, from his early work on, the significance that social context has in shaping the theological task. In a paper presented at a meeting of theologians in Mexico City, in 1975, Sobrino put forward two pivotal questions to frame his chief concerns regarding the meaning and purpose of theology: How does Christian reality influence theological understanding? And what is the ultimate concern that moves us to understand things theologically?[62] His response to the first question sketches the profound impact that the liberating characters of Jesus's revelation, the promise of God's kingdom, and the presence of sin have on theological reflection. Sobrino's response to the second question complements the first by turning to the theological subject in order to elucidate the proper relationship between theology and reality. He stresses that all thinking, including theological thinking, emerges from a particular interest, bears a particular perspective, and has an ultimate purpose. As such, the distinctiveness of this theology resides in its liberating character: in how it seeks to foster the eradication of sin in order to transform and heal sinful reality.[63] In the language of Ellacuría, theology is not only tasked with realizing and shouldering the weight of reality, but also with taking charge of its weight—that is, with transforming it.

Like other liberation theologies that emerge from situations of oppression, Sobrino's theology is shaped by and responds to an immediate situation of conflict and widespread suffering. Reflecting on this situation, and on that of most of the Third World, Sobrino insists that "theology must understand itself as an intellectual exercise whose primary purpose is to eliminate [historical] suffering. . . . [S]uffering in today's world means pri-

marily the suffering of people who are crucified, and the purpose of theology is to take these people down from the cross."[64] This long-held concern
for the victims and their liberation inspires, initiates, and permeates all
of Sobrino's theological reflections. It gives a soteriological structure that
provides a comprehensive guide and direction to his theological project.
In what follows, I enlist the three dispositions of Sobrino's fundamental
theologal spirituality to organize his methodological presuppositions and
to examine his prescription for the theologian's disposition as he or she
engages in the theological task.

A Theology That Engages Reality with Honesty and Compassion

If theological knowledge is to function as a principle of liberation (and reconciliation), it cannot confine its task to the examination of scriptural texts
and other traditional sources, but must also turn toward historical reality,
wherein God continues to make Godself present today. After all, revelation,
which constitutes the basis for theological reflection, can always be traced
back to personal or communal experiences of God's manifestation in historical reality. It is no surprise, then, that Sobrino ascribes great methodological significance to properly grasping and engaging the lived context
that facilitates our religious experiences because it is by interpreting these
that theology first emerged and continues to renew itself.

Theology must confront reality and allow reality to speak for itself and
unveil its truth. Indeed, Sobrino is mindful that "the theological enterprise, in so far as it is a public product presented in and to society, can
hide, cover up, and even justify society's evil."[65] Thus, he insists that theology must manifest a fundamental spirit of honesty in its engagement and
interpretation of reality. Such honesty is essential if theology is to access
the truth that will lead to liberation and reconciliation. This spirit of honesty is concretized through three interrelated elements in the noetic dimension of the theological task: first, the commitment to a preferential
option for the poor, which leads the theologian to interpret reality from
the perspective of the victims; second, the discernment of the victims of
history as "signs of the times," and thus as the manifestation of God's presence and purpose in historical reality; and third, an understanding of
theology as *intellectus amoris* that underscores that compassion is the only
honest and appropriate reaction to a suffering world.

THE OPTION FOR THE POOR AND THE SIGNIFICANCE
OF PLACE TO THE THEOLOGICAL TASK

The place or setting from which theologians exercise their task has a decisive role in shaping their work, since their reflections and interpretations will be informed by the reality that they inhabit and engage directly. Following Ellacuría, Sobrino contends that in order to properly confront reality, theological thinking—like any other type of thinking—must be grounded and active in the midst of reality. The theologian cannot be a distant observer or pretend to be an impartial witness of reality, but must engage reality as one who is embedded and active within its dynamism. Moreover, because all actions carry within themselves a particular interest, and because not all locations offer the same access to reality, the theologian must take a particular stance before the world and actively situate herself in the place from which she can best grasp the truth of reality.

For Sobrino, the proper stance for the theologian to adopt before a suffering reality is best captured by the preferential option for the poor—a solidarity that leads the theologian to enter into the world of the victims and thereby share their perspective. In his view, the option for the poor provides, among other things, a pre-understanding that disposes the human person to properly grasp and interpret God's revelation, and thus functions in a manner akin to other existential pre-dispositions such as openness to and trust in God's revelation.[66]

To the extent that this pre-understanding emerges from both the universal human capacity to engage the world with attitudes that either foster or hinder our comprehension of reality and from an implicitly or explicitly spiritual perspective that seeks to grasp reality honestly, the option for the poor can be understood as a pre-theological or even pre-religious stance. From a historical and existential viewpoint, to make an option for the poor is "simply the most reasonable conclusion to draw from the cruelty and universality of [the poor's] suffering,"[67] and thus, for Sobrino, it is the natural and compassionate reaction of any human being who seeks to honestly respond to the victims of history and oppose their suffering.[68] In a similar vein, but now speaking from an explicitly Christian perspective, Sobrino contends that the scriptures confirm this compassionate response as paramount because the preferential option for the poor captures "the fundamental attitude of Jesus and God toward the world: Godself sees the totality of this world from the perspective of the poor, God's primal reaction toward this world is to save the lives of the poor."[69]

Sobrino insists that there are some places, situations, or settings "in which important elements in the 'sources' of revelation, which had been buried, are rediscovered."[70] In certain situations, both the Christian sources and the theological interpretation of reality yield more insight than others, in part because God's revelation is more clearly manifested in them. In this sense, "the place of theology is first and foremost something real, a particular historical situation in which God and Christ are believed to be continuing to make themselves present; this is therefore a theologal setting even before it is a theological setting, a setting from which the texts of the past can be read more adequately."[71] Hence, for Sobrino the place of theology and the "sources" of revelation are conceptually distinct but not mutually exclusive.[72] The place of theology is in its own way a source of revelation as well as an aid to better understand the traditional sources of revelation and their relevance for the present time.

For Sobrino, the world of the poor is the best theological place and situation to guide and inform a theologian's reflection. The world of the poor "gives food for thought" in that it reminds us that Christ's gospel— God's kingdom—is God's response to the situation of the poor. It "gives power for thought" insofar as their situation, although not the only vantage point, provide theological thinking with a light and a perspective from which one can better grasp God's revelation and the whole of reality. It "teaches thought" in that the world of the poor unmasks false ideological thinking and thus protects the truth from our tendency to manipulate it, which in turn enables a theology informed by a spirit of compassion.[73] Sobrino acknowledges, however, that it is only *a posteriori* and through personal experience that theologians can justify this initial epistemological stance because only after being engaged in the process of interpretation do theologians come to realize that they can "obtain a wider and sharper view of everything from the perspective of the situation of the poor."[74]

Doing theology from the perspective of the poor can and should promote a profound transformation—a conversion—of how the theological task is carried out. Sobrino notes that an honest appreciation of the situation of the poor causes an epistemological break in our analogical way of thinking about God because such a situation confronts the theologian with a reality of injustice and suffering that is different from and even contradictory to God's revealed will.[75] This reality of suffering calls for the theologian's personal conversion and the urgent transformation of reality.[76] For Sobrino, the radical contradiction that ensues in our theology from the power of sin underscores that our confrontation with the suffering of others cannot be resolved conceptually but only through our compassionate solidarity with the victims, the eradication of their suffering, and our willingness to engage in the task of constructing a world that is in harmony with God.

In the final analysis, to make an option for the victims and to interpret reality from their perspective offers the theologian a privileged perspective that illuminates God's revelation and reality anew and can foster a transformation in the way the theological task is put into practice. Indeed, it is by reflecting from the perspective of the poor that liberation theology has been able to rediscover and better appreciate important theological concepts, including, for instance, the social character of sin, God's gratuitous and nonexclusive partiality towards the victims, the liberating nature of Jesus and the salvation he brings, and the centrality of God's kingdom and why this is good news first for the poor and then for everyone.

THE IRRUPTION OF THE POOR AS THE SIGN OF THE TIMES

Once the theologian has committed herself to exercise her task from the perspective of the poor, the need to properly discern the presence of sin and grace in reality demands that she allow herself to become available and vulnerable to the reality that impinges upon her.

In addition to the social sciences and other analytical instruments that help us describe and interpret historical reality, Sobrino notes that the theologian should always engage reality with a certain degree of openness and an epistemological modesty that does not assume *a priori* that she already possesses the necessary categories, theories, or texts to make sense of reality. This attitude of humility instills in the theologian an inclination to always analyze and actively reinterpret reality in new ways. The theologian must allow herself to risk being truly affected by the situation of the victims in which she has chosen to place herself and thus to confront this situation with an honesty that "identifies as its primary interest the objective service of reality, not the service of the thinking subject."[77] Such a spirit of honesty enables the theologian to grasp what is novel in a given reality and properly discern how this newness may be a bearer of sin or grace in that particular situation.

Sobrino deems this spirit of honesty with reality to be crucial if theology is to detect in the present what the Second Vatican Council defined as "the signs of the times." He explains that Vatican II offered two meanings for the signs of the times that may be discerned in light of revelation: First, it advanced a historical-pastoral understanding of these signs as the historical "events that characterize a period" and whose identification and discernment are critical for the effective pastoral ministry of the church.[78] Second, and more relevant for our purpose, the council also offered what Sobrino defines as a historical-theologal conceptualization that states that these signs are "happenings, needs and desires . . . authentic signs of God's presence and purpose."[79] As Sobrino points out, "history is seen here, not just in its changing and dense novelty, but in its sacramental dimension, in its ability to manifest God."[80] Hence, he argues, theology must be open to these historical manifestations of the divine and make of them a constitutive hermeneutical principle in order to understand other revelations from God.[81]

Sobrino's sacramental understanding of history explains his concern for the proper engagement and interpretation of reality in the theological enterprise. When a particular reality is understood as a sign of the times in which God becomes manifested—a reality in which historical reality and God actually converge—then we must begin to consider historical reality as a theological concept. For Sobrino, this is indeed what the task of theology formally entails: the elevation of historical reality to the status of a theological concept insofar as this manifests God and offers a guiding response to our faith.[82] In this sense, theology "seeks to be not only a *real* theology, but also a *theo-logal* theology that grasps the presence of God within reality in such a way that the identity of neither dimension is diminished, but strengthened."[83]

For most Latin-American liberation theologians there is today one reality, a historical sign of the presence of God in history that overshadows all others and requires our immediate attention. Gustavo Gutiérrez refers to it as the "irruption of the poor," which gives rise to his central theological question: "How is it possible to tell the poor, who are forced to live in conditions that embody a denial of love, that God loves them?"[84] Leonardo Boff alludes to this when he asks "What does it mean to be Christian in a world of the oppressed?"[85] And Sobrino, following Ellacuría, asserts "that the sign of the times . . . par excellence, is the 'existence of a crucified people' . . . and that the prime demand on us is that we 'take them from the cross.'"[86] Hence, the "crucified people" with their sufferings as well as their hopes have irrupted as the chief historical event through which God becomes present and denounces the injustice of poverty, offers the hope of liberation, and encourages humanity to live in a more humane way.[87]

That liberation theologians have made of historical reality a primary "text" through which they seek to reflect on God's revelation and advance their theological argument should not lead one to infer that they have rejected the teaching of the church or the sacred scriptures.[88] As Dean Brackley has rightly noted, while liberation theology ascribes a certain methodological priority to God's revelation in the present reality— particularly in the reality of the poor—over authoritative texts (God's revelation in the past), "[t]his does not mean that it ranks 'reality' as an authority superior to Scripture. The priority is methodological."[89] This methodological choice underscores liberation theology's concern to discern God's revelation in the present and articulate a faithful and timely human response to such revelation.

Nonetheless, Sobrino is mindful that discerning the signs of the times is a delicate and risky undertaking. Thus he argues that these signs must be assessed against scriptural revelation, which serves as the ultimate norm and corrective for partial and false interpretations of God's presence in the present.[90] Indeed, his experience in Latin America has shown him how the interpretation of both theological concepts and reality can be grossly distorted and manipulated. Just as Sobrino asserts that the signs of the times must be critically evaluated before they are raised to the status of theological concepts, he also contends, following Ellacuría, for the need to historicize theological concepts through Christian praxis as a means of establishing their proper relationship to history.[91]

This is particularly evident in Sobrino's Christology, where the story of Jesus—as presented by the synoptic gospels—emerges as the point of departure and as a corrective response to the abstract, dogmatic, and sometimes distorted images of Christ often advanced by popular religiosity and traditional Latin American Catholicism.[92] His condemnation of the uncritical appropriation of these images stems partly from the fact that as idealized portrayals of Jesus's divinity they minimize his actual humanity and thus promote an exclusively transcendent and ahistorical understanding of salvation. Perhaps more importantly, Sobrino notes that they have had an alienating and soporific effect on Latin American Christians in such a way that "centuries of faith in Christ have not been able to respond to the distress of the continent, nor even to suspect that there was something scandalous in the coexisting of unjust poverty and Christian faith."[93]

This Christian failure to effectively address injustice and conflict or to begin creating more harmonious and humane social arrangements on the Latin American continent highlights the deep interrelation that exists among the fundamental dispositions of honesty with the real, fidelity to the real, and letting ourselves be carried by the real. A theological approach that offers a dishonest and therefore distorted understanding of reality precludes us from properly discerning the presence of sin and grace within it. At the same time, it prevents us from taking an ethical and thus faithful stance before it. In the end, such theology renders us unable to respond to reality's demands or be empowered by the grace present therein.

For Sobrino, even those theological approaches that have benefited from what he calls the first or Kantian phase of the Enlightenment—"the movement of depositivation (abandoning a theology based on Denzinger), the new historical-critical work in exegesis, the interpretation of dogma, the development of the various hermeneutics"—fall short of their authentic purpose if they limit their task to giving meaning to or offering an accurate interpretation of reality, while neglecting the transformative and liberative dimension of theological understanding.[94] "Theological understanding is thus inseparable from the practical and the ethical and cannot be reduced to giving explanations."[95] What is needed, claims Sobrino, is a theology that "in its theoretical thinking [is] moved by the suffering of the victims, and that this suffering direct the praxis of taking the crucified down from the cross"—that is, a theology that understands itself as *intellectus amoris*.[96]

THEOLOGY AS *INTELLECTUS AMORIS*

As noted, an honest encounter with suffering elicits in the human person a primordial compassionate reaction that seeks to eradicate this suffering and liberate its victims. This response is reflective of how God reacts in salvation history to the plea of human suffering.[97] Hence, Sobrino identifies compassion as both the fundamental Christian reaction to a world of victims and the reality that draws us closer to the revealed God.

In line with Vatican II and following the insights of Rahner and Ella-curía, Sobrino argues that the centrality and relevance of God's self-communication to the world is best expressed in the actual reception of and correspondence to God loving self-donation in our lives.[98] Conse-quently, our relationship to this God who freely and lovingly gives Godself away should be manifested primarily in our willingness to be configured according to God's will, and not only in the formal revelation of propositional truths about God.[99] So, too, theology must seek first to understand God's love and how we respond to that love. Particularly in a world characterized by conflict and massive suffering, compassionate love becomes the honest and primary reaction required of the theologian as a human being, believer, and theologian, and this compassion ought to inform and direct his theological task. Again, for Sobrino, "theory and praxis, intellectus and mercy, cannot be understood as parallel or disparate elements [in the theological process]. Moreover, the fundamental way to relate them is by making of theological theory the *intellectus misericor-diae*."[100] In this sense, theology is best understood as compassionate love seeking understanding—*intellectus amoris* and *amor quaerens intellectum*.[101]

In Sobrino's theology, theory and praxis are dialectically related and their interrelationship functions in two distinct ways. First, praxis is a key element in the process of cognition that enables the deepening and develop-ment of theological concepts and ideas. For instance, in explaining his christological approach Sobrino affirms that "knowing Christ is, in the last resort, following Christ."[102] In other words, we grasp who Jesus is not only through our theoretical knowledge of him, but first and foremost by the extent to which we choose to live and actively engage reality in a man-ner analogous to his. These praxical (and ethical) aspects of knowing and their contribution to acquiring theological knowledge also underline the significance that Sobrino ascribes to *orthopraxis*, without which, he af-firms, "we simply do not enter into a right relationship with God and the Bible."[103]

Second, although theology is a theoretical reflection, it must nonethe-less question itself as to how it both relates and reacts to a suffering world. "Ethically and praxically," Sobrino affirms, "honesty with the real means responding primarily to the demands of reality itself."[104] Thus, theology must understand itself as the intellectual task that illuminates and advances the most important undertaking in a world riven by oppression and violent conflict; namely, it must exercise compassion as a way to eradicate oppression and advance the construction of a world that fosters life and fraternity.[105] Hence, while Sobrino's understanding of theology as *intellectus amoris* emphasizes its noetic character, his own theology also strives to compassionately respond to a conflicted and suffering world by functioning as a noetic element within the larger Christian task of transforming and reconciling reality according to God's will. In Ellacuría's words, this theology sees itself as the "ideological moment of ecclesial and historical praxis . . . the conscious and reflective element of praxis."[106]

It is important to note that Sobrino does not advance his understanding of theology as *intellectus amoris* as an alternative to or replacement for the more traditional interpretation of theology as *intellectus fidei*. For him, this latter understanding of theology rightly recognizes both the human predisposition to receive the mystery of God and theology's critical task of deepening our knowledge and our interpretation of the faith revealed to us. He likewise welcomes the effort to conceive theology as *intellectus spei* (the understanding of hope) as a way to stress the significance of promise in God's revelation and in the human response to it.[107] However, within the triad of hope, faith, and love, Sobrino argues for the priority of love (compassion) as the reality that best enables Christian theology—and the praxis that ensues from it—to make God's will present both in the personal life of Christians and in the history they endeavor to construct.

A Theology That Faithfully Perseveres in Its Honesty Toward Reality

The theologian's decision to engage reality with a disposition of honesty sends her on a prophetic and perilous journey to nurture that which is helpful and positive within reality and to transform the weight or negativity therein. To sustain this initial honesty with reality in the midst of challenges, doubts, and rejections, Sobrino tells us, the theologian must appropriate a spirit of faithfulness—that is, she must be faithful to the real.

Sobrino describes this spirit of faithfulness as the Socratic dimension of the intellectual task, because like Socrates's life, it expresses the "will to transform reality, to bear its burden, without evading the consequences of direct confrontation with the powers of the world."[108] Hence, a theologian who would shoulder the burden of reality in order to redeem it must choose to stand with and faithfully exercise her task from the perspective of those who already bear the consequences of personal and structural sin today. Faithfulness to this option then involves a willingness to face persecution, even martyrdom.

Sobrino advances the understanding of theology as *intellectus amoris* as the most appropriate response to a suffering world. He further explains that the type of suffering confronted by theology in any particular context will determine the type of merciful praxis that theology should foster. In the face of the oppressive situation of the Latin American continent, for instance, he argues that love (compassion) must take the form of justice and liberation. Theology, in this case, takes the form of *intellectus justitiae* and *intellectus liberationis*. In this regard, Sobrino understands theology as

> a specific and autonomous undertaking insofar as it is an exercise of logos, but not as completely autonomous with regard to the fundamental human-Christian task. Within and alongside other historical activities (social, cultural, political, economic) and ecclesial tasks (pastoral, liturgical, prophetic, catechetical), the theology of liberation understands its purpose as the authentic liberation of crucified people.[109]

In this sense, theology must become a source of salvation not only through its contents but also *in actu*.[110] Hence, a theology that understands itself as *intellectus justitiae* "seeks to operate within reality in order to save it, incarnating itself within humanity as it is, responding from an original compassion. In this way theology realizes, in its very theological activity, the fundamental demand of God to love and save the world."[111] This ultimate goal largely explains why Sobrino locates the reconciling reality of God's kingdom as the central, fundamental content of theology. He reminds us that this kingdom is not only to be understood eschatologically as an object of hope and gratuity, but also as a reality that must inform every aspect of Christian praxis today. In his words, "the end purpose of theology . . . is that the Reign of God be realized in this world, and the specific role of the theological logos is to illuminate, promote, and direct the formation of this Reign."[112]

As noted already, Sobrino argues for the priority of love (in the form of compassion) over hope and faith as the reality that best enables Christian theology to fulfill its task in a world of victims. Sobrino's main argument on behalf of love—a love that, in order to become effective in an oppressive world, must take the form of justice—is twofold. First, he contends that when theology understands itself as *intellectus justitiae*, it better avoids the dangers of falling into the error of retreating from reality into an abstract and idealized world and thus failing in its responsibility to honestly confront and faithfully transform reality in accordance with God's will.[113] Second, he argues that love concretized in the practice of justice can provide an interpretative stance that opens up access to the mystery of God and to a deeper understanding of our faith and hope. As such, it also helps us persevere in our original honesty and our commitment to serve reality despite the difficulties that we may encounter in the process. The practice of justice invariably confronts believers with history's most urgent and disheartening realities, which in turn radically question the initial hope and faith of believers. By provoking these questions, Sobrino argues, the practice of justice "maintains believers in a fundamental honesty and thus in a fundamental truth," and demands that "if hope and faith are to be real, they have to take concrete shape. They have to be fashioned into Christian hope and faith."[114] In other words, because the practice of justice prompts believers to take a stance with God in spite of being confronted with a reality that appears to deny God's presence, and because such a practice demands an absolute de-centering of the self, it ultimately subverts believers' limited grasp of hope and faith and gradually shapes their understanding of these realities into a Christian form.[115]

Hence, a theology that understands itself as *intellectus justitiae* radically opts to respond to the suffering of reality by transforming it through a praxis that takes charge of and is willing to bear its burden. This praxis makes God present in history, brings us closer to the transforming presence of God, and strengthens our commitment to Christian truths by helping us question, discern, and deepen our understanding of hope and faith even in the face of the challenges that history introduces.

By advancing a salvific encounter with God in history, theology becomes, in a manner of speaking, a mystagogy—an encounter and initiation into the mystery of God—that facilitates our transformation into a new creation capable of likewise transforming this world according to God's will.[116] In fact, Sobrino further contends that by informing a liberating praxis, theology leads believers to understand their life as a journey with God and toward God in which they begin to realize that just as they must faithfully engage the burden of reality, the grace of reality also carries them along through the mysterious power of God's gratuity.

Letting the Grace of Reality Carry Theology

Up until this point, I have examined how the fundamental dispositions of honesty with reality and fidelity to the real help to integrate and structure Sobrino's theological task. There is, however, an additional spiritual attitude that is essential in shaping his methodological approach: letting the theological task be carried by the grace of reality. While Sobrino notes that his understanding of this disposition or spirit results "more from experience and intuition than from theoretical reflection,"[117] it stands in continuity with his own spiritual interpretation of how the human person (including the theologian) should properly engage reality.

To be sure, a suffering world demands that theology engage the negative aspects—the weight—of historical reality, but a theologal understanding of the latter also tells us that, in engaging reality, theology encounters both the weight of the world and that which is ultimate in reality: God's grace. Sobrino argues that insofar as theology engages reality with honesty and compassion and faithfully perseveres in this original honesty, it discovers that reality not only extends difficult challenges but also offers something good and unexpected that is given freely to theology in a gratuitous manner.

In our encounter with the poor, Sobrino tells us, something positive has irrupted in our consciousness and this irruption has the structure of grace, insofar as something positive and undeserved has been given to the theological task.[118] The reality of the poor challenges the theological task and compels the theologian to reconsider the identity, relevance, and ultimate purpose of her discipline. This questioning is something that theology should welcome as positive and necessary. But beyond that, when theology recognizes the crucified people as the sign of the times, opting to stand with them and against that which oppresses them, and seeks to participate in the transformation of reality by informing a praxis of mercy, it begins to realize that "there is 'grace' in the crucified people, that is, that the crucified people bear us as their burden."[119] As noted previously, for Sobrino, God's grace becomes manifest most clearly in the lives of the victims of history who offer us, in a manner of speaking, a "light" that helps theologians penetrate the contents of theology and rediscover theological themes that had otherwise gone unnoticed in revelation and in reality. More precisely, the victims of history function as a *"medium in quo who* are instrumental to know and to grasp the contents of faith."[120] Drawing from the Third Latin American Conference of Bishops in Puebla, which states that the poor evangelize theology, Sobrino adds that "the poor do not give intellectual capacity to theology, but offer light and contents that really enable the intellectual task."[121]

The central idea behind "letting ourselves be carried by reality," then, is twofold. First, within reality there is something positive—a hope, a grace—that breaks in amidst a historical landscape burdened with the negativity of sin. When theology opts to bear the weight of the latter, it finds itself inspired, and thus empowered, by the dynamism of the former. Second, as theology, understood as *intellectus amoris*, engages in the justice-love praxis of transforming reality, it also undergoes its own process of conversion and transformation. To the extent that theology seeks to become a bearer of grace for the poor, these poor in turn become bearers of grace for theology. And because theology is a discipline whose task is to interpret reality in order to change it according to God's will, it must also engage in the reflection of that grace and good news that it has received. Theology then not only takes the form of *intellectus amoris* and *intellectus justitiae*, but must also incorporate into its own task this new dimension of gratuity and thus become *intellectus gratiae*. The definitive reason to define theology as *intellectus gratiae*, Sobrino asserts, "is that God is present, explicitly or in a hidden manner, in the victims of this world. Hence, to do theology from, for, and with them is to do theology while we are being carried by reality."[122] While Sobrino initially stresses the necessity that theology be informed, structured, and oriented according to the demands that a suffering reality imposes upon it, it is this same broken but graced-filled reality of the victims with their oppression and hopes that, ultimately and paradoxically, liberates and transforms theology and leads it properly in its task.[123]

In the end, Sobrino affirms that "*intellectus amoris* and *intellectus gratiae* are the two specific forms that configure a theology that assumes the irruption of the hopeful and suffering poor as the sign of the times today."[124] Although Sobrino claims that conceiving theology as *intellectus amoris* is the most important innovation that liberation theology offers to the theological task, he nonetheless insists on the need to incorporate into this task the understanding of theology as *intellectus gratiae*. Taken together, these two ways of envisioning theology protect it from fostering a

Christian praxis devoid of gratuity or a Christian gratuity that never concretizes itself in the practice of love. Finally, they show how theology must engage the totality of revelation and seek to unify God's closeness with God's otherness as well as the transcendent with the historical.[125]

Conclusion

As this chapter has shown, Sobrino's spiritual perspective provides us with a lens that illuminates and integrates his theological thought. Building on Ellacuría's interpretation of reality and his three dimensions in which the human person confronts and apprehends it, Sobrino's fundamental theologal spirituality outlines the most basic dispositions—or spirit—that actualize any human person's fundamental relationship with God as he or she engages a historical reality that bears both the burden of accumulated sinful human choices and the grace of a hidden God: honesty with the real, fidelity to the real, and letting oneself be carried by the real.

The previous sections focused on how these same dispositions structure the manner in which Sobrino approaches the theological task. Confronted by a suffering world and informed by a theologal spirituality, Sobrino contends that theology must engage this conflicted reality with a spirit of honesty, fidelity, and trust. Theology must apprehend and interpret reality with honesty and compassion, not by attempting to manipulate it but rather by taking a stance before it, discerning the presence of grace and sin in it, and reacting with mercy to its demands. This compassion becomes manifest in theology's preferential option for the poor and calls on theology to take the form of *intellectus amoris*. Moreover, theology must remain faithful to its initial apprehension of reality by persevering in its commitment to serve it. Theology must assume a mode of operation that advances the liberation of the victims and the humanization of the victimizers. Its love-compassion becomes practical by taking the form of justice, and theology itself takes the form of *intellectus justitiae*, nurturing a praxis willing to transform and bear reality's burden. Because theology recognizes the presence of God's self-communication in the midst of the world's negativity, it disposes itself to be carried by the dynamism of the former and takes the form of *intellectus gratiae*. As such, theology also seeks to inform a transformative praxis rooted in the recognition of God's gratuitous love.

As noted earlier, Sobrino acknowledges that his formulation of funda-mental theologal spirituality is rooted in the revelation that emerges from Jesus Christ. In the following chapter, I turn to Sobrino's Christology—his treatment of Jesus's incarnation, mission, death, and resurrection—in order to examine how this theologal spirituality correlates with and be-comes explicitly historicized in Jesus's life. The final chapter will then as-sess how the spirituality that unfolds from Sobrino's Christology contributes to fostering a discipleship and a theology of reconciliation.

4 Life and Spirit of the True Human Being

Jon Sobrino's fundamental theologal spirituality establishes three basic and interrelated dispositions that every human being should appropriate in order to engage reality properly. Sobrino proposes that *every human person* should embrace a spirit that seeks to be honest with reality and faithful to the real, a spirit that allows him or her to be carried by the "more" of reality. Moreover, for Sobrino, the fundamental act of the Holy Spirit is to actualize and shape these dispositions according to the *principle of mercy*. It is through these dispositions that human persons develop and actualize their human nature, respond to the invitation and the demand that historical reality places upon them, and embark upon a process that may be aptly described as divinization.[1] In turn, these dispositions lay the foundation upon which an explicitly Christian spirituality must be built, because Jesus's life and practice model within their own historical context how an authentic and compassionate human being should engage reality.[2]

For Sobrino, then, Christian spirituality entails embracing the fundamental theologal spirituality instantiated by the concrete manner and spirit with which Jesus lived. It means living a life focused on following Jesus and thus "journeying with, being and doing—in today's terms—what Jesus was and did."[3]

Moving from Sobrino's theologal spirituality toward a spirituality concretely rooted in Christian tradition, this chapter identifies who this Jesus is that we are to follow and then considers the meaning and the manner of our following. It argues that Sobrino's interpretation of Jesus's life and spirit from the standpoint of the victims provides the proper place from which to best appropriate Christ's reconciling revelation. This analysis of the structure of Jesus's life and the manner in which the Spirit enabled and disposed him to engage and confront his historical circumstances will establish the agenda for the book's final chapter: the development of a Christian spirituality and theology of reconciliation that engage the conflicted reality of the Latin American continent. Before we consider those elements in Jesus's life that offer the theological resources to work toward social reconciliation, it is necessary to consider, at least briefly, Sobrino's approach to Christology and the significance that he assigns to following Jesus. This is necessary because in some Latin America ecclesial circles, the understanding of Jesus Christ and the discipleship to which he invites us remains a much disputed question.[4]

Sobrino's Approach to Christology: From Jesus to Christ

For centuries, the Latin American church has largely sanctioned those dogmatic formulations of Christ that stress his divinity over his humanity, and the transcendent significance of his salvation over the historical. As I indicated in the previous chapter, this abstract understanding has generated apolitical and pacifying images of Christ that ignore Jesus's historical existence and obscure his significance for the situation of the continent. Indeed, the promotion of these alienating portrayals of Christ has often been used to legitimize oppressive social and political structures, making Christology an unwitting accomplice in the victimization of the Latin American people. In short, these biased interpretations of Christ have turned a narrative of liberation and hope into one of oppression and loss.

As an example of these images that separate Christ from Jesus and the historical liberation he brings, Sobrino points to the abstract depiction of Christ as "The Reconciler."[5] He and other liberation theologians do not take issue with the fundamental truth that this image conveys. What they reject is how it has been enlisted to generate a naive and innocuous image of Christ, one that is entirely divorced from the prophetic Jesus who was put to death by a sinful and conflicted world. "Historically," Sobrino asserts,

> it is dangerous to profess faith in Christ the reconciler without having Jesus of Nazareth firmly in mind, and it is dangerous, when remembering him, to present a peaceable Jesus with no prophetic condemnation . . . a Jesus who loves everyone, but without specifying the different forms this love takes, defending the poor and issuing a radical call on their oppressors to be converted.[6]

Sobrino insists that such understandings of Christ deform the proclamation of the Christian faith and undermine its capacity to address the glaring conflicts in Latin American society. As a corrective, he proposes a Christology that seeks to become a mystagogy—an introduction into the mystery of Christ. His is a Christology that draws on the church's doctrinal wealth and the powers of the human intellect, as well as one whose "deepest essence lies in being something 'spiritual,' in that it should help persons and communities to meet Christ, to follow the cause of Jesus, to live as new men and women and conform this world to the heart of God."[7] To this end, Sobrino adopts a chronological logic of Christological reflection analogous to the one deployed by the New Testament Christian communities.[8] Methodologically speaking, his Christology takes the study of Jesus of Nazareth as its point of departure, and enlists an epistemology rooted in the principle of discipleship—that is, in the following of Jesus— as the means to enable Christian believers to grasp and encounter the Christ.[9]

For Sobrino, the recovering of the historical Jesus is essential to "safeguard the true faith in Christ" and to prevent its manipulation.[10] The manner in which we understand Christ and his reconciling mission cannot be arrived at independently of Jesus, but must be illuminated by the particularity of his historical life. Sobrino's understanding of the term "historical Jesus" owes little to the "quest for the historical Jesus" in recent biblical scholarship or to its usage by contemporary historians. He recognizes the theologized character of the New Testament accounts and the impossibility of gaining full access to the Jesus of history, but nonetheless accepts the fundamental structure of Jesus's life as portrayed by the gospels. He defines the historical Jesus as the sum of "the life of Jesus of Nazareth, his words, his actions, his activity and his praxis, his attitudes and his spirit, his fate on the cross (and the resurrection)."[11] Thus, the historical Jesus comprises that which is at the core of the Christian mission and tradition, in particular those aspects of his life that had the greatest impact on history and best explain the whole of his life—his "practice, and . . . the spirit with which he engaged in it and . . . imbued it."[12]

Sobrino acknowledges the importance of historical-critical research, but his concern is not mainly whether it is reasonable (or not) to believe in the historicity of certain events, nor is it whether our interpretation of Jesus Christ is freed of mythological elements that may obscure our understanding. Rather, in light of the conflicted Latin American situation, Sobrino enlists historical tools to remove the ideological baggage attached to Christ, baggage that prevents Christians from developing a discipleship that can effectively confront and engage historical reality in their time. Beginning with the "historical Jesus" is a sound epistemological move that makes possible both a richer theological reflection and a more authentic following of Jesus. It does so by leading to an encounter with the Christ who sends us to transform an ailing reality.[13]

That Sobrino's Christology takes as its methodological point of departure the recovery of the historical Jesus does not mean that it disregards the divine and transcendent Christ, although he has certainly been criticized for doing just that.[14] Indeed, as Sobrino notes, "[Christology's] real starting point is always . . . overall faith in Christ."[15] He further acknowledges that the contents and the expression of our faith must constantly illuminate one another, since the faith that becomes practical in the following of Jesus both precedes the quest for the historical Jesus and benefits from it.[16] But he is also very clear in his insistence that "only in the following of Jesus do we become like unto the reality of Jesus and only on the basis of this realized affinity does the internal knowledge of Christ become possible."[17] In other words, our notional faith must always be complemented by our effort to remake Jesus's life in terms of our present demands. Only by being like Jesus can we gain a connatural understanding of Jesus—"an inner knowledge" that introduces us into the mystery of Christ and enables us to surrender our lives to the ultimate meaning of his existence.

Not everything that Jesus did is normative, however, nor do all elements of his historical life offer us equal access to him. To apprehend the reality of Jesus, Sobrino argues, one ought to be particularly attentive to Jesus's practice and the spirit in which he carried it out. In broad terms, then, our following of Jesus has to take into consideration two distinct dimensions that respond to two interdependent spheres of his existence: one pneumatological and the other christological. The pneumatological dimension refers to the Spirit that strengthened Jesus and enabled him to actualize his fundamental dispositions vis-à-vis reality and undertake the journey of realizing God's will. In turn this Spirit enables us to faithfully follow Jesus in our own historical reality.[18] The previous chapter largely focused on the pneumatological dimension, as Sobrino acknowledges that his fundamental theologal spirituality is implicitly developed with Jesus's spirituality in mind. The christological dimension, on the other hand, points to the structure of Jesus's life and to the path or channel (*el cause*) that his life lays out for us: incarnation, mission, cross, and resurrection. These two dimensions mutually inform one another and converge in generating a way of being in the world that seeks both to recreate Jesus's life and to respond to the movements of the Spirit today. Thus, Sobrino describes the whole of Christian life as " 'carrying out Jesus with spirit.' The 'carrying' refers to the channel of the authentic life mapped out by Jesus' life; the 'out' refers to the perennial need for bringing up to date and openness to the novelty of the future; the 'with spirit' refers to the strength needed to undertake this journey in the actual situation."[19]

The remainder of this chapter thus examines the structure of Jesus's life as empowered by the Spirit and focuses on the reconciling elements revealed therein. While it suggests that each one of the fundamental dispositions that constitute the core of Jesus's pneumatological existence can be correlated with a particular moment in the overall structure of his life (the disposition of "honesty with the real" with the incarnation, "fidelity to the real" with his mission and cross, and "letting oneself be carried by the real" with the resurrection), it is important to keep in mind that they are intimately interrelated with each other and that it is the Holy Spirit who actualizes them.[20] But because the following analysis seeks to illuminate the relevance of Jesus's life for Christian discipleship, it takes the incarnation—and the confession that the very Word became flesh—as its point of departure. It underscores the centrality of Jesus of Nazareth, but also assumes the disciples' overall faith in Christ and God's revelation.

Incarnation: God Being Honest with Reality

In line with the Christian tradition, Sobrino embraces Jesus as the incarnation of God, who reveals reliable insights into who God is and what matters to God. He upholds that the incarnation illuminates, in a sacramental manner, the active presence of the transcendent in human history: God places Godself in the midst of human reality to be known by it, to fully engage it, and ultimately to save it.[21] In this, Sobrino affirms that Jesus Christ is the definitive mediator of God in history. But he also acknowledges that the incarnation does not exclude the significance of other revelatory events. He thus stresses the fundamental continuity between the revelations of the Old and New Testaments, as both testaments evince a soteriological structure in which God repeatedly reveals Godself in response to the suffering that some human beings inflict upon others.[22] God's actions confront those forces that oppress humanity and reject God's will. Indeed, as Sobrino notes, "it is in and through partiality toward [the oppressed] that God reveals God's proper reality."[23]

Such partiality is evident in key salvific moments of the Hebrew Scriptures. In the exodus narrative, for instance, the Yahwist tradition explains God's intervention as a consequence of God knowing and having observed the misery of God's people (Exod. 3:7). Similarly, in the Elohist tradition God tells Moses, "The cry of Israel has come to me; I have also seen how the Egyptians oppress them. So come, I will send you to Pharaoh to bring my people the Israelites out of Egypt" (Exod. 3:9). According to Sobrino, the reason for this partiality lies in the "mercy that God feels for the poor, the small, the victim, without there being anything anterior or posterior to the simple reality of the poor that moves God to compassion."[24] This partiality forms a consistent pattern throughout the Old Testament, where Yahweh is depicted as the father of orphans, the protector of widows (Ps 65), and "the defender of Israel, the Go'el that 'defends the poor.'"[25] God's compassion is the principle that "remains present and active throughout the [revelatory] process, providing it with its basic direction and content; that is, an origin that *originates* important and lasting realities."[26] This same principle of mercy becomes historically manifested in Jesus Christ's preferential option for the victims and guides and informs all aspects of his incarnation.

In this, the incarnation reveals that an honest engagement with historical reality calls for utmost mercy. God engages the human condition so as to liberate humanity and enter into communion with it. God's closeness does not impose itself extrinsically upon creation. Rather, to use the language of Ignacio Ellacuría, in the incarnation God "realizes the weight of reality" and thus becomes fully embedded in midst of the human condition—that is, God takes on humanity in the flesh. In this "becoming flesh," Sobrino tells us, God has lowered Godself in a twofold manner: "[God] has come down to the human level and, within the human, to what is humanly weak. To express it more precisely, *transcendence* has become *trans-descendence*, benevolent closeness, and thus has become *condescendence*, affectionate embrace."[27]

For Sobrino it is not random or inconsequential that Jesus was born in the unimportant town of Nazareth, which lay in the hills of the marginal province of Galilee, or that the gospels present Jesus "as a person of the poor, surrounded by the poor, and serving the poor."[28] Analogous to the paradigmatic salvific events of the Old Testament, the incarnation evinces God's constitutive partiality for that which is small and weak. As Sobrino asserts, "From the standpoint of the transcendent, we may say that Jesus is the maximal historicization or concretization of God's option for the poor."[29]

Understood within its specific historical context, the event of the incarnation shows how, in a world framed by the mighty and oppressive power of the Roman Empire and in a nation where religious leaders either accommodated religion to the demands of the oppressor or created an ideological system of purity that discriminated against most of the population, God chose to pitch God's tent among the oppressed and the marginalized. God's action can be understood as a rejection of the trappings of tyrannical power and of the illusion of self-protective purity. It underlines God's determination to overcome that which is artificial, self-serving, and unreal in history. Thus, God's option highlights God's commitment to engaging reality honestly and attests that merciful immersion within a suffering world is the only honest response to such a world.

Sobrino sees in the incarnation further affirmation of God's preferential preoccupation with those who suffer. He points out that the New Testament narratives disclose different forms of poverty, including persons who were socially excluded, religiously marginalized, economically oppressed, and socially dependent. Drawing on the insights of biblical scholar Joachim Jeremias, Sobrino uses contemporary categories to conceptually divide the New Testament poor into the two basic categories of the economically and the sociologically poor.[30] The former are those described in Matthew 25:40–45 as the "least" of Jesus's brothers and sisters—those who go hungry, naked, sick, and for whom life itself has become a great burden and survival is by no means guaranteed. The sociologically poor, on the other hand, are those who are marginalized by the ruling society that excludes them from the community because of their ignorance, profession, or social behavior. Scripture presents the poor as standing in a dialectical relationship with the rich, who actively push them to the underside of first-century Palestinian society: "The poor," Sobrino tells us, "are those who are at the bottom of the heap in history and those who are oppressed by society and cast out from it; they are . . . those at the bottom, and being at the bottom in this sense means being oppressed by those on top."[31]

Within the world of the poor, human suffering and injustice abound, and the failure of the human family is most starkly revealed.[32] It is within this world and the lives of the victims that the mystery of God has most clearly irrupted, and within its negativity that the transcendent God is both perplexingly hidden and radically present.[33] To be sure, God's free and graceful presence is not limited to any particular reality or moment in history. Yet the dynamic of the incarnation stresses that God has taken a primordial decision to become preferentially present in those places where suffering most prevails. In the event of the incarnation, spirit and action converge in such a way that God's compassionate reaction becomes manifest in God's solidarity with those who struggle to survive—and to embrace life—under the weight of oppression.

Jesus's Mission and His Spirit of Faithfulness to Reality

To address Jesus's mission is to speak of that which gave meaning and shape to his life—that which concerned, motivated, and directed him. It is also to speak of Jesus as the one who mends and transforms a reality that exists in a state of crisis and conflict.[34] The synoptic gospels present Jesus as a deeply relational being who found the meaning of his existence by living a de-centered life focused on two fundamental realities that became central in his life: the kingdom of God, and God as Father. These two themes, Sobrino tells us, "are all-embracing, since by 'kingdom of God' Jesus expresses the whole of reality and what is to be done, and by 'Father' Jesus expresses the personal reality that gives final meaning to his life, that in which he rests and what in turn does not allow him to rest."[35] They point to what is ultimate in Jesus's life—God and God's plan for humanity. In turn they illuminate the relational character of Jesus's God: God never reveals Godself as a God in *Godself* but rather as a God *in*, *of*, and *for* the people.[36] Although "kingdom" and "Father" are not identical, they complement one another in that Jesus's experience of God leads him to engage historical reality with the purpose of doing God's will—namely, to engage in the mission of the kingdom—and this mission correspondingly refers Jesus continually back to God.[37]

Although God's kingdom primarily refers to an eschatological reality that points to the end of history, when God will fully reign over God's people, it also entails a historical dimension that is already present in an anticipatory and partial fashion as something that can be verified in history.[38] Sobrino suggests that Jesus must have understood God's kingdom "as a dual unity, a God who gives himself to history or a history that comes to be according to God."[39] Jesus's mission consists of his faithful response to these two interrelated dimensions—the historical and the transcendent—of God's kingdom.

In the following sections, I examine how Jesus sought to historicize God's kingdom in first-century Palestine—that is, how he strove for the greatest realization of God's kingdom within his own historical-cultural context. This process of historicization required the dispositions elaborated in the last chapter: a spirit of honesty that enabled Jesus to grasp the meaning of the kingdom and its relationship to history, a spirit of faithfulness to respond to the demands that the kingdom placed upon him, and a spirit of trust that allowed him to be carried by the grace of the kingdom. Jesus's mission was empowered by a merciful spirit that enabled him to realize and effectively respond to the possibilities and challenges that the kingdom discloses. The treatment of Jesus's mission is thus divided into three subsections: Jesus's understanding of the kingdom, Jesus's main activities on behalf of God's kingdom, and the God that Jesus encountered in his striving for the kingdom.

JESUS'S UNDERSTANDING OF GOD'S KINGDOM

Although the concern for God's kingdom or reign occupied the center of Jesus's preaching and activity, Sobrino concurs with other scholars who note that he never offered an explicit definition of what constitutes this kingdom.[40] He does examine how Jesus and many of his contemporaries must have understood this in light of their Hebraic tradition, most particularly the apocalyptic current that had emerged in Israel after the failure of its monarchy and its ensuing exile.

While the term "kingdom of God" is "a late apocalyptic formulation" that expresses Israel's hope for a reign of justice, "the confession of the kingship of Yahweh is basic to Israel and runs right through its history; it is another way of saying that God acts in history and takes Israel's side."[41] This kingdom had two basic connotations: "that God rules in his acts," and that the kingdom "exists in order to transform a bad and unjust historical-social reality into a different good and just one."[42] It follows that God's reconciling reign is not ushered into a neutral or receptive landscape but rather breaks into the world over and against a reality that is infused with the effects of sin. God's reign was not just a symbol that condemned the present situation and evoked God's concern for God's people. It also expressed the conviction that God will act in the future. The people of God in the Hebraic tradition expected God's kingdom to become a historical reality (even if this would occur at the end of history) that would transform the whole of society according to God's will. In Sobrino's words:

> The Kingdom of God is a utopia that answers the age-old hopes of a people in the midst of historical calamities; it is then, what is good and wholly good. But [the Kingdom] is also something liberating, since it arrives in the midst of and in opposition to the oppression of the anti-Kingdom. It needs and generates a hope that is also liberating, from the understandable despair built up in history from the evidence that what triumphs in history is the anti-Kingdom.[43]

In continuity with this tradition that expresses the hopes of the oppressed throughout history, Jesus proclaims the imminence of God's decisive irruption in history. He simultaneously stresses that the kingdom is solely God's initiative and something God gives completely and freely. While this gratuitousness implies that the coming of the kingdom cannot be rushed or forced by human action, Jesus's life and mission show that such gratuitousness is not opposed to human activity on the kingdom's behalf. In fact, God's free, loving initiative places a claim on human cooperation and conversion.[44] Without negating his own Hebraic tradition, which understood the coming of God's kingdom as an imminent judgment of the world, Jesus underscores that the kingdom is good news. As Sobrino summarizes it, "God is coming close; God is coming close because God is good, and it is good for us that God should come close."[45]

While Sobrino does not question the universality of God's salvific will or the inclusive character of Jesus's mission, he insists on a fact that, though plainly revealed in scripture, continues to be a source of difficulty and scandal for many followers of Jesus—namely that the kingdom of God is primarily addressed to the victims of history. That Jesus conceives of God's kingdom as "good news" to the poor and the victims of history provides us with some insight into its content because it represents a positive alternative to the oppressive conditions under which they barely subsist. While the life that the kingdom offers entails far more than mere survival, Sobrino argues that at its minimum it must include what is the greatest necessity for history's victims: the basic possibility of life.[46]

Conversely, the essential relationship between the kingdom and the poor also sheds light on those on whom the kingdom is bestowed. This is perhaps nowhere more evident than in Jesus's proclamation of the Beatitudes, which describe the "mindset of a person of the Reign": the pure of heart, the merciful, the peacemakers, those who are able to forgive, and the poor.[47] For Sobrino, the beatitudes call the members of the kingdom to adopt a measure of austerity or material poverty (Luke 6:20–26), as well as an attitude of absolute dependence on God. To be a poor person "with spirit" (Matt 5:3), Sobrino tells us, is "to believe that in weakness there is strength, [that] poverty is the locus of the spirit."[48]

JESUS'S ACTIVITIES ON BEHALF OF GOD'S KINGDOM

Jesus's mission reveals that God's kingdom is more than a notion pregnant with hopeful meaning; it is an event, one that demands and generates activity.[49] Sobrino groups Jesus's activities into two general categories: his messianic practice and his prophetic praxis.[50] The former involves signs that illuminated the contents of the kingdom but neither make it fully present nor seek the total transformation of society. His praxis, on the other hand, refers to the activities he engaged in with the aim of transforming Palestinian society, largely his denunciation of the forces that opposed the kingdom (what Sobrino calls the "anti-kingdom"). As we study Jesus's activities, especially his practice, I will pay attention to identifying how Jesus's particular way of being was good news to those who encountered him, because, according to Sobrino, this "way of being" is the most basic way to connect Christology and spirituality.[51]

Jesus's Messianic Practice: The Miracles and the Welcoming of Sinners. Within the context of first-century Palestine, Jesus's miracles provoked awe, reverence, and hope, but not necessarily surprise. Their witnesses would not have understood these miracles as violations of the laws of nature or as supernatural displays of power that set Jesus apart from his contemporaries. Rather, they would have perceived his miracles as evidence that God was acting through Jesus—that something had changed and that something powerful and new was happening. While these miracles do not transform the structure of society or establish God's kingdom in totality, they are nonetheless "signs" of the closeness of God's reign.[52] They suggest what this kingdom will be like in contrast to the context of suffering and oppression within which they occur: "the blind receive their sight, the lame walk, the lepers are cleansed, the deaf hear, the dead are raised, and the poor have good news brought to them" (Matt 11:5).

Jesus's miracles underscore his utter compassion and signal the fundamental spirit of honesty that shaped his mission. To Sobrino, Jesus "appears as someone deeply moved by the suffering of others, reacting in a saving way and making this reaction something first and last for him, the criterion governing his whole practice."[53] With a few exceptions Jesus's miracles were directed to the marginalized and toward those who suffer. These people found in him someone who loved and defended them, while those who followed him were drawn by his integrity, his freedom to serve, his fidelity to God and his mission, and especially his goodness.

Sobrino cautions, however, that Jesus's miracles should not be reduced to mere "works of mercy" that have an end in themselves. Just as they bring the necessary help to the recipient and help reincorporate him or her back into communal living, these miracles "are at the same time works that arouse hope in the possibility of liberation."[54] The liberatory aspect of Jesus's miracles is particularly evident in his exorcisms, which illustrate that he struggles against the negative forces that keep historical reality in a state of conflict.

In the midst of an oppressive situation, Jesus's actions inspire in others a spirit of love and hope that affirms that change is possible and that God's reign is a feasible reality. With his practice Jesus "gave spirit" to those who put their trust in him.[55] He transformed the beneficiaries of his miracles by granting them a new disposition with which they could more fully engage reality. Thus Sobrino ascribes the epithet of "good news" not only to Jesus's mission and the kingdom that it brings forth, but also to Jesus himself, as a key and revealing christological title.[56] Jesus is good news because of what he did and proclaimed, but even more so because of the manner in which he did these things. Jesus's actions and words effectively begin to mediate the kingdom, and his manner of being shows that "he was a *good* mediator because he *loved with kindness*."[57] In his delicate interaction with the recipients of his actions, Jesus conveys a profound sense of self-worth and personal agency. With statements such as "Your faith has made you well" (Mark 5:34) or "Do not fear, only believe" (Mark 5:36), Jesus recognizes the presence of God's grace already dwelling in others and underscores that it is the recipients' faith that makes the miracle take hold. His practice generates a power—a spirit—that does not impose in an extrinsic or authoritarian manner upon those who receive it. Rather, it encourages and empowers them from within to trust—to let themselves be carried by the "more" of the real—and thus to personally appropriate the faith that "God is good to the weak and that this goodness must triumph over evil."[58] This theologal faith, Sobrino tells us, is a gift from God, "so that believers, now healed, are converted so as to become themselves principles of salvation for themselves."[59]

Early in the gospel of Mark, Jesus declares, "I have come to call not the righteous but sinners" (Mark 2:17). Often depicted as blasphemy by his enemies (Mark 2:7), Jesus's reconciling of sinners is central to his mission. Sobrino notes, however, that more than just "forgiving" sinners, Jesus is often portrayed as talking, eating, and comingling with them: "[R]ather than pardon—rather than a mere quasi-juridical absolution—it is Jesus' welcome and acceptance of the sinner that stands forth."[60] For those who have been traditionally ostracized and marginalized from society by their religious leaders, Jesus's sharing of himself—and of his spirit—fostered both a restoration of dignity and an interior renewal that empowers a new life. Such renewal anticipates the coming of the kingdom and captures the experience of the sinner in light of God's initiative and gratuitous self-giving.[61] Jesus's welcoming actions assume the absolution of sinners and generate within them the conviction that their own conversion is possible. Hence, analogous to his miracle-working, through Jesus's merciful hospitality change is nurtured and enabled within those who encountered him.[62]

To be sure, Jesus, who engaged reality with a spirit of honesty, recognized the seriousness of human sinfulness and the need for conversion. But in the gospels, the sinners' acknowledgment of their shortcomings is accompanied and effected by Jesus's affectionate solidarity. In Sobrino's words, "The conversion demanded so radically from Jesus is preceded by the offer of God's love. It is not conversion that requires God to accept the sinner; rather, just contrawise, it is God's acceptance that makes conversion possible."[63] It is only in light of God's acceptance and forgiveness that the recognition of one's own sin and the call to engage one's reality anew no longer represent a source of bleak impossibility but instead one of gratitude, hope, and ultimately, liberation.

Jesus's approach to sinners largely depended on the nature and the degree of their sinfulness. As Sobrino notes, his interactions clearly differentiate between those who "sin 'from weaknesses' or those 'legally considered sinners' according to the dominant religious view of the time," and those who today we would call "oppressors."[64] From the first group, which includes prostitutes, the poor, and the sick, Jesus asks for a conversion in their understanding of God and of themselves—one that rejects the distorted images that their oppressors have imposed upon them, which they in turn have internalized. Above all, Jesus wants them to recognize that "The God who is coming is a loving God . . . one who seeks to welcome all those who think themselves unworthy to approach because of their sinfulness."[65]

From the "oppressors," Jesus requires a radical conversion and an active cessation from oppressing. As exemplified in the story of the chief tax collector, Zacchaeus, Jesus's welcoming of sinners is offered freely and prior to the sinners' repentance. But this welcoming can also prompt them to conversion and to establishing a new relationship with him, with God, and with those against whom they previously sinned. Expressed in terms of Sobrino's "theologal spirituality," we can say that by allowing themselves to be carried by the grace that Jesus mediates, sinners can move from a state of manipulating reality in a self-serving fashion to one in which they honestly engage it. This, in turn, leads them to join others in taking responsibility for its welfare. "The freely forgiven one is the grateful one," writes Sobrino. "And it is *the gratitude of knowing oneself to be accepted* that *moves a person to a de-centering from self*, to generous action, to a life of eager striving that the love of God that has been experienced may be a historical reality in this world."[66]

Sobrino acknowledges that the gospels offer few accounts of Jesus succeeding in converting oppressors. This does not mean he did not persist in trying. As Sobrino's examination of the manner in which Jesus directly engaged his adversaries shows, Jesus enlisted the kingdom's positive message to unmask the hypocrisy of those who rejected his welcoming. Jesus lifts up God's unbounded goodness, which inherently questions and challenges their false sense of security and their self-serving view of God.[67] In his desire to awaken the conscience of his adversaries and foster their transformation, Jesus goes so far as to issue forth warnings and at times direct condemnations. He speaks clearly and even harshly, but never rules out the possibility of their future conversion. Hence, he outlines for them the path that leads to salvation: you must be merciful to the needy (Luke 10:29–37) and do things for them (Matt 25:36–46).[68]

The welcoming of sinners therefore reveals a compassionate and tender Jesus who frees himself from the distorted religious conventions of the time to draw closer to sinners, where he mediates a spirit of honesty, fidelity, and trust that can liberate them from their own enslavement and incorporate them into a reconciled community. With these actions, Jesus stresses the kingdom's grace over its judgment and points to a God who is good beyond measure. And yet these reconciliations, though enabled by God's merciful grace, are not mechanical or automatic. They call for a response—a conversion—from the sinful subject to freely accept the grace being offered through Jesus. By welcoming sinners, Jesus prompts others to undergo a profound transformation in their lives and embark on a lifelong journey of faith.

Jesus's Prophetic Praxis: Confronting the Anti-Kingdom and Defending the God of the Kingdom. If Jesus's messianic practice stresses his positive contribution to the coming of the kingdom, his prophetic praxis underscores both his direct confrontation with the forces that reject the kingdom and his struggle to proclaim the features of a society that reflect the promises of God's reign.[69] To explain Jesus's praxis and its consequences, Sobrino relies on what he describes as the *theologal-idolatric* structure of reality. As noted in previous chapters, the theologal dimension of reality refers to that aspect of historical reality that effectively mediates God's grace and presence. In contrast, the idolatric dimension of reality points to a historical reality that has, for the time being, become unable to mediate God's presence because it has been deformed by the human person's sinful choices. On the one hand, history encompasses "the true God (of life), God's mediation (the kingdom) and its mediator (Jesus)," and on the other it includes "the idols (of death), their mediation (the anti-kingdom) and mediators (oppressors)."[70] The idols are those realities, like power or riches (*mammon*), to which the oppressors have wrongly ascribed the ultimate-ness and absolute-ness that correspond only to God. The anti-kingdom largely refers to unjust social structures and false ideologies rooted in idols and distorted visions of God: for example, the manner in which the system of ritual purity was manipulated in Jesus's time. Thus, Jesus's ministry takes place within a reality that, in its present condition, is so deeply divided by deception and conflict that Jesus himself cannot remain indifferent to it, but rather must take a side so as to uphold the true God.

Jesus's praxis is largely found in those activities, particularly verbal ones, in which he confronts, unmasks, and denounces the dominant groups and their misuse of power. "In modern terms," Sobrino explains, "Jesus [was] doing something like carrying on an ideological, de-ideologizing, and denunciatory struggle."[71] For instance, Jesus denounces the use of wealth that dehumanizes the rich (Matt 6:21), leads them to tolerate the inhumane poverty of others (Luke 16:21), and places them in opposition to God's will (Luke 1:53).[72] In light of the theocratic nature of first-century Palestinian society, Jesus seems particularly concerned with confronting those groups who manipulate religion to defend their interests and oppress others. This is most evident in Jesus's confrontation with the Pharisees and the temple priests.

For Sobrino the gospels' typical example of Jesus unmasking an oppressive image of God occurs around the tradition of ritual purity (Mark 7:1–23). Confronted by some Pharisees and scribes on the subject, Jesus exposes how purity has, in fact, been used to justify the practice of children ignoring and abandoning their parents in need (vv. 9–13) in direct contradiction to God's command to "Honor your father and your mother" (Exod 20:12). While Jesus is not against the development of religious traditions, he wants to uphold both God's integrity and God's support for human life and thus "cannot allow God to be used to defend the opposite to what is clearly God's will."[73]

Jesus also addresses the real meaning of purity and declares that "there is nothing outside a person that by going in can defile, but the things that come out are what defile" (Mark 7:15). Subverting the presuppositions of the system of ritual purity, Jesus asserts that "purity" is a function of how the human person exercises his or her freedom in relationship to others, since "it is from within, from the human heart, that evil intentions come: fornication, theft, murder, adultery, avarice, wickedness, deceit, licentiousness, envy, slander, pride, folly" (Mark 7: 21–22). As Sobrino writes, "Jesus exposes the fact that these real evils are those that God condemns unequivocally . . . because their effect is, directly or indirectly, to inflict harm on one's neighbor."[74] In short, Jesus condemns this piety because its practice obscures God's will, generates a social mechanism that distorts the proper relationship between humans and God, and ultimately preserves a structure that enslaves people.[75]

Similar concerns frame Jesus's conflict with the temple priests. Sobrino draws from two events that illuminate Jesus's confrontation with the Sadducees: his cleansing of the Jerusalem temple (Mark 11:15–19; Matt 21:12–17; Luke 19:45–48) and his threat to destroy it (Mark 13:2; Matt 24:2; Luke 21:6). Although it is difficult to determine whether Jesus was opposed to the temple itself or rather against the abuses committed therein, Sobrino suggests that Jesus was likely proclaiming a new setting for the human encounter with God (Matt 18:20, 25:31–49; John 4:21–23).[76] Even beyond that, he notes that the mere act of cleansing the temple points to Jesus's condemnation of priestly corruption. In fact, the two Old Testament citations that the three synoptics ascribe to him in their accounts—Isaiah 56:7 and Jeremiah 7:11—clearly indicate that Jesus's followers understood his actions to be directed against the dishonesty of the priests. From this Sobrino concludes that in this action, "Jesus distances himself from and criticizes alienating and oppressive worship."[77]

Jesus's critical stance was not limited to the religious sphere but extended to the negative role that the temple played in Palestinian daily life and in civil society because this institution was also at the center of Israel's economic, political, and social life: It contained the treasury, all major decisions were made there, and while it offered employment to many in the city, it also exacted heavy taxes from the peasants in the countryside. Sobrino writes, " 'Destroying the temple' is a symbolic expression denouncing the reality of the false god and the oppressive structure of society, upheld by religious power and justified in the name of religion."[78]

Jesus responds to the manipulation of reality by upholding the true nature of God and denouncing the forces of the anti-kingdom. Through his prophetic praxis, which is animated by a spirit of fidelity, Jesus implicitly reveals "what a society in accordance to the Kingdom of God should be."[79] Thus, for Sobrino, Jesus underscores that God's reign is not only an eschatological symbol, but also an ethical-praxical symbol that calls for conversion and the practice of love concretized in actions of justice that seek the eradication of historical injustice.[80]

JESUS'S RELATIONSHIP TO A LOVING FATHER
WHO IS AN UNGRASPABLE MYSTERY

Sobrino proposes that the God in whom Jesus placed his trust was, above all, goodness and mystery—"absolute intimacy and absolute otherness."[81] Although a detailed and systematic study of Jesus's conception of God is beyond the scope of this book, the preceding examination of Jesus's activities reveals some aspects of his interior life. They illuminate his relationship to God and the main features of the God who revealed and commanded his mission.

Through his miracles and his welcoming of sinners, Jesus expresses his conviction about the utter goodness of a God who is "kind to the ungrateful and the wicked" (Luke 6:35) and who makes the welfare of humans God's ultimate cause. For Jesus, Sobrino tells us, God's goodness is best expressed in terms of *agape* love, "that is, a love that rejoices in the well-being of others and only on account of the well-being of others."[82] This experience of God as "loving tenderness" energizes the core of Jesus's mission and underlines the relationship of openness and trust that Jesus has with the God whom, with all intimacy, he calls *Abba*, Father.

This term of endearment also shows that for Jesus, God is not just abstract goodness but rather someone deeply personal: a good Father in whom he can trust and rest.[83] As Sobrino writes, "This experience of God's goodness permeates Jesus' activity of doing good and bestows final meaning on his person, because he sees that reality itself is charged with God's goodness. His trust, then . . . stems from the primary experience that at the back of reality there is something good, that God is Father."[84] The gospels attest that such goodness generates a deep joy in Jesus's life, which he manifests in his propensity to celebrate. This inclination is expressed in his joyful prayers (Matt 11:25) and particularly in his celebratory meals, as illustrated by the multiplication of the loaves, his eating with sinners and the marginalized, and the last supper, as well as in several resurrection narratives.[85]

Nonetheless, the synoptic gospels also intimate that Jesus's trust in and closeness to God did not "guarantee him continual clarity of vision with regard to the Father's will."[86] Indeed, a number of passages portray Jesus as ignorant or actually mistaken regarding central aspects of the kingdom, such as the time of its coming (Matt 10:23; Mark 9:1, 13:10, 13:32; Luke 9:27).[87] In a similar vein, the gospels depict Jesus, from early on in his public life, engaged in discerning the nature of his mission. The difficulty of this process is amply demonstrated in the synoptics' treatment of Jesus's temptations (Matt 4:1–11; Mark 1:12–13; Luke 4:1–13) and becomes increasingly pronounced as his ministry draws him closer to the cross.

For Sobrino, the temptations are not so much related to the type of power—political, ideological, religious—that Jesus might enlist to bolster his ministry. Rather they seem to be connected to the manner in which Jesus would use any power at his disposal in order to conduct his messianic mission: "whether to carry this [mission] out with the power that controls history from outside or with immersion in history, with the power to dispose of human beings or with self-surrender to them."[88] In other words, the temptations directly impinge on the manner in which Jesus sought to engage historical reality. They reflect Jesus's limitations as a human being and especially focus on "what is more specific to and typical of Jesus: his relationship to the Kingdom and his relationship to God. The temptations therefore bear on Jesus' messianism and sonship. In this sense . . . [they concern] what is deepest in Jesus, his ultimate attitude to God."[89]

For Sobrino, this lack of knowledge regarding certain aspects of the kingdom, God, and even himself "is the noetic precondition for [Jesus's] unconditional openness to God."[90] Noting those scriptural passages that suggest Jesus's miracles as expressions of the power of his faith (Mark 9:23, 11:22), Sobrino invites us to consider Jesus as a man of faith.[91] Indeed, he argues that "faith was Jesus' mode of being."[92] This faith, understood in its scriptural sense as an absolute trust and openness to God, lays the foundations for the grace-filled relationship that Jesus, and in an analogous manner, all human beings, establish with God.

As Jesus's public ministry developed in the midst of temptations, conflicts, and crisis, there seems to be a progressive development in his overall vision. His understanding of his mission, and even of the God who sent him, begins to expand and change. If, during the early part of his career,

Jesus's life of faith was grounded in his absolute trust in the goodness of the Father, the later part shows that this trust was complemented by an active openness and faithful availability to God, who reveals Godself as wholly other. Jesus, who had neither possession nor control of God, seeks and finds God's unexpected will, molds himself according to it, and allows God to be God. Thus, Sobrino writes, "The personal ultimate for Jesus is, then, God-Father, and his relationship with him is one of trust-availability."[93]

In concluding this section on Jesus's mission, it is important to reiterate the significance of Jesus's compassionate spirit in the struggle to historicize God's reconciling kingdom. Mercy is both what "relates Jesus with the divine Parent and the reign of God"[94] and that which "shapes [Jesus's] life and mission."[95] His mission, which unfolds through his messianic practice and prophetic praxis, conveys Jesus's apprehension of the ultimate goodness of God and of reality, and his simultaneous recognition of the negative forces that mediate conflict in the world. Jesus struggles to unmask and denounce the different manifestations of the anti-kingdom and seeks the transformation of society in order to concretize the presence of God in history. Our treatment of the cross will show that, as Jesus's mission unfolds in ways unforeseen to him, he strives to remain open to the divine mystery that at times reveals itself as utter otherness. His trust and obedience to God are certainly tested by a mission that in the end will determine his fate. Nevertheless, Jesus's faithful receptivity to his mission time and again deepens his trusting surrender to the God who is not only goodness but also infinite mystery.[96]

The Cross: Remaining Faithful to the End

All four gospels attest to the fact that Jesus died a violent death. They lavish so much attention on Jesus's passion and crucifixion that Christian tradition has often overemphasized the importance of his death at the cost of his life and ministry. Sobrino rejects any attempt to isolate the cross from Jesus's life, and instead insists that his death was a direct consequence of his mission and the way in which he lived his life. "Jesus," he affirms, "was faithful to his incarnation and his mission, and that led him to persecution and the cross."[97] Like other shocking events such as the Shoah, El Mozote, and the massacre in Rwanda, the cross unveils the *mysterium iniquitatis* that generates the unjust murder of innocents, questions the sovereign power of God and the goodness of humanity, and obscures the fundamental truth of this world. For Christians, the cross is particularly scandalous because the one put to death was the Son of God, who was faithful to the demands of the kingdom and thus willingly bore the negative reaction and weight of the anti-kingdom.

The gospels portray Jesus's mission as threatened by hostility and persecution. These negative elements appeared at the beginning of his public life and progressively increased until his death in Jerusalem. Such a hostile climate suggests that Jesus must have been keenly aware that his life was at risk. He was certainly mindful that John the Baptist had been violently executed and that murder was the common fate of the Israelite prophets (Luke 11:50; Matt 23:34, 37). Jesus knew well the costs of siding with the weak and denouncing the forces of the anti-kingdom, and the manner in which the latter part of his ministry unfolded clearly suggests that he eventually came to foresee his violent death.

Sobrino divides Jesus's public ministry into two main chronological periods separated by what he calls the "Galilean Crisis" (Mark 8:11–38; Matt 13:54–58; John 6:60–66).[98] While Sobrino acknowledges that the historical details of this specific crisis are a source of debate among scholars, he associates it with a turning point that marks both a significant shift in Jesus's understanding of his mission and a new emphasis in his relationship with God. Up to this point, Jesus's activities had stressed the imminent coming of the kingdom and his intimacy with God. He performed miracles, welcomed sinners, and challenged his adversaries. But the Galilean crisis clearly confronted Jesus with the apparent failure of his enterprise. In spite of Jesus's efforts, the kingdom had not come in its fullness, the leaders of the people had utterly rejected him, many of his followers were beginning to desert him, and his disciples seemed unable to understand his ministry: "In short, his early mission had failed and he had to ask himself whether and how to continue."[99]

Jesus faced up to the need to reassess his expectations. He left the heart of Galilee, withdrawing north to Caesarea Philippi and the Syro-Phoenician border, "which," Sobrino notes, "could be interpreted as a temptation to shun publicity and reduce his following to a small group with the characteristics of a sect: limited numbers, with a strong cohesion."[100] In the borderlands, Jesus was likely enticed to continue his mission in an uncontroversial and narrowly focused manner, operating at a safe distance that might protect him and his inchoate community from direct confrontation and from retaliation by his opponents.

Soon after, however, Jesus turned around and began his journey toward Jerusalem. While it is clear that Jesus retained his trust in the Father and in the values of God's kingdom, Sobrino intimates that there was an apparent shift in Jesus's implementation of his mission—a shift that became progressively more evident as he drew closer to the cross. Jesus began to emphasize that he would inevitably suffer and die, and he invited his followers to deny themselves and take up their cross (Mark 8:34). Moreover, in the latter part of his life he no longer stressed the closeness of the kingdom; although he still prayed for it during the Last Supper, he did not clarify how it would come, nor did he perform miracles and exorcisms, and in his discourses he now concentrated on defending himself while attacking the corrupt Jewish and Roman leaders.[101] Jesus's words and actions not only focused on a prophetic praxis that vigorously defended the true God and God's reign; they also highlighted the fact that such a stance would likely result in the loss of his life.

Even though Jesus foresaw his impending death, there is no evidence that he ever violently retaliated against his persecutors. Instead, he remained faithful to the values that the kingdom generates—truth, justice, and forgiving love—and to the alternative that this peaceful utopia offers against the never-ending cycle of violence and vengeance. Jesus not only rejected the allure of the sword, but chose to absorb its weight and thus present himself as defenseless against his enemies. He turned the other cheek, loved his persecutors and, in the end, forgave his executioners.[102] Hence, while the formal content and purpose of his mission remained the same after his retreat from Galilee, the manner in which Jesus embodied this mission now stressed a dimension of sacrificial self-surrender. It is as if history had led him to the profound realization that standing for and defending the kingdom's addressees necessarily implies full participation in their vulnerability and even their probable fate. As Sobrino notes, for Jesus, "Sin is no longer something to be simply denounced and castigated, but something one has to bear."[103]

Even when Jesus could not completely grasp the when and how of God's kingdom, his commitment to serve others and his loyalty to a God who is both "Father" and "mystery" drove him from the periphery of Israel

toward Jerusalem. This journey, which placed Jesus at the center of a society that generates conflict and death, unveils his spirit of fidelity to the
real: "It reveals him as a human being who not only announces hope to
the poor and curses their oppressors, but persists in this, despite persecution, because this is God's will."[104]

JESUS OFFERS HIS LIFE IN SERVICE OF OTHERS

It is impossible to accurately determine every factor that motivated Jesus to
risk his life. However, one can assume that like any other human being in
a similar situation, he must have asked himself what his possible death
might signify and what role it might play within the overall mission of the
kingdom. Although Sobrino finds no evidence that Jesus attributed an absolute transcendent meaning to his death akin to what the New Testament
authors would later propose, he argues that Jesus most likely ascribed a
positive meaning to the offering of his life and that he likely saw such an
offering as standing in continuity with his cause.[105] He underscores that
Jesus did not see his fate as something that represented a total rupture
with his foregoing mission, but rather as its culmination.

Sobrino admits that most New Testament texts do not offer a clear answer as to how Jesus may have understood his death since they already
assume a post-paschal perspective. Nevertheless, he suggests that Jesus's
words in the accounts of the Last Supper (Matt 26:26–29; Mark 14:22–
25; Luke 22:14–20; 1 Cor 11:23–27), though liturgical in form, hold a historical core that sheds light on the manner in which he faced his fate and
interpreted the offering of his life.[106] As Jesus anticipated his imminent
capture, he organized a solemn farewell meal. During the meal, Jesus acknowledged the closeness of his death and reaffirmed his eschatological
hope for the coming of the kingdom. He stated, "Truly I tell you, I will
never again drink of the fruit of the vine until that day when I drink it new
in the Kingdom of God" (Mark 14:25 par.). These words, Sobrino asserts,
do not betray desperation but rather Jesus's unrelenting trust in God and
his hope that the kingdom would emerge triumphant and make things
new. In spite of the opposition that surrounded him and even mindful of
the inevitability of his death, Jesus continued to be convinced of the righteousness of his mission.

According to Sobrino, Jesus's understanding of his own death may be
further elucidated from the passages that narrate the institution of the

Eucharist. Although this understanding is not explicitly stated, in general terms these texts express that "[Jesus's] death will be something 'good' for others, for all."[107] Indeed, "they tell us that the bread—Jesus's body—is given 'for you' and that the wine—his blood—is 'shed for many,' 'for the forgiveness of sins,' as a 'new covenant.' "[108] In their historical core, then, these texts portray Jesus's understanding of his death as something that stands in continuity with a life of service on behalf of others—a life that has produced "positive fruits" in those it touched and one that will culminate in a final act of sacrificial service.

If early in his ministry Jesus called his disciples to follow him in proclaiming and bringing about the reality of the kingdom, and on their way to Jerusalem he summoned them to deny themselves and take up their own cross, just hours before his death he put forward the offering of his life—lived for the sake of others—as an example to be imitated by those who would continue his legacy.[109] This is evident in the Pauline and the synoptic accounts of the Lord's Supper, where Jesus calls his disciples to share in his cup as a symbolic way to invite them to participate in his approaching death.[110] Hence, Sobrino writes:

> Jesus goes to his death with clarity and confidence, faithful to God to the end and treating his death as an expression of service to his friends. . . . Jesus saw with clarity right to the end what God demands of every human being: "you must go on doing justice and loving tenderly." . . . He saw that this is good and required of him, and that it is good, and so required, of others.[111]

THE CRUCIFIXION

For Sobrino, it is the Gospel of Mark that best captures Jesus's experience of the last moments of his life. Mark conveys like no other witness the theological discontinuity that the cross imposed between Jesus's final hours and his pre-crucifixion life. As we have seen, in the latter part of Jesus's life, he seemed to recognize that the kingdom might come in a different way than he expected. He also seemed to apprehend that his closeness to the Father coexisted with God's mysterious otherness, to which Jesus responded with the obedience that led him to Jerusalem.[112] On the cross, Jesus no longer experienced God's closeness and, as Sobrino puts it, "sin appears with greater power than the Father."[113] As expressed in Mark, Jesus's words on the cross—"My God, my God, why have you forsaken me?"—suggest a different quality in the relationship between God and Jesus, one characterized by God's silence, abandonment, or inaction.[114]

Nonetheless, drawing on St. Paul, Sobrino insists that God *was* on the cross (2 Cor 5:19) and speculates that silence and inaction might be the "negative way in which the cross affects God himself."[115] More significant, for Sobrino, is God's willingness to participate in Jesus's passion and in the suffering of the victim's world. The cross, Sobrino argues, is not the result of God's rightful punishment upon Jesus, but rather the direct consequence of God's incarnation in a conflicted world: "a radical drawing near for love and in love, wherever it leads, without escaping from history or manipulating it from the outside."[116] Through the cross God reveals Godself as a "God of solidarity" willing to love in a human way—that is, willing to bear history's suffering.

Even if we affirm, with Sobrino, that on the cross Jesus felt abandoned by God, we must also insist that he firmly held on to his own poverty and to the hopeful memory of his loving Father. Jesus kept turning toward God with cries that question and protest God's silence and never accepted God's apparent absence. In the end, and despite God's mysteriousness, Jesus died in the same faithful manner in which he lived: placing his will, suffering, and ultimate hope in God.

While the New Testament offers various legal reasons for Jesus's death, as I have insisted, his crucifixion was the direct outcome of his mission and the faithfulness with which he chose to live his life. Such faithfulness in part explains Sobrino's assertion that Jesus's passion and death were the culmination of a life pleasing to God.[117] By identifying the totality of Jesus's life as that which is agreeable to God, Sobrino encompasses both Jesus's actions and his manner of being and living. In other words, he underscores the spirit with which Jesus related to all of reality, including God and other human beings. In a summary statement that recapitulates Jesus's life, Sobrino affirms that the New Testament portrays Jesus as "one who 'went about doing good,' who was 'faithful and merciful,' who came 'not to be served, but to serve.'"[118]

In the end, we can say that Jesus's entire life is salvific because it reveals what God wants human beings to be. As Sobrino notes, Jesus is not only truly human (*vere homo*), possessing all of the characteristics of human nature, but first and foremost he is the revelation of the true and complete human being (*homo verus*).[119] He has fulfilled what the Lord requires of all humans: "to do justice, and to love kindness, and to walk humbly with . . . God" (Mic 6:8). For our purpose, it is important to remember that implicit in Jesus's manifestation of true humanity is the open invitation for others to follow him in walking with and toward God. After all, it is in this encounter with Jesus that "human beings have been able to see love on earth, to know what they are, and what they can and should be."[120] This following of Jesus is indispensable if Christians are to grasp and appropriate the graces of the resurrection.

The Resurrection: Letting Ourselves Be Carried by the Real

Sobrino's treatment of the resurrection responds to what he sees as two important omissions in recent theological treatments of the subject: their disregard for God's partiality toward the victims implicit in the resurrection, and the limited relevance they ascribe to the resurrection for Christian discipleship today. As with the other facets of Jesus's experience, Sobrino approaches the resurrection from the perspective of history's victims. This perspective illuminates the essential relationship between the cross and the resurrection, and reminds us that the exalted one was also an innocent victim. Building on this oft-ignored insight, Sobrino asserts that the hope generated by the resurrection not only affirms both God's defeat of death and the future restoration of those who have died, it also proclaims the victory of God's justice over human injustice. As a hope that underscores the triumph of God over the forces of the anti-kingdom, the resurrection vindicates Jesus's reconciling vision and ushers in a promise that is offered to all, but that is primarily directed to those who have been trampled by history's injustice.

Sobrino also insists that, although Jesus's resurrection was a unique eschatological event that took place beyond history, it impacted human history and must not be considered something extrinsic or only incidental to it. On the contrary, the power of the resurrection must continue to strengthen the present lives of Jesus's followers, and their discipleship must be "shot through with the triumphant aspect of the resurrection"[121] in such a way that Christians may begin to live as "risen beings" today.[122] Thus Sobrino daringly proposes that insofar as Christians follow their crucified victim—Jesus—the "risen Christ can become victoriously present in their lives."[123] By stressing the essential relationship that exists between the resurrection and the cross, Sobrino alludes to the relationship between Jesus's resurrection and the totality of his life. This relationship suggests that, if followers of Christ seek to replicate within their own context the structure of Jesus's life and engage reality with a spirit analogous to his, they will also find themselves carried by the graces of the resurrection.

This section does not offer a comprehensive treatment of Sobrino's interpretation of the resurrection but focuses on the faith claim that Jesus was risen by the "more" of reality—that "God raised [Jesus] from the dead" (Rom 10:9)—and on how his disciples today can begin to live a life of eschatological fullness within the contingencies of their time and place.

THE FIRST EXPERIENCES OF THE RESURRECTION

In a manner analogous to the kingdom, the resurrection points to what is "more" and final in reality. As Sobrino writes, it "is the action of God by which the eschatological irrupts into history and in which the true reality of Jesus begins to be made plain."[124] With the resurrection an anticipatory glimpse of what is ultimate suddenly appears on the horizon of humankind. In God's raising action, Jesus's entire life is vindicated and the gospels describe him as being introduced into a new, exalted, and definitive life. Jesus's resurrection is the direct consequence of God's acting on his behalf. God responded to the unjust and meaningless reality of a crucified victim, revealing Godself as a just liberator of victims and ushering in a reconciling hope for all, most particularly for the least of this world. These faith claims were attested by the first disciples, who were given the grace to experience the resurrected Christ.

The New Testament writings enlist different types of language in their attempt to articulate the reality of Jesus's resurrection, including resurrection, exaltation, and life. This multiplicity of efforts highlights the difficulty of their task and, for Sobrino, confirms that there is no one language adequate to express the unique and eschatological character of such an event.[125] In fact, these writings never explicitly describe what happened at the actual moment of Jesus's resurrection, but rather treat it as a matter of fact and refer instead to the experiences of the first disciples and their encounters with the risen Jesus. Although the accounts of the empty tomb seem to have been written early on and appear in all four gospels, the New Testament does not ground its claim of a resurrected Christ on them but instead on the appearance narratives. Sobrino notes that, while the "appearance" of Christ can also be understood as "*understanding* in depth, a *knowing* that they have met [the exalted] Jesus," what is most significant is not so much the fact that the disciples "saw" Jesus as that they were given the grace to see him.[126] This grace was accompanied by the disciples' strong affinity to Jesus, and by some type of human expectation—a hope—that predisposed them to experience and recognize him as risen.[127]

At its core, the content of the post-resurrection appearance narratives centers on the disciples' encounter with the risen Jesus and on how that experience transformed their lives. Although the disciples' difficulty in recognizing the risen Jesus attests to the novelty of his risen reality, it is clear to them that the resurrected Jesus is the same crucified one who forgave sinners, performed miracles, and ate with them. In spite of the essential discontinuity that Jesus manifests in his risen existence, the resurrection did not transform him "in such a way as to make his earthly life something merely provisional; rather, the resurrection gives definitive and lasting validity to that life."[128]

And yet, Sobrino argues that the Easter event created a new faith in the first disciples: one that recognizes Jesus's *absolute* and *definitive* character while also incorporating the scandalous revelation of the cross. Sobrino explains that while the disciples likely accepted Jesus as the Messiah, and took the values of the kingdom he preached to be something ultimate, there is no clear evidence that prior to the resurrection they acknowledged Jesus as ultimate in himself because their faith was not focused on Jesus but instead upon God. Indeed, "[e]ven if they thought of Jesus as the Messiah, they would mean by this rather the closeness of the Kingdom than the unrepeatable and ultimate reality of Jesus' person."[129]

The Easter event not only upholds the disciples' understanding of Jesus and of his pre-crucifixion message, it goes qualitatively further in that it reveals the totality of Jesus. The resurrection generates a faith that places Jesus himself at its core. Moreover, because this new faith had to contend with the fact that the risen Christ was none other than the crucified Jesus and thus that God acts unexpectedly, it calls Jesus's disciples to incorporate into their faith a dimension of openness and self-surrender before the mystery of God.[130] Indeed, Sobrino claims that without the experience of the resurrection, "it is difficult to think that there would have been such conviction and self-surrender on the part of Christians—often to death itself—not only for Jesus' cause but for his person."[131]

After the resurrection, what Jesus had said and done became normative in the disciples' lives. They began to shape their own existence according to his and took up his mission, even at the cost of their own lives.[132] Jesus's resurrection was understood as a prefiguring and "first fruit" of a universal resurrection—as a constitutive part of God's future re-creation of reality and definitive salvation of the world.[133] It would be difficult to overestimate the impact of the resurrection and the extent to which it radically changed how the disciples understood and related to Jesus, and how they grasped *all* of reality. The resurrection completely transformed both what they believed and the way they lived. Sobrino writes that

> when the New Testament speaks of Jesus' resurrection, it relates it to all dimensions of the believers' situation. So it states that on the basis of Jesus' resurrection believers know who God is, who Jesus Christ is, how we have been justified and saved, what baptism means, what makes the new Christian liturgy possible, where the possibility of forgiving sins in the community comes from, and many other things.[134]

Although an eschatological event, the resurrection was encountered and perceived in history and is thus capable of transforming the lives of past and present Christian disciples.[135] Sobrino argues that the experience of the resurrection is not only handed down to us in the testimony of the first disciples as an offer to be accepted. It is also extended to those who follow Jesus, as an invitation of the Spirit to analogously remake such experiences today.[136] Hence, Sobrino claims that in some similar and limited way we must be able to share in the present the experiences enjoyed by the witnesses who first encountered the risen Christ.[137] It is to this possibility that we now turn.

GRASPING THE RESURRECTION: THE CONTOURS FOR A CHRISTIAN ANTHROPOLOGY TODAY

In order to live as risen beings in our place and time, we must first grasp the meaning of the resurrection. This is no simple undertaking. In addition to the inherent limitations of the scriptural language that attempts to capture the temporal and metaphysical complexity of the resurrection, we must contend with the novel content that the Easter event introduces into our understanding of the reality of God, Jesus, and humanity. As Sobrino observes, further reflection on this triple reality would eventually lead Christians to understand God in Trinitarian terms—to recognize that Jesus is in indissoluble unity with God, and to regard the human person of the Trinity as having received the Holy Spirit.[138]

According to Sobrino, it is this novel revelation that provides the means to properly grasp the resurrection, since "the 'new' God makes the reality of the 'new' human being possible, and it is this 'new' human being who can know the 'new' God."[139] This "knowing" of the resurrected Christ that the grace of the Spirit empowers is not only an intellectual endeavor akin to the hermeneutical one that takes place when two different cultural or historical horizons come together. Rather, it also entails the fusion of the whole reality of the human person.[140] As Sobrino writes, "The resurrection is . . . linked in the New Testament with fundamental human realities, and if this linkage is not seen in a purely arbitrary way, then these realities, duly actualized, will not only have light shed on them by Jesus' resurrection but will also, in turn, help us to understand it."[141]

Sobrino argues that the meaning of the resurrection is most fully unveiled when we assume a particular hermeneutical stance that predisposes us to grasp and be transformed by the reality of the risen Christ.[142] Moreover, because faith in the resurrected Christ impinges on how we engage reality in its totality, this stance must be as encompassing as possible and must include the different human dimensions in which we confront reality. Here, Sobrino adapts Immanuel Kant's three famous anthropological questions that map out the whole field of reality—What can I know? What ought I do? For what can I hope?—in order to identify the proper stance that allows the human person to grasp the resurrection and thus live as a risen being.[143] To Kant's questions, Sobrino adds one of his own: What can we celebrate in history today? Sobrino's response to each one of these questions refers us to the Easter event, and also back to Jesus's life and the spirit with which he engaged reality through his incarnation, mission, and cross. Through them, Sobrino illustrates the human stance that enables us to be open to the transcendent in history—that is, to God's self-communication—and explicates how our reception of and correspondence to God's self-communication can transform us into new, resurrected Christic beings who are capable of engaging reality as Jesus did.

Hope: The Power of God and Justice. To the question of what kind of hope allows us to grasp the resurrection, Sobrino insists that it is ultimately a *"hope in the power of God over the injustice that produces victims."*[144] He explains that the Israelite notion of the resurrection emerges from the Old Testament apocalyptic tradition. Surrounded as they were by oppressive empires, the Israelites understood that the Lordship of God and their communion with God had to extend beyond death, because neither the passage of time nor death could obstruct God's justice. Imbued with a concern for ultimate justice, the Israelites' concept of the resurrection emerges as a communal hope rooted in the conviction that God is just and that God always takes the side of the victims.[145]

Building on this insight, Sobrino insists that our hope in the resurrection cannot be a hope just for "me"—for my own survival—but must also (and first) be a hope that includes the present and past victims of history. From a Christian perspective, this de-centered hope calls for a profound personal conversion that links our capacity to share in the hope of the resurrection with our participation in the life and death of Jesus. In other words, we may share in the hope of the resurrection insofar as our hope resembles the type of hope that Jesus manifested for the kingdom during his earthly mission: one that responds with honesty and mercy to the just aspirations of the victims and actively anticipates God's eschatological justice in the world. Sobrino claims that "the Christian courage to hope in one's own resurrection depends on the courage to hope for the overcoming of the historical scandal of injustice."[146] Indeed, only a de-centered hope that places us in solidarity with the hope of the victims can predispose us to grasp the resurrection and empower us to live as risen beings today.

Praxis: Living the Cross and Resurrection. Moving now to the question of what type of praxis allows us to grasp the resurrection and live as risen beings, Sobrino answers that it is a praxis constituted by actions that concretize the hope ushered in by the Easter event. Just as the risen Christ entrusted the disciples with the mission of witnessing with word and action the hope unleashed by his resurrection, those who strive to grasp Jesus's resurrection today are also called to proclaim with their lives the good news that God's justice prevails. Thus they are to engage in the mission of being in some way "raisers" who cooperate through the power of the Spirit in God's project of lifting up the victims of this world.[147]

More specifically, Sobrino tells us that our actions must be, in their formal and substantial dimensions, analogous to God's raising Jesus from death.[148] Formally, our actions are analogous to God's when they are rooted in eschatological ideals—that is, when we try to make possible what seems impossible in this world, for instance by attempting to overcome structures that perpetuate oppression and conflict. In terms of substance and content, our actions are analogous to God's resurrecting action when we seek justice for the victims of injustice.

Sobrino is mindful that humans are unable to replicate God's eschatological action, but he argues that our actions can be similar to those of Jesus in their sacramentality.[149] Like Jesus's activities on behalf of the kingdom, our actions can function as historical signs of God's eschatological reality and therefore be understood as partial and limited resurrections that disclose God's preferential love for the victims and generate hope in the final resurrection. Sobrino thus concludes that "the course of action needed today to grasp Jesus' resurrection is nothing other than carrying out Jesus' mission, with the *form* of the impossibility of the Kingdom becoming real and the *content* of giving life to the poor."[150] It is to those who act in this way that the risen Christ allows himself to appear.

Knowledge: Knowing and Accepting the Promise of Reality. This leads to the third question regarding the type of knowledge that allows us to grasp the resurrection and live as risen beings. Sobrino contends that this knowing is one that accepts reality as a mystery that is graciously shown to us.[151] As a reality that is offered to us unexpectedly and undeservedly, the resurrection is best understood as God's definitive and eschatological promise: the offering for an eternal and just life that does not yet exist.[152] The resurrection links us to the future, helps us ascribe meaning to history, and opens a space for the exercise of human freedom between its offering and fulfillment.[153]

The promise of the resurrection also means that we cannot understand reality's future as a simple extrapolation of the present with all of its conflict and negativity, but must make room for a hope that defies and confronts such negativity. Indeed, grasping reality as a promise demands both that we relinquish the desire to fully control how reality unfolds, and that we remain open to and hopeful for God's unexpected grace. While we are called to accept reality honestly, as it is given to us, and while we must be faithful to this reality by assuming responsibility for it, we are also called to be mindful that there is a "more" to reality that we cannot fully grasp in the present.[154]

For Sobrino, such a stance before reality opens us to God's grace and prevents us from attempting to manipulate God. It also hearkens back to the manner in which Jesus engaged reality, which in turn disposes us to grasp his resurrection today. In other words, we are to engage history as Jesus did, particularly during the early part of his ministry, with a spirit of honesty and trust in the ultimate goodness of reality, because behind it resides a God who is a good Father. Like Jesus on the cross, we must remain faithful and available to this reality even when we do not understand its unfolding because behind it there is a good God who is also unsurpassable mystery.

CELEBRATION: LIVING AS RISEN BEINGS WITH A NEW LIFE IN FREEDOM AND JOY

In identifying the particular hope, praxis, and knowledge with which we are to follow Jesus, Sobrino is outlining the necessary hermeneutical stance that enables us to grasp the resurrection. He is at the same time sketching the core of a Christian anthropology renewed by the spirit of the resurrected Christ. In their engagement with reality, these renewed human beings mediate the presence of the risen Christ within the contingencies of their historical context and allow themselves be carried by the graces of the resurrection. They begin to live as risen beings who take on "the burden of history in a 'risen manner.'"[155] "Living in this way," Sobrino tells us, "is a form of living adequately our creatureliness in accordance with the Creator. In this way we experience the inrush of what is true, good, and saving, of something final on the historical level."[156] But what does this goodness of the resurrection—this "more" of reality—add to our following of Christ? And what can we celebrate in history today?

Instead of removing Christians from history and from the anguish, grief, and hopes that history entails, the capacity to live as risen beings encourages them to a fuller incarnation in history. What this capacity consists of, Sobrino tells us, is the addition of a dimension of victory to the love expressed in our following of Jesus and to our stance on behalf of the victims of history. Ultimately, it transforms us by disposing us to follow him and to engage reality with a new freedom and a new joy.[157]

Our following of Jesus elicits a radical love that is let loose by a bound-less freedom. Despite this, different kinds of historical attachments—some more legitimate than others—often impair the effectiveness of our love. In contrast, Sobrino suggests that Christians who have appropriated in their lives the power of the resurrection manifest a freedom that enables them to love without limits, becoming utterly available to God's will.

These exemplary witnesses, among whom Sobrino singles out the mar-tyrs, tell us that our Christian freedom is always a freedom to love. Their willingness to surrender their lives for the sake of others "shows the most radical meaning of Christian existence as a journey," since "that walking toward God—if it is like Jesus' journey—follows the pattern of liberation-martyrdom, of kingdom-cross."[158] Hence, a Christian discipleship that manifests the triumph of the resurrection involves appropriating a radi-cal and heroic freedom that enables us to love others without limits, even when this love will invariably lead us to the cross.

For Sobrino, living with joy that overcomes sadness is the second di-mension that reflects the victory of the resurrection. Such joy, central to our living as risen beings, implies that even today Christians have reason to celebrate life, not as a mere diversion or entertainment that also alien-ates us from reality, but in a way that is deeply mindful of the grace-filled mystery life offers us. This joy refers to our being able to celebrate all that is positive in the world, for even in the midst of conflict we can celebrate the presence of grace manifested in the lives of our martyrs as well as in partial moments of justice, forgiveness, and fraternity. In Sobrino's words, "It is the joy of communities that, despite everything, come together to sing and re-cite poetry, to show that they are happy [when] they are together, to cel-ebrate the Eucharist."[159]

The celebrations that express the joy of the resurrection are inherent to a Christian spirituality that generates solidarity, strengthens Christian hope and identity, and anticipates our eschatological communion. More-over, such celebrations are rooted in a joy that recognizes with the deep-est gratitude that, alongside the negativity and conflict of reality, there is also goodness—a grace—actively present therein that carries us and draws us to itself.

In the end, for Sobrino, to live as risen beings who have grasped the resurrection means to live as beings who are open and receptive to Christ's grace and who thus allow themselves to be carried by the "more" of reality.

In permitting themselves to be carried by his grace, they begin to configure themselves according to God and to appropriate God's reconciling promise for their personal lives and for all of reality.

Conclusion

This chapter examined the christological and pneumatological dimensions of Jesus's life in order to better grasp who the Jesus is that we are to follow and what it means to follow him. It began by recalling the three basic and interrelated dispositions that encapsulate the requirements for a fundamental spirituality capable of fostering the proper relationship between the human person and reality. Following Sobrino, I asserted that every human person should be honest with the real, faithful to the real, and allow him or herself be carried by the real. Because I defined Christian spirituality as informed by the concrete manner and spirit with which Jesus lived, the chapter examined how Jesus actualized these dispositions within the structure of his life.

As noted earlier, Jesus's incarnation among the poor highlights his honest and compassionate response to a reality that is both riddled with negativity and pregnant with promise. His mission reflects the life of a contemplative in action who is mindful of God's graceful presence within our conflicted history. Above all, it underscores his faithfulness to his initial apprehension of reality by proclaiming the news of God's goodness and mediating in concrete ways the ultimate reality of God's kingdom, while at the same time struggling against the negative forces of the antikingdom. Jesus's engagement with historical reality is informed by his relationship with a God who manifests Godself both as a good Father and as ungraspable mystery. In both of these relationships, Jesus displays the fundamental attitudes of honesty, trust, and faithful availability that enabled him to properly grasp and respond to the whole of reality.

The cross clearly conveys the extent of Jesus's faithful perseverance in God as well as the ultimate goodness of reality. It reveals that a life of service entails not only witnessing to this goodness, but also a willingness to bear the same negativity and injustice borne by the victims of history. Thus, it calls for a spirit of radical solidarity as the distinctive Christian way of overcoming injustice. Finally, the resurrection shows how Jesus was swept up by what is ultimate in reality—that is, by God. While in the resurrection Jesus's life is vindicated by a God who establishes justice and lifts up the crucified, in his appearances the risen Jesus extends to his followers the spirit that enables them to live as new and risen beings in history. It is in the following of the crucified Jesus that the risen Christ lets himself be "seen" and pours his Spirit upon us, transforming us into renewed human beings capable of living as risen beings today with a newfound freedom and joy.

This chapter examined how Jesus's life and spirit instantiate the appropriate manner in which Christians should engage reality. This instantiation models, in general terms, what Christians should do as they strive to live a life of discipleship. It is good to remember, however, that Christian spirituality is the creative following of Jesus in our historical context and that it is the Spirit who enables us to discern how the general features of our following of Jesus must be incarnated in a particular situation of enmity and conflict.

While Sobrino does not explicitly articulate a spirituality of reconciliation, the general structure of his Christian spirituality—in its fundamental theologal and christological dimensions—invites us to extrapolate such a spirituality. Hence, in the final chapter, building on Sobrino's work, I offer a constructive proposal that illustrates how following the structure of Jesus's life—his incarnation, mission, cross, and resurrection—while informed by his Spirit enables us to be open and respond to the "more" of reality. These two dimensions in our following of Jesus constitute a Christian spirituality that can effectively begin to heal and reconcile our conflicted reality. This Christian spirituality of reconciliation, in turn, lays the groundwork for the development of a Christian theology of reconciliation.

5   Reconciling Reality

In the past century, humanity has achieved much by way of technological advances, leading to a great concentration of wealth and a high standard of living in certain regions of the world. Yet injustice, conflict, and suffering continue to be the predominant experience for the majority of people sharing our historical landscape. Such an ambiguous, if not outright negative, legacy is acknowledged in the writings of European and Third World thinkers alike. Walter Benjamin, for instance, reminds us that "There is no document of civilization which is not at the same time a document of barbarism."[1] Benjamin's famous dictum describes a reality that, although often glossed over by the more industrialized nations, is easily confirmed by the experience of those throughout Africa, Asia, and Latin America who live in nations with a colonial past. Considered from the viewpoint of these nations, it becomes clear how, for most of human history, the manner in which we have come to organize ourselves and structure our relationships has meant that the well-being of some has come at the expense and misery of others. As the Uruguayan novelist Eduardo Galeano observes, "Our defeat was always implicit in the victory of others; our wealth has always generated our poverty by nourishing the prosperity of others—the empires and their native overseers. In the colonial and neo-colonial alchemy, gold changes into scrap metal and food into passion."[2]

From this conflicted reality of our making emerge the myths of the victors and the stories of the vanquished; the contrived innocence of those who can afford to remain oblivious to this situation, and the hope of the oppressed. While plural experiences and a fragmented history offer competing narratives as to the *what* and the *why* of our circumstances, liberation theology avers that it is from the perspective of the victims and survivors that we can best grasp what this reality—in its historical and sacramental dimension—seeks to communicate to us, and what it demands from us as well.

Karl Rahner asserted that reality wants to express itself—that it wants to have a word.[3] This theological intuition, picked up by both Ellacuría and Sobrino, is confirmed by Vatican II's call to discern the authentic signs of God's presence and purpose in the events, needs, and longings of God's People.[4] Indeed, God manifests Godself through creation, in the voices of the prophets, in the life of Christ and his disciples, and far beyond the porous boundaries of our churches, temples, and mosques. But reality does not only proclaim. Weighed down by the effects of sin, it also cries out history's negation of God's communication. This complaint is what the Latin American bishops, assembled in 1968 at the Medellín Conference, heard in their continent's situation. They thus spoke of a "deafening cry from the throats of millions of men asking their pastors for liberation."[5] Ten years later, the bishops at the Puebla Conference began their analysis of Latin America by noting that "misery, as a collective fact, is an injustice that cries out to heaven."[6] If these bishops and theologians are right and God continues to communicate through historical reality, then letting reality speak freely and listening to its word from the vantage point of those who suffer are indispensable both for our human realization—to become "hearers and doers of the word"—and for the reconciliation of this same reality.

Our proposal for a Christian discipleship and theology of reconciliation takes as its point of departure Sobrino's claim that reality itself can be articulated as a theological concept. Hence, this chapter enlists his theologal-idolatrical interpretation of historical reality, briefly noted in the christological treatment of Chapter 4, to frame its final reflections on reconciliation. Sobrino's interpretation of reality describes in historical-theological terms the root causes that account for the conflicted situation of reality, pointing the way toward a discipleship of reconciliation. This chapter is structured in four parts. First, it sketches Sobrino's construal of reality, in both its theologal and idolatric dimensions. Second, it examines the negative or idolatric aspect of his analysis of reality—that is, the mystery of sin that grounds and largely explains historical conflict. The third and fourth sections draw the varied strands of this book together to give an account of the role of reconciliation in the larger dynamic of salvation. Building on our previous work, the third section turns to reality's sources of reconciling grace and hope (the theologal dimension) to propose a Christian discipleship of reconciliation. Finally, the fourth section

gathers, in a systematic manner, the insights from the proposed discipleship and complements them with other elements of Sobrino's soteriology
to offer a liberationist theology of reconciliation structured around the
three indispensable features in a process of reconciliation: truth, justice,
and forgiveness.

The Confrontation of Sin and Grace in History

Drawing from imagery contained in New Testament apocalyptic writings,
Sobrino articulates his sacramental understanding of reality as open to
the transcendent but weighed down by the effects of sin. His interpretation, influenced by the situation of the Latin American continent, depicts
historical reality as a battlefield on which the God of life confronts the
idols of death. For Sobrino, the division and conflict that currently afflict
human history are the result of what he describes as the theologal-idolatric
structure of current reality. As briefly noted in the previous chapter, Sobrino explains that, on the one hand, history's structure encompasses
"the true God (of life), God's mediation (the Kingdom) and its mediator
(Jesus)," and, on the other hand, "the idols (of death), their mediation (the
anti-Kingdom) and mediators (oppressors)."[7]

The idols are those finite realities, like power or riches (*mammon*), to
which their human mediators have wrongly ascribed the ultimateness and
absoluteness that are properly applicable only to God. The anti-Kingdom
largely refers to systemic forces, such as unjust social structures and false
ideologies that advance and perpetuate the values inherent to the idol of
choice. These idols and their structures dehumanize the mediators who
put their hopes in them, just as they generate innumerable victims through
exclusion and oppression. In Sobrino's dialectical interpretation of reality, the fundamental line of demarcation is not between history and the
transhistorical or between nature and grace. Rather, it is between sin and
grace—evil and hope. "These two types of realities," he explains, "are not
only distinct, but conflictually disjunctive, so mutually exclusive, not complementary, and work against each other."[8]

While the conflicted nature of historical reality transcends temporal
and cultural boundaries, we must keep in mind that the causes and modalities of conflict can take numerous forms, such as ethnic wars, gender-based
abuses, nation-state rivalries, interreligious conflicts, or unequal distribu-

tion of resources. Indeed, as we have repeatedly noted, the intelligibility and relevance of any theology of reconciliation largely depends on how attentive it is to its particular context and how appropriately it responds to the challenges that a given conflict poses. Drawing on Christian resources, Sobrino's account offers a condensed snapshot of history's present state of affairs, one that sheds light on both the negative forces that introduce enmity into reality as well as the sources of healing and hope present therein.

At the same time, Sobrino's portrayal of history's current situation poses a number of hazards for developing a discipleship and a theology of reconciliation. Even if we insist that Sobrino is *not* advancing an ontological dualism or some type of Manichaean understanding of reality that questions the goodness of creation and God's ultimate sovereignty over it, other questions remain. Drawing on the insights of theologians such as Miroslav Volf, one may rightly argue that Sobrino's portrayal of reality does not account for the dynamism and the moral ambiguity of the human condition. Instead, his static distinction between "victims" and "oppressors" may foster ill-fated reconciliation projects constructed around moral polarities that pit "just" groups against "unjust" ones.[9] Such an antagonistic vision could easily lead to the demonization of oppressors and thus forestall a complete reconciliation. Despite this tension, even Volf acknowledges that we cannot completely dispense with the categories of "oppressed" and "oppressors" because that would be "a mockery of the millions who have suffered at the hands of the violent—battered women, exploited and dehumanized slaves, tortured dissidents, persecuted minorities."[10]

Sobrino himself is mindful of the limitations of binaries such as victims and oppressors, poor and non-poor. He realizes that when the poor make an authentic option for themselves, and the non-poor draw closer in solidarity with the poor and in some fashion join them in their pursuit for justice—just as Monsignor Romero and Ignacio Ellacuría did—both groups transcend the limits of the dialectic portrayed by this snapshot of reality and actively participate in the process of reconciliation.[11] In a similar vein, Sobrino concedes that, as interpretive frameworks that claim to offer the absolute and ultimate meaning of reality, religions "can generate and have generated fanaticism and violence," but he also reminds us that within religion itself we can find the resources to overcome these dangers—that at least in principle, "religions also contain self-correcting mechanisms."[12]

It is important to keep in mind that Sobrino's binary interpretation refers to historical reality's present condition, not its ultimate nature. He is, in fact, describing the deforming consequences that the presence of sin effects in history. Insofar as this interpretation reflects an accurate appreciation of the world's current negativity, which evokes an honest indignation and elicits compassion, it anchors a more authentic Christian praxis—one that rejects a naïve and "cheap" understanding of reconciliation while at the same time recognizing the unavoidability of conflict. The point is not *whether* reconciling Christians will encounter conflict, but rather *how* they will respond, and what theological resources they will have at their disposal to successfully engage a conflicted world.

A central feature of the Christian discipleship of reconciliation proposed here is its capacity to effectively respond to our fractured reality without becoming hostage to the limits imposed by the conflict itself. It is a discipleship receptive to the transcendent present *in* history and inspired by the reconciled understanding of reality as revealed to us in the eschatological promises of Christ. It is indeed a discipleship whose partiality for the victims is neither exclusive nor rooted in their moral merits, but rather is informed by the gratuitousness of God's mercy, which is bestowed on all and guided by the eschatological values of fraternity and communion. Nonetheless, before we turn to the grace-giving dimension of Sobrino's interpretation of historical reality, it is first necessary to identify and examine, from a systematic theological perspective, the sources of conflict: the *mysterium iniquitatis* with its idols, mediations, and mediators.

Approaching the Source of Conflict and the Mystery of Sin

Evil, at both the natural and the human level, is all that opposes the good and the flourishing of the human person and creation. It is, in Sobrino's words, "physical and psychical, factual and moral, historic and transcendent, individual and societal, avoidable and unavoidable, committed and endured."[13] What is specific to human evil is that it is the product of sin. It is not something natural that manifests the limitations of creation, but has a moral character that involves the human intellect and will.[14] Sin corrupts the human person and disfigures history, thereby preventing both from exercising their sacramental function. It alienates us from God and one another, and creates victims.

For Sobrino, sin is humanity's fundamental failure—the misuse of freedom and the product of human *hybris*. It is the fruit of a willful and profound, self-serving deception whereby the human person places his or her own personal interests above all else. While a proper level of self-care is a necessary feature in the development of every healthy human being, a radical self-centeredness fosters "lack of empathy" toward others and prevents us from developing appropriate relationships with them or God.[15] By blindly placing ourselves at the center of life, we disavow our essential dependence on God. This rejection of our condition of creaturehood, in turn, betrays the relationship of interdependence in which we are called to exist with other creatures. We disregard or objectify others and desire to reconfigure reality according to our will. Sobrino writes, "This culpable blindness leads to the falsification of reality, to the lie; existentially it leads to a self-interested way of understanding reality, to *self-ishness*."[16]

Human sinfulness, though ultimately a mystery, has its own inherent dynamism and twisted logic that demonstrates a tendency toward death and the suppression of truth. As Sobrino notes, "The violation of the eighth commandment (against lying, concealment) necessarily follows the violation of the commandments that protect life: not to steal, not to kill."[17] Sin's dynamism, which defies the possibility of personal and social reconciliation, is most evident in social relationships. Like most other liberation theologians who seek to offer a corrective to Christianity's traditional emphasis on the personal (and thus private) character of sin and its effect on the individual's relationship with God, Sobrino underscores the objective and social dimension of sin—its historical objectification and its consequences, which are "something visible and verifiable, something of which one can and should have an awareness."[18]

The forces that generate and abet sin on the social level are the idols. Taking a biblical perspective and building on the work of other Latin American theologians such as Juan Luis Segundo and Pablo Richard, Sobrino argues that idols are not a thing of the past or the invention of primitive people.[19] Idols are "actual realities that shape society and determine the life and death of the masses."[20] They are god-like substitutes in which we place our trust and to which we ascribe ultimate and transcendent value. These idols become, in a manner of speaking, the gods and objects of an inauthentic faith that gives a distorted meaning and purpose to our existence.

Any element of the created order can become an idol (for example, a particular gender, or a racial or ethnic identity). In El Salvador and most of the world, the pursuit of wealth has become the great idol served by those who viciously prey upon the vast majorities. More than twenty years after they were first written, the words of Monsignor Romero's final pastoral letter remain insightful and relevant: "The absolutization of wealth holds out to the persons the ideal of 'having more' and to that extent it reduces interest in 'being more.' . . . [It] encourages the selfishness that destroys communal bonds among the children of God. It does so because the idolatry of riches prevents the majority from sharing the goods that the Creator has made for all, and in the all-possessing minority it produces an exaggerated pleasure in these goods."[21]

The idolatry of wealth, which characterizes much of Latin American reality, perpetuates unjust economic arrangements around the globe. It becomes concretized through an array of social structures, organizations, and juridical systems that foster its existence and enable the powerful to protect their privileges.[22] These arrangements are justified through deceptive ideologies that perpetuate the status quo and promote cultural values that encourage an unbridled lust for personal consumption and the gratification of the self.[23] For Sobrino, these structures and ideologies embody and actualize the forces of the anti-kingdom in which personal sin has become crystallized.

In these idols and the forces that mediate them, sin and concealment come together to produce two types of victims: the worshipers and mediators, who become dehumanized by the idols of their own creation, and the millions of innocent victims "whom [the idols] dispatch to the slow death of hunger and the violent death of repression."[24] For Sobrino, therefore, "*Sin is what brings death*, violently (repression, wars) or slowly (injustice): sin is what brought death to the Son of God and what goes on bringing death to the sons and daughters of God. . . . [It] is at the same time *what generates division and antagonism*."[25]

While the mystery of sin explains why historical reality is currently riddled by conflict and crisis, this state of affairs is not the last word on human reality and history. The God of life has never abandoned creation. As you saw in the last chapter, God has sent a mediator who sets the path that we are to follow. God's reconciling kingdom empowers us with the spirit that transforms us and enables us to begin transforming our conflicted reality.

The Mystery of Salvation I: A Christian Spirituality of Reconciliation

Any authentic expression of Christian spirituality will contribute to healing historical reality and foster reconciliation among human beings and with God.[26] But a spirituality that defines itself as a Christian spirituality of *reconciliation* must explicitly attend to the demands that ensue from injustice, oppression, and enmity in a particular context. As the previous chapter established, Jesus's life and spirit model the appropriate manner in which Christians should engage reality. Here we begin our exploration of the theologal dimension of reality by examining how we experience and participate in it. This will allow us to develop a Christian discipleship of reconciliation that, nurtured by God's grace, seeks to become available to the mystery of salvation.

The spirituality of reconciliation presented here has several characteristic features. First, because it is rooted in Sobrino's Christology, it is most relevant to situations of socioeconomic injustice, notwithstanding the fact that several of its insights are of universal significance. Second, because Sobrino's theology explicitly seeks to respond to the Latin American situation and his methodology incorporates a critical reflection on Christian praxis therein, the Christian spirituality that ensues from his Christology largely describes the reality experienced by Christian disciples in Latin America. Nevertheless, and without denying the many challenges and complications that such a life entails, it must be noted that the spirituality advanced here is primarily prescriptive: It outlines the kind of life to which Jesus is calling Christian disciples in the midst of a situation of conflict. Third, this discipleship is carried out within the context of Christian communal life and not by isolated individuals. It constitutes a comprehensive ecclesial praxis that fulfills the church's mission to serve God's reign. As Sobrino rightly notes, "Faith and the substance of the Christian faith are lived in a group."[27]

Fourth, this spirituality addresses the main challenges encountered by those who work toward effective processes of reconciliation—the sometimes competing quests for truth, justice, and forgiveness. More specifically, this spirituality attends to the three indispensable dimensions in any process of reconciliation noted in the first chapter: the truthful uncovering of the events and sources of conflict, and the responsibility to attend to the memories and help restore the agency of those victimized by these events; an expression of justice that responds to the claims of the victims and seeks to construct a more harmonious socioeconomic order; and the forgiveness necessary to restore communal life and construct a different kind of future.[28]

Fifth, this spirituality guards against the temptations and distortions to which the practitioners of reconciliation are subject. Here I am not simply concerned with insincere attempts at reconciliation that, out of personal interests or political convenience, willfully disregard the need for truth, justice, and forgiveness. More challenging are those distortions that were not anticipated in the agents' original plans. Sobrino's close witnessing of the movements of liberation in Latin America and particularly in El Salvador demonstrates that even Christian-inspired pursuits of a society's liberation and reconciliation are always subject to human limitations and sinfulness. Even the best-intentioned attempts at reconciliation are commonly derailed by, among other things, the gradual displacement of the victims and their demands as the central concern of the reconciliation process; the mystification of violence as the most effective means to transform society; the tendency to demonize the oppressor; the oppressors' unwillingness to take responsibility for their actions; and the victims' understandable difficulty in forgiving their perpetrators, which closes off the possibility of social reconciliation and their own liberation.[29]

Finally, any rendering of a Christian spirituality of reconciliation must demonstrate how following Jesus within one's own context and individuality can effectively inform the manner in which Christians seek to overcome situations of enmity. Here I propose a spirituality of reconciliation that can be best understood as a process organized around the essential moments that structured Jesus's life and the Spirit who animated it. This spirituality illustrates how the creative following of Jesus can help overcome enmity and conflict within the general conditions of socioeconomic injustice and oppression that characterize the situation in most of Latin America, but also elsewhere.

Constructing a Christian Spirituality of Reconciliation

According to Sobrino, our following of Jesus has to take into consideration two distinct dimensions that respond to two interdependent spheres of his existence: one christological, the other pneumatological. These dimensions mutually refer to each other and converge in generating a way of being in the world that seeks to conform itself to Jesus's life and respond to the movements of the Spirit today. The christological dimension points to the structure of Jesus's life and the path or channel his life lays out for us: incarnation, mission, cross, and resurrection. The pneumatological dimension refers to the Spirit, who strengthened and enabled Jesus to undertake the journey of bringing God's will to fruition within the challenges and opportunities of his historical situation. This Spirit likewise enables us to realize the dispositions of honesty, fidelity, and trust that empower us to creatively follow Jesus in our contemporary world.[30]

As in the previous chapter, I propose that each of these fundamental dispositions correlates to a particular moment in the overall structure of Jesus's life: honesty with the real correlates with his incarnation, fidelity to the real correlates with his mission and cross, and letting oneself be carried by the grace of reality correlates with his resurrection. While these three fundamental dispositions are deeply interrelated and always present in each moment of Jesus's life, different moments of his life more clearly manifest a particular disposition: Jesus's incarnation stresses his honesty with reality, his mission and crucifixion evinces his faithfulness to the end, and his resurrection confirms his trust in a reliable God and ushers in a hope offered to all.

In an analogous fashion, the honest appreciation and engagement of our situation requires that we immerse ourselves in it. Only such an "incarnation" enables us to consider the different forces that shape a particular situation, discern the presence of sin and grace therein, and compassionately respond to the demands that this situation places on us. In turn, the realization of the task before us sends us on a long and difficult mission—collaborating in the advancement of God's kingdom—that calls for a spirit of fidelity. This fidelity to persevere in our original honesty and compassion is especially needed in those moments when the cross looms, when we risk our lives by acting in the knowledge that we will be forcibly opposed by those who benefit from the current state of affairs. All of this we are able to do insofar as we appropriate the graces of Jesus's resurrection and rely on a spirit that affirms our transcendence, strengthens our hope, and empowers us to trust in God's graces.

In enlisting the structure of Jesus's life to systematize a Christian spirituality of reconciliation, I will treat the key events in chronological order, but I am also mindful that Jesus's resurrection already impacts all aspects of Christian discipleship. Thus, in a larger or smaller measure, the insights and graces derived from this event inform every aspect of our following of Jesus.

INCARNATION: THE HONEST AND COMPASSIONATE ENGAGEMENT OF CONFLICTED REALITY

In Sobrino's Christology, the incarnation models the honesty and compassion with which Christians are to engage their historical reality. Jesus's life shows that compassionate engagement is the only adequate response to a suffering and conflicted world. His kenotic movement illustrates God's loving solidarity with humanity and invites us to take a similar turn toward the other, particularly toward the suffering other.[31] In a historical context permeated by conflict and injustice, an honest apprehension of reality elicits a compassion that compels the subject to stand in solidarity with the victims of oppression, and against the forces that oppress them.

Yet reality is not always easily apprehended. The truth that is able to challenge the inadequacy of our social arrangements is all too often obscured and manipulated by those in power. Regarding the situation of Latin America and El Salvador in particular, Sobrino writes: "We live in a culture of concealment, of distortion, and thus in effect we are living in a lie. There is not only *structural injustice*, not only *institutionalized violence*—as the bishops emphasized in Medellín—but also *institutionalized concealment, distortion, and lies*. And vast resources are used to maintain that structure."[32]

This deceptive varnishing of reality is the product of many national and international organizations, governments, corporations, and other powerful minorities (for example, national oligarchies) who profit from the country's status quo and the suppression of truth. Following Ignacio Ellacuría, Sobrino adopts the term *civilization of wealth* to describe the cultural values, beliefs, and socioeconomic and political arrangements sustained by the network of powerful national and transnational organizations that control most of the Western nations.[33] These powerful players have taken advantage of technological advances in organization, information, and transportation to structure a market-oriented economic order whose main goal is the accumulation of capital and the maximization of profit for the elite.[34] This economic order has increased the gap between rich and poor nations, reduced the great majorities to poverty and marginalization, and undermined local cultures, creating conditions that consistently lead to violent conflict between the powerful and the powerless.[35]

This culture of deceit begs for a spirit of honesty that can enable us to overcome our tendency to place our own interests above the truth that reality mediates. Appropriating that spirit marks the beginning of a process of conversion toward Christian discipleship—the start of a new life journey that seeks to follow Jesus's way of being in the world. We are urged to attend to conflicted reality by entering into the world of those who bear the negative consequences of enmity. There we can establish relationships of friendship and solidarity and take an ethical stance against the social and economic forces that enforce poverty. "This incarnation," Sobrino states, "is hard, but it is a conversion which leads to solidarity with the poor and seeing reality in a very different way, overcoming the mechanisms we use to defend ourselves from reality."[36]

The core of a liberationist spirituality of reconciliation is the encounter with God in the world of the victims. The world of the poor communicates two essential insights: It implicitly denounces those who reject God's plan and perpetuate the sinful causes of conflict, and it discloses God's healing presence and will for a reconciled world.

The situation of the victims renders transparent the complex economic and social structures that conceal vast mechanisms of oppression, exposing the agents behind their victimization. By revealing exploitative processes, the victims condemn the counterfeit narrative of the oppressors and the bogus justifications of passive spectators who would like to prolong their comfortable blindness to reality. More importantly, the victims bear a truth that demands the recognition of their grievances and the restoration of their dignity.

While the world of the oppressed is certainly not exempt from the presence of sin, the poor and the victims nonetheless stand as a privileged locus within which to encounter God. As the bishops at the Third

General Conference at Puebla attested, the poor have an "evangelizing potential. . . . For the poor challenge the church constantly, summoning it to conversion; and many of the poor incarnate in their lives the evangelical values of solidarity, service, simplicity, and openness to accepting the gift of God."[37] These are the humanizing values evident in the experiences of the base communities and in the spirit of renewal they have brought to the broader church as they have worked to transform the oppressive political reality in which they live.[38] Out of all of the values illustrated by the lives of the victims, I want to underscore why solidarity is so crucial for a spirituality of reconciliation.

The murder of Archbishop Óscar Romero and priests, religious, and lay ministers attracted worldwide attention to the Salvadoran civil war in the 1980s. Indeed, Sobrino tells us that Romero's death elicited a call for solidarity to which many people from relatively affluent backgrounds around the world responded with material aid and concrete actions that sometimes led them to participate directly in the lot of the victims. In these encounters, the life of the victims prompted many non-victims to re-examine the purpose and meaning of their lives: These non-victims "under[went] the experience of being sent to others only to find their own truth. At the very moment of giving, they [found] themselves expressing gratitude for something new and better than they [had] been given."[39] For many Christians, examining the world from the perspective of the poor led to new insights into their faith and new ways to respond to the mystery of God.

These relationships between victims and non-victims illustrate the type of solidarity needed in an unequal and conflicted world—that is, a solidarity rooted in friendship. In other words, a solidarity that is capable of generating a profound sense of shared responsibility among victims and non-victims alike, and of fostering a mutually beneficial sharing of gifts among them.[40] This understanding of solidarity defies the traditional notion that assistance always flows in one direction—from the non-poor to the poor—and thus undermines existing patterns of social paternalism and domination. While this solidarity among unequals must acknowledge the vast gap that separates victims from non-victims, it ultimately reaffirms the true communal and interrelated nature of humankind. For Christians, it models how we are called to mercifully bear with one another.

Solidarity thus is the reconciling praxis that emerges from compassion, and bonds the followers of Christ in communities of mutual accompaniment and co-responsibility. Such solidarity reflects the distinct memory and hope that constitutes these communities: the Christ event. The memory of Jesus Christ, which roots their identity, is continuously mediated by the narratives of the gospel, sacramental celebrations, and the liberating praxis of the local church. It is within these communities of solidarity, all too often forged by oppression and persecution, that the victims of conflict can find healing and meaning for their own memories of suffering. Here survivors find a hospitable place to share, examine, and work through their painful stories by placing them within the salvific narrative of Jesus's life, death, and resurrection. Here is also the place where repentant oppressors, now forgiven, are welcomed to begin a new life. Indeed, for Sobrino, this memory of having been forgiven is something the perpetrators can contribute to the process of reconciliation. Somewhat analogous to the healing memory of Jesus, "[this memory] is a salvific recollection . . . [that] pulls us back to the truth, back to honesty with the real . . . and helps us minimize the hubris that comes into the practice of liberation."[41] Above all, these communities are sustained by hope and stand as sources of hope for others. Their hope manifests a mode of living with a renewed imagination and with confidence in the promises of God revealed in Jesus: that the reign of God is at hand (cf. Luke 10:9), and there will be "a new heaven and a new earth" (2 Pet 3:13; Rev 21:1).

But the kingdom is both "here" and "not yet." While we may say that reconciliation takes place in a partial and limited manner whenever the kingdom becomes sacramentally present in history, a fully reconciled humanity will only come at the end of time and will include the living and the dead. What is more, the coming of the kingdom and the historical task that its coming bestows upon Jesus's followers is one riddled with conflict. It invariably places the victims and those in solidarity with them in opposition to the oppressors and the structures they maintain. As I show in the following section, it is in the midst of the conflict between victims and oppressors that Christian spirituality calls for perseverance in one's honest apprehension of reality by proclaiming the reconciling promise of God's kingdom, denouncing and forgiving sinful reality, and remaining available to the mystery of God's will.

GOD'S KINGDOM: A RECONCILING MISSION ANIMATED
BY A SPIRIT OF FIDELITY

Jesus's followers today are entrusted with the same mission he inaugurated: to pursue the fullest realization of God's reconciling kingdom in history at both the individual and social level. Through our personal actions of solidarity with the victims of history, we proclaim the values of God's kingdom and strengthen the hope that such a reign is possible. Through our denunciations of oppressive structures—whether religious, social, economic, or political—and our efforts to build a more just society, we witness to the sociopolitical implications of this reconciling reign. By working on behalf of the kingdom, Christians enact their fidelity to God's revelation and persevere in their initial compassionate response to a world of suffering.

In Sobrino's view, compassion is the principle that elicits, grounds, and informs all our efforts to transform sinful reality and forgive the oppressor. Our efforts on behalf of the kingdom concretize a mission of mercy that becomes practical in the pursuit of both social justice and interpersonal forgiveness. Sobrino affirms that Christians are called to both "forgive sinful reality" and "forgive the oppressor."[42] Following the insights of the Latin American bishops' conferences at Medellín and Puebla, he argues that a Christian praxis must first focus its efforts on the eradication of structural sin and the corresponding humanization of its victims, and then attend to the personal rehabilitation of the oppressor.[43]

While the social and interpersonal dimensions of the reconciling mission are deeply interrelated and equally important, the chronological priority given to the struggle for social justice underscores that our efforts must begin with what is most urgent—addressing, albeit imperfectly, the structural causes of widespread oppression, conflict, and affliction. As we will see, seeking justice first does not relax the tension between the pursuit of justice and the offering of forgiveness, nor does it assume that full social justice must be achieved before forgiveness can be extended. Rather, it presumes that our pursuit of justice is already informed by a profound compassion that is always willing to extend forgiveness.

Forgiving Sinful Reality: From a Civilization of Wealth to One of Poverty. The problem encountered by Jesus's followers in most of Latin America is not merely that the kingdom is "not yet"—i.e., that it does not exist in its fullness. Rather, this kingdom and the fullness of life it brings are actively denied by the presence of sin, which in turn spawns conflict and death.[44] Hence, the task of "forgiving reality"[45] in pursuit of a reconciled society entails the profound transformation of the socioeconomic structures, institutions, laws, and cultural values that generate sin and promote enmity among human beings.

While complete reconciliation among human beings and with God will come only with the fulfillment of God's kingdom, the values that we can draw from Jesus's proclamation of the kingdom offer us a basic standard from which Christians can both prophetically evaluate the prevailing conditions of injustice and envisage an alternative. God's kingdom establishes the fundamental values to which humanity must aspire and thus provides an overarching vision for a society rooted in truth, human dignity, and fraternity.

Thus, God's kingdom provides the basic direction for a historical project: a utopia that both denounces all that stands against the integral flourishing of the human person and realizes Christian hope in the public sphere.[46] This utopia must not be hijacked by a set of otherworldly platitudes that make its historical realization, at least in its initial stage, an impossibility. At the same time, grounding Christian praxis in the vision of God's gratuitous and eschatological kingdom is essential because it protects the end purpose of this praxis from being reduced to what is politically efficient and feasible at a given point in time. Indeed, as a rational and viable historical project, a Christian utopia enables the mediation of Christian faith into the indispensable political praxis that seeks the renewal of the human person and society.

Though inspired by the values of the kingdom, this utopia is a human project that is vulnerable to human sinfulness and fallibility. Thus it must not be conflated with the kingdom. God alone will ultimately fulfill God's kingdom; meanwhile the Christian utopic vision takes shape through our continuous, imperfect, and provisional attempts to make the kingdom present in history.[47] Because of the inherently provisional character of any Christian utopia, our reconciling praxis must remain open to the unforeseen possibilities of God's grace while taking into consideration the limitations and opportunities present in a particular context.

When speaking about the characteristics of a viable Christian utopia that aims to historicize the reconciling values of God's kingdom, Sobrino consistently relies on Ellacuría's formulation of the civilization of poverty.[48] Far from proposing a society of "paupers," Ellacuría proposes a civilization of work, love, and austerity structured according to Jesus's beatitudes. This discipline would be the Christian alternative able to supplant the civilization of wealth described above. Citing Ellacuría, Sobrino describes the civilization of poverty as one that "rejects the accumulation of capital as the engine of history, and the possession-enjoyment of wealth as the principle of humanization; rather, it makes the universal satisfaction of basic needs the principle of development, and the growth of shared solidarity the basis of humanization."[49]

Like Ellacuría, Sobrino acknowledges the numerous and important advances achieved by the civilization of wealth among First World nations in the sciences and culture, as well as its recognition (at least in theory) of the dignity of the human person.[50] However, mindful of the human and material cost that has accompanied the pursuit of wealth and power by Western nations, Sobrino argues that converting historical reality into a more humane civilization requires a U-turn and a profound transformation of the world at the global and local levels. As Sobrino writes, "We must fight against sin by destroying and building. We must destroy the idols of death, that is, we must destroy the structures of oppression and violence. We must build new structures of justice."[51]

Because the kingdom was first offered to the poor, Sobrino argues that it is the poor—particularly those who have made an option for themselves and their fellows—who offer the most adequate utopian vision: one that is not conceived from the illusionary world of abundance and self-gratification, but rather one that envisions "the existence and the guarantee of an essential core of basic life and of human family."[52] Thus a Christian ministry of reconciliation will strive to develop new economic, political, and cultural projects that guarantee basic human needs and enable a more humane civilization rooted in simplicity and solidarity.[53]

Although informed by faith values, these projects should not contradict the rational order, but rather enlist reason in order to be persuasive in a pluralistic society. This reliance on reason is indispensable both in determining how faith claims are to be transformed into political action and in seeking the collaboration of non-Christian partners. Hence, insofar as these projects seek to mediate the Christian faith in the public sphere, they need to understand themselves as rational enterprises open to the examination and evaluation of the members of this same sphere and willing to engage the secular world in a dialogue that is fruitful to all. Indeed such dialogue requires, from all involved, an attitude of humility that makes room for a diversity of voices within civil society, chiefly those of the poor.

Whether labeled a "civilization of poverty" or not, any working utopia should guarantee the minimum material necessities, uphold the values of human fraternity, and aim at a new social paradigm that incorporates the noblest human traditions, both Christian and non-Christian, around which the different elements of society can come together to create a more humane and reconciled world.[54]

Forgiving the Oppressor: The Stubbornness of Love. Integrally related to the mission of transforming reality and promoting God's kingdom is the delicate and difficult task of forgiving the oppressor. Sobrino describes oppressors as mediators of the anti-kingdom and agents of the idols who bring about death.[55] By extending forgiveness to their persecutors, victims introduce the possibility of restoring broken relations and begin to concretize the promises of the kingdom. Such fidelity, Sobrino tells us, presupposes a particular vision of God as the "transcendent beginning of reconciliation."[56]

Sobrino notes that the Christian God has been revealed as a wholly decentered God who loves and forgives us first, and who stands on our side even when we stand against God. This is a God who seeks no retribution even as the Son is put to death. God's act of raising Jesus is not accompanied by reprisals against those who abandoned or betrayed the crucified one, and God does not wait for their conversion before acting. Instead God forgoes God's rights before humanity and "remains at their mercy and offers them a future."[57]

For Sobrino, Christian forgiveness is an expression of a deep love that never gives up on the persecutors' potential to be humane. This love seeks to convert and recreate sinful humans for the ultimate purpose of bringing them into loving communion with God and others. In his ministry, Jesus loved the oppressors by confronting and unmasking them and even by warning them of a final condemnation.[58] Although the oppressors repeatedly rejected him, Jesus never gave up on them and cried out for their forgiveness even as he was hanging on the cross. Indeed, Jesus the forgiving victim is animated by his hope in the conversion of sinners and the miracle of reconciliation. "From this hope," Sobrino claims, "arises the attitude of forgiving up to seventy times seven, hoping for the triumph of love, or—when hope seems to be totally against hope—leaving eschatological forgiveness to God."[59]

Forgiveness is necessary for both victims and victimizers, but the former are the only ones who, in history, can extend pardon to their oppressors. For the victims, offering forgiveness opens the possibility that they themselves might be liberated from a reality that is often characterized by understandable but poisonous feelings of resentment or, worse, by a crippling internalized sense of worthlessness that the oppressors have projected onto them throughout their prolonged victimization. For the victimizers, asking for and receiving unconditional forgiveness begins to liberate them from their guilt and restore their human dignity. "We come to be truly human," Sobrino writes, "not only by making our own selves— often in Promethean fashion—but by letting ourselves be made human by others."[60] In allowing themselves to be carried by the grace mediated by the victims, the victimizers encounter salvation and an invitation to become co-responsible for the well-being of reality.

As we have seen, a Christian spirituality of reconciliation is rooted in and shaped by compassion, which moves us to forgive reality through achieving justice and to personally forgive the sinner. In fact, Sobrino insists that strict justice, without forgiveness, would lead personal and social relationships into a state of chaos. This is the case not only because of justice's inability to effectively deal with countless offenses, but particularly because forgiveness is indispensable to "break the vicious circle of offense and retaliation" that usually characterizes conflicted situations.[61] Put bluntly, how can justice alone redress murder and years of oppression, or undo the suffering that has already been inflicted?

This is not to say that forgiveness erases the recognition of past injustices or the possibility of compensation for the victims, or that it prohibits holding the perpetrators to account. On the contrary, offering or accepting forgiveness already assumes that a wrong is being acknowledged. Indeed, though the willingness to forgive is neither prior to nor dependent on achieving justice, there will be no lasting historical reconciliation unless there is repentance, justice, and accountability for previous injustices.

But unlike justice, forgiveness underscores the gratuitous dimension of love through which the victim is willing to renounce his or her legitimate rights for the sake of the sinner and the hope of reconciliation. In Sobrino's words, "If forgiveness of reality stresses the efficacy of love, forgiveness of the sinner stresses the gratuity, unreason, and defenselessness of love. We do not forgive out of any personal or group interest, even a legitimate one, but simply out of love."[62]

The victims certainly cannot be forced to extend forgiveness; the capacity to forgive is a gift and a grace accepted in gratitude by those who know themselves to have been forgiven.[63] When offered freely, Christian forgiveness is a radically generous praxis that facilitates the sinner's conversion and makes us images of God. Forgiveness, however, is a risky endeavor. The victims' extension of forgiveness can always be ignored, rejected, or, even worse, manipulated against the victims themselves. But our pursuit of reconciliation requires not only truth and justice but also the victims' forgiveness and the perpetrators' repentance.

A REDEMPTIVE CROSS: LIVING WITH A SPIRIT OF FIDELITY TO THE END

For Sobrino, Jesus's crucifixion was a direct consequence of his honest and compassionate incarnation in a conflicted world. Jesus did not seek the cross as such, nor was the crucifixion part of some divine plan that required his suffering in order to expiate human sin and satisfy a judging God. Rather, it was the historical outcome of loving others without limit in a sinful world.[64] Thus, Jesus's cross reveals the extent of his fidelity to God and to the mission that God entrusted to him. In an analogous manner, those who follow Jesus today and take up the cross by engaging in a compassionate praxis that seeks to eradicate evil are likely to endure a fate similar to that of Jesus.

When Sobrino describes the Christian task of taking responsibility for the sinful and conflicted character of reality, he makes a distinction between *overcoming* and *redeeming* its evil.[65] He suggests that we should try to *overcome* violence's evil through all legitimate and effective means, such as confronting injustice and the original causes of the violence, assisting those in need, and proposing negotiations and dialogue between the conflicting parties. In contrast, *redemption* emphasizes that eradicating the sin and injustice that permeates our social relationships cannot be accomplished indirectly. It requires from us a solidarity that is willing to take up and endure the consequences of sin. "What is most distinctively Christian,"

Sobrino writes, "is to redeem violence. This only takes place when we eradicate it, and in order to achieve that we must not only struggle against it from outside [violence itself], but we have to bear with it from within. To do this—and to do it for love of the victims—is what exemplifies the love of the martyrs."[66] For Sobrino, the suffering of Jesus—and that of the martyrs—has a redemptive dimension insofar as it stops, absorbs, and reverses the inherent tendency of evil and violence to generate even more violence.[67]

RESURRECTION: LETTING OURSELVES BE CARRIED BY A SPIRIT OF TRUST

Jesus's resurrection ushers in the promise of final justice and an offer of forgiveness that is the product of a love tested by suffering and death. In the resurrection, God responds to the unjust execution of the innocent victim Jesus and reveals Godself as a just liberator, thereby renewing our hope in a future that is God's. But it is Jesus's post-resurrection appearances that help model a discipleship of reconciliation: They convey God's forgiving love and function as commissioning events in which the disciples are welcomed back into the community and entrusted with Jesus's reconciling mission. The appearance stories underscore how Christ, the sinless victim, offers perfect forgiveness and teaches us to forgive. His pardoning is entirely a gift and potentially transforming; its purpose is none other than the purpose of all love: "to come into communion."[68]

Although freely offered, Christ's forgiveness urges us all to examine and accept our complicity in a broken reality that continues to produce victims. To be sure, we do not all bear equal degrees of responsibility for the conflicted nature of reality, for although we are all sinners some sinful actions are qualitatively more serious and yield greater negative effects than others. Yet sober acknowledgment of the current human condition demands that we avoid any idealization that might place a particular group above accountability, for an integral part of following the crucified and sinless victim is the call to continuous conversion. This conversion is enabled by the Spirit, who makes Christ's risen life present in history. It is this same Spirit of the resurrected Christ who empowers us to live as persons raised to life amid the very brokenness of history.

Sobrino approaches the resurrection with an eye toward how it may affect our lives and discipleship today. The fact that the eschatological event of the resurrection was perceived in history and that it transformed the lives of Jesus's disciples, he argues, indicates that at least in some analogous and limited way, we must also be able to share today the experiences enjoyed by those first witnesses.[69] In the resurrection all initiative and agency rests solely in God, who raised Jesus from the dead and gave the disciples the necessary grace to experience the risen Christ. This gratuitous bestowal of grace was accompanied by the disciples' receptivity and affinity to Jesus and by a hopeful expectation that predisposed them to experience and recognize him as risen.

As we saw in the previous chapter, to explicate how followers of Jesus today might analogously grasp the Spirit of the resurrected Christ, Sobrino adapts Immanuel Kant's three anthropological questions to map out the Christic stance toward reality: What can I know? What ought I to do? For what can I hope? To these questions, Sobrino adds one of his own: What can we celebrate in history today?[70] For Sobrino, appropriating the manner in which Jesus hoped, acted, and knew predisposes the disciple to encounter and be transformed by the risen Christ. Sobrino claims that inasmuch as we follow the crucified Jesus, the risen Christ becomes present "so that this following can here and now be shot through with the triumphant aspect of the resurrection of Jesus."[71]

In the following pages, I examine how the Christic stance of hoping, acting, and knowing as Jesus does enables us to appropriate the graces of the resurrection. Building on Sobrino's work, my analysis stresses how the appropriation of Jesus's resurrection drives this spirituality of reconciliation and how the Spirit of the risen Christ molds and renews those who follow Jesus with the same honesty, faithfulness, and trust with which he lived. As I will show, in this discipleship the Spirit of the resurrected Christ allows us to be carried by the "more"—that is, the grace—of reality.

The resurrection, Sobrino affirms, "introduces a hope into history, into human beings, into the collective consciousness, as a sort of life experience capable of giving shape to everything."[72] This hope is staked on the promise of a reconciled eschatological community rooted in God's merciful justice where the victims of history will be restored to life—a community constituted above all by the poor and the victims and, by extension, the forgiven victimizers.[73] In Sobrino's words, "the utopia of Jesus, the kingdom of God, can be properly described as the ideal of reconciliation, especially because in that kingdom will be present those who are always absent—the poor and the weak. And they will be there with their oppressors, now forgiven and converted; in other words, as a new world."[74] The promise of the kingdom not only refers to our hope in God's victory over death, but also comprises our hope in God's power over injustice and in God's eagerness to forgive the victimizers.

Sobrino maintains that hoping as Jesus did entails a willingness to participate in the hope of those who are crucified today. Indeed, while the hope generated by the resurrection is available to all, it responds in a particular manner to the aspirations of those who unjustly bear the consequences of oppressors' sins. Sobrino explains that "the hope of the poor focuses on a future grasped simultaneously as gift and promise, and as a call to action."[75] It looks forward to life, not simply in the sense of guaranteeing basic rights and livelihood, but also in the sense of becoming a person—"a genuine creature of God and no longer the perennial victim of idols."[76] While this hope is nurtured by the poor's partial triumphs against injustice and by their active solidarity with one another, its roots are in God. In the ultimate analysis, the hope of the poor can be understood as "a primordial act of confidence in reality despite all, a hope explicated as confidence in a God who is Father."[77]

It is only by partaking in the victims' hope and situation that non-victims can claim such a hope as their own; the victims' hope is thus also a "decentering" hope that calls us to loving actions on behalf of the other, as it invites us to trust in the "more" of reality.[78] On the other hand, it certainly risks presumption for a non-victim, including me, to speak of the significance that the resurrection has for the victims. One must speak with care and humility, mindful that the victims are, as Sobrino writes, "the great 'other' for us."[79] Speaking, as it were, from the "outside," one may say that their hope is first a hope for an end to suffering. This hope nurtures their conviction that God is on their side and that justice will be done, which strengthens the struggle against the negativity of this world.

While hope in the resurrection aids victims to hold on to their aspirations for justice, it also enables them to reject the alienating values of the dominant group, including the desire for retribution—that is, the desire to impose upon their former oppressors the conditions they themselves were made to endure. Confidence in the promise of the resurrection fosters both a sense of gratitude to God and the conviction that a just future is possible. This prospect in turn frees former victims to extend to their persecutors the forgiveness that Christ offers to all in the cross and the resurrection. "Positively speaking," Sobrino writes, "the experience of gratuity entails gratitude to something greater than oneself, and the response of the one who has been forgiven and 'graced' multiplies spirit and practice exponentially."[80] The experience of knowing ourselves as accepted and forgiven moves us to conversion and to extend the same forgiveness to others.[81] In this sense, the hope of the resurrection implicitly demands that we not abandon the oppressors trapped under the weight of sin, nor reject the possibility of their eventual conversion.[82]

For those who strive to grasp Jesus's resurrection today, the fact that Jesus was raised by God not only entails the expectation that one day they will be raised, but also calls them to engage in the mission of lifting up the victims of this world.[83] By engaging in a praxis that seeks to make the resurrected hope a reality, we gain a better grasp of the resurrection and extend to others its hope in practical and credible ways. In a striking comparison, Sobrino argues that if we are to grasp the resurrection, our actions must be analogous to God's action of raising Jesus from death.[84] In other words, for Sobrino, we ourselves should become "raisers" who seek justice for the victims, and people whose actions are inspired by transcendent values rooted in eschatological ideas such as justice, peace, and reconciliation.

Even when our actions are limited and fallible, the discipleship of reconciliation that unfolds from the resurrection is one that seeks to anticipate and make present, even if in a provisional and imperfect manner, the eschatological promise of God's kingdom. As Sobrino notes, "We have to take all possible steps, limited and even ambiguous though they may be, to achieve minimum but important and necessary objectives—agreement, cease fires, etc.—but these have to be guided by the utopia of the shared table."[85]

Our acceptance of Christ's resurrection has a profound effect on how we relate to historical reality, for it prompts us to comprehend history as a promise—a gratuitous mystery in which the future is not conceived as a mere extrapolation from the present. Grasping the resurrection requires a spirit of trust and openness toward God's grace. Such a disposition rejects the tendency to try to control reality and instead fosters an attitude that acknowledges that we do not have all of the answers. This epistemological humility both makes room for the newness that comes from God's unexpected grace and, in a manner of speaking, allows us to be carried by the "more" of reality. As Sobrino writes, "only an intelligence that does not want to seize everything, decide on everything, accept as possible only what it can know by extrapolating from what it already knows, can be shot through with grace."[86]

This attitude of epistemological modesty and openness to grace is relevant particularly for a Christian spirituality of reconciliation. As stressed earlier, no human project can be identified with God's kingdom, and all efforts toward reconciliation must by their very nature remain ambiguous and incomplete until the end of time. Although our efforts are certainly important and made urgent by the suffering of history's victims, they remain anticipatory and hopeful signs of God's ultimate reconciliation. Appropriating the power of the resurrection enables us to engage in a praxis of reconciliation that, because it is mindful of its limitations, opens itself up to the unexpected gifts of God's reconciling grace.

Celebrating Life as a Reconciling Risen Being. To live as risen beings means living as new creatures who are receptive to God's grace and thus committed to following Jesus and making God's reconciling promise a tangible reality in the world. This way of life is animated by a spirit of gratitude and trust in God, which infuses our following of Christ with a dimension of victory that, in turn, enables us to engage reality with a new freedom and joy. This freedom, Sobrino tells us, "expresses 'fullness' when it introduces us into history in order to 'love' and . . . expresses 'triumph' when 'nothing is an obstacle' to it."[87] As noted earlier, such freedom is most clearly manifested in Christian martyrs whose lives bore and absorbed the effects of a conflicted world. Paradoxically, lives that willingly bear the weight of sin usually express the extraordinary freedom of Christians who have appropriated the power of the resurrection and who thus live as risen beings today.

Christian joy is usually expressed and nurtured through celebrations—especially the Eucharist—that recall our Christian identity and the triumph of the resurrection. With their rich symbolic rituals and the active participation of the community, these celebrations generate solidarity, strengthen Christian identity, and anticipate our eschatological communion. Deceased victims are honored and remembered anew against the legacy of hope that is nurtured by the liberating events and people through whom God has manifested salvific love for us. These ritual gatherings keep alive the memories of past challenges and sufferings endured by the community; they help us remember rightly and in a forgiving way. They also provide an opportunity for the victimized community to share its stories and grieve its losses. It is within the safe context of community life and celebrations infused by the community's faith, hope, and love that victims are often afforded the possibility to begin reconstructing the shattered sense of meaning that usually ensues from violent and traumatic experiences of loss.[88]

In a world of pervasive conflict, these celebrations are fueled by the recognition—and the joy—that the reality of the resurrection has somehow reached us, and that our reconciling efforts are guided by the promise of a "more," by a hope and a grace that appear to carry us. Thus, they help us recognize what is good and positive in the *present* and keep our hope in God's promise for a reconciled *future* alive. While their main purpose is to express joy and gratitude to the living God, these celebrations help the community remain receptive to what is ultimate and true in reality—the gratuitousness of God's merciful love. In turn, they encourage us to respond with a gratitude that extends to others the same love and forgiveness that has been offered to us.

Building on Sobrino's Christology, I have argued that our following of Jesus, in order to appropriate his way of being within the context of our conflicted reality, must attend to the structure of his life and to the Holy Spirit who empowered him. As has been true for two thousand years, disciples of Jesus today must enter into the world of the victims to better grasp the truth of their situation and to establish relationships of solidarity between victims and non-victims. Thus, solidarity characterizes the compassionate response that ensues from an honest appreciation of a conflicted reality. The spirit of honesty and faithfulness that enables the followers of Jesus to address the demands of their conflicted reality converges with a spirit of trust that empowers them to be carried by Christ's resurrected spirit and his grace, also present within the dynamisms of reality. Each new situation challenges Jesus's disciples to remain available to this "more" of reality in order to discern both God's will and the most appropriate response to the opportunities and constraints of a given situation. This sobering stance is accompanied by the conviction and hope that such provisional steps will be eventually surpassed—if not by us, then by those who come after us.

The following section continues our examination of the mystery of salvation. Moving from praxis to theory, the discipleship of reconciliation that we have just proposed serves as the foundation for a more systematic theological reflection. Thus, the following section outlines a theology of reconciliation from a liberationist perspective organized around the three key moments in the reconciliation process: truth, justice, and forgiveness.

The Mystery of Salvation II: Toward a Liberationist Theology of Reconciliation

As Sobrino's idolatric-theologal portrayal of reality indicates, God has taken the initiative and is already engaged in the project of overcoming evil and division. In spite of all its brokenness, history bears the accumulated goodness and hope of God's healing presence that bestows upon it its most defining feature and fundamental orientation.

God's revelation and commitment to humanity enables us to take an imaginative glimpse at the final and reconciled nature of reality. Free of sin and conflict, reality may be conceived as a dual unity that manifests the communion of the divine and non-divine—that is, "a God that gives himself to history or a history that comes to be according to God."[89] Indeed, the God who grounds history's origin also draws it to its ultimate fulfillment. Thus, the future belongs to God and to the promise that at the end of time the conflict between sin and grace will be overcome. "Only at the end of the ages," Sobrino affirms, "will the tension between the 'already' and the 'not yet' be resolved, and this tension will be resolved in the form of salvation, God's triumph, God's definitive manifestation."[90]

While one may speak of reconciliation as an expected positive state of affairs—that is, as a goal, theology is most relevant and useful when it articulates reconciliation as a revelation to be appropriated from a human perspective: as a long and difficult historical process that entails liberation from the causes of conflict and oppression, be they social, personal, or spiritual. Such a process intimates that " 'God needs time' for history to overcome the ambiguity inherent in it so that God can show himself as pure positivity."[91] Thus, theology ought to recognize that the quest for reconciliation unfolds historically in opposition to other realities and processes. In fact, that quest involves overcoming the sources of antagonism introduced by other realities just as it also calls for new forms of relationship.

At the beginning of this project, I noted that the process of liberation that leads to reconciliation requires three interrelated moments that include the pursuit of truth, justice, and forgiveness. "Each one of them," Sobrino avers, "finds its transcendent expression and rooting in God," and becomes historically embodied "in its truest form in Jesus of Nazareth."[92] Enlisting the three moments to guide our reflection will enable us to underline both the soteriological structure and the eschatological orientation implicit in the grace-bearing side of Sobrino's idolatric-theologal interpretation of reality. Sobrino's approach helps us grasp reconciliation as a process that begins with and is grounded in the transcendent God of life, becomes definitively mediated through the life and mission of Jesus Christ, is furthered through the Holy Spirit's empowerment of Jesus's disciples and other men and women, and will be fully accomplished with the final establishment of God's kingdom. While the following reflections systematically expound how God's revealed truth, justice, and forgiveness advance the human task of reconciliation, they also address the God who originates them. The emphasis here is on theology—God talk, and as such they speak of the God whom liberation theologians have helped us better understand in the context of situations of endemic conflict.

God's Reconciling Truth

Although pure otherness and inexhaustible mystery, God becomes available to us in God's Trinitarian economy. God's actions in history provide the basis for God's revelation and the promise of a reconciled reality. Even if Sobrino speaks often of God's reign and the "God of the kingdom," his conception of God is far from that of an absolute monarch who rules over his subjects. Rather, Sobrino intimates that God's activity reveals a radically relational God who wills to be a God of, for, and with people.[93] This fundamental truth lies at the core of a Christian theology of reconciliation. Through Jesus and the Spirit, God seeks to draw near us, offer Godself to us, and enter into communion with humanity to bestow upon us the love that constitutes us as children of God and makes us whole. As Sobrino notes, "To be encountered by the Lord is the experience of the love of God. Indeed it is the experience of the fact that love is the reality that discloses to us, and makes us able to be, what we are. It is God's coming to meet us, simply because God loves us, that renders us capable of defining our very selves as who we are, in order, in our turn, to go forth to meet others."[94]

As we have seen, the possibility of human flourishing is rejected when human persons move away from God and subordinate themselves to idols of their own creation. Human sinfulness ruptures our relationship with God and introduces into history the forces that deform it with inauthentic and oppressive relationships that bring about conflict and ultimately death. Because sin seeks to conceal itself, the primary demand that ensues from our conflicted reality is the willingness to seek the truth. God's revelation both grounds the ultimate truth of human existence and denounces its sinful proclivity to cover up and distort the truth of reality. In this regard, Sobrino often reminds us of Paul's words: "For the wrath of God is revealed from heaven against all ungodliness and wickedness of those who by their wickedness suppress the truth" (Rom 1:18).[95]

To argue along with Sobrino and the Christian tradition that God grounds the truth implies that God's revelation and our experience of theologal reality can offer us the resources to honestly engage the different complexities of human existence. While those resources do not afford us the capacity to grasp God's encompassing view, they enable us to affirm certain normative truths critical for any process of reconciliation. For Christians, the universal God is revealed in the particular person of Jesus of Nazareth. His life may not set specific moral norms, but it does establish a truthful and meaningful way of being in the world that provides the pattern for the discipleship to which we are invited. Without denying the difficulty of finding the truth behind any particular conflict, the capacity to discern truth from falsehood presupposes that an honest engagement with reality should enable us to distinguish between oppression and liberation, victims and oppressors. Sobrino therefore writes, "it is good to turn again and again to a God who denounces the . . . evil of lying, who 'begins' truth, and who thereby makes the truth needed for reconciliation more possible."[96]

Jesus embodies God's truth in history and reveals it as "good news." As noted in the previous chapter, Jesus reveals the true and authentic human being who manifests the type of life that is pleasing to God. His life proclaims the goodness of God and the coming of God's reconciling kingdom. But his actions and words also reveal a deep awareness of the conflicted nature of reality. Thus, Jesus upholds the true God before the idols that generate conflict and unmasks the mechanisms of oppression that oppose the coming of the kingdom. Jesus's prophetic denunciations seem to indicate that he evaluated the existing social arrangements and discerned the presence of grace and sin therein, aided by God's prophetic assurances of a future reconciled reality and by the immediate perspective afforded by the poor. Examined against the utopic vision of a just and fraternal community proclaimed by the kingdom tradition, the situation of the poor exposed the lies that oppress the truth and helped Jesus set the direction of his ministry. Indeed, "the human being, living and living fully, was a clear-cut criterion of Jesus' course of action."[97]

Although one may rightly state, in ontological and doctrinal terms, that "[God's] Word, being revealed, communicates the truth,"[98] Sobrino's more historical and relational approach to Christology stresses Jesus's honesty, faithfulness, and trust as the historical dispositions actualized by the Holy Spirit that manifest both God's compassionate nature and Jesus's unique relationship with the Father. These dispositions disclose "the divine filiation of Jesus—that is, of his being Son of God, consubstantial with God."[99] While God is the initiator and end subject of human salvation, God's Son, Jesus, is its mediator.

For Sobrino, "Jesus stands in the line of the God of truth" not only because his revelation conveys unmatched liberating insights and possibilities, but first and foremost because Jesus makes God present to us.[100] As he elsewhere explains, "Jesus is not merely one who talks wisely about God . . . or even only one who carries out the will of God . . . but is the flesh of God in history."[101] Thus we have stressed how the mediator's honest and compassionate way of engaging others in the world—his manner of being— was decisive in healing their fragmented relationships, reconstituting them as persons with agency and self-worth, and enabling them to become recipients of God's merciful love. Indeed, Jesus's life not only bears the truth of a sound noetic claim, but also reveals Jesus himself as liberating.[102] He conveyed the experience of salvation that heals, generates hope, and leads to reconciliation.[103] Thus, it is his life—incarnation, mission, death, and particularly the resurrection—that allows us to arrive at the truth of Christian dogma: "*Jesus Christ is verus Deus et verus homo*."[104] And it is this same life that enables us to assert that God's truth and God's self-giving in Jesus are indispensable and "good news" for a world in conflict.

God's Merciful Justice

God's own honest engagement with a humanity afflicted by suffering and conflict explains why Sobrino insists that compassion abides as the origin and principle of God's engagement with the world: "Mercy is the absolute beginning of the history of salvation, and this mercy abides as constant in God's salvific process."[105] The display of divine mercy evinces a transcendent God-in-relationship who does not remain indifferent to the human condition, but allows Godself to be vulnerable and affected by humanity.[106] In a reality riven by oppression, God's disclosure is at once revelatory and liberating. God mercifully reacts to the suffering of humanity through liberating actions that free us from the oppression of sin and restore our relationship with others and God. Just as God's honesty liberates our cognitive truth from sinful distortion and concealment, God's justice liberates the victims from oppression, and God's forgiveness liberates oppressors from their guilt. These merciful and liberating actions have as their end purpose our incorporation into God's life.

Because God's justice ensues from God's mercy and seeks to bring about God's unity with and within creation, it is best understood not in juridical but in relational and interpersonal terms. In fact, God's justice may be described as the restorative modality that God's love takes in order to confront the current lordship of the idols over history, heal our fragmented relationships, and effectively attend to the suffering victims. God's mercy becomes justice to recreate the "whole human being and all human beings"; it is a love aimed at the transformation of the whole of society.[107] This renewed state of affairs that will fully arrive through God's final intervention in history reflects the ultimate reigning of God. As Sobrino writes, God reigns when "human beings reproduce in their lives the goodness and the compassion, the justice and the reconciliation of God."[108] And only when God thus reigns will the world be transformed into God's kingdom. Through the eschatological establishment of the kingdom, God both eradicates the division that sin had introduced into the world and overcomes the separation (but not the distinction) between transcendence and history. God enters into indissoluble communion with humanity and "without ceasing to be human, we are taken up into divinity."[109]

Jesus's proposal for justice is grounded in the gratuitous promises of God's kingdom because the kingdom mediates God's will for justice and reconciliation in the world. It is important to note, however, that while Jesus and God's kingdom are essentially related and inseparable, they are not absolutely the same. The mediator (Jesus) must be distinguished from the mediation (God's kingdom). Although God's eschatological justice has *already* become historically present in Jesus and in his practice and praxis (and, in a derivative way, in the actions of men and women of good will), the fullness of God's justice is *not yet*. In fact, this justice is being actively denied. Thus, Sobrino asserts, God's will "is not simply that the mediator appear in history, but also that the divine will for the world be realized in history."[110]

In proclaiming God's kingdom, Sobrino argues, Jesus not only announces the advent of justice but the coming of the "reign of life."[111] This analogy comparing God's reign with human life offers an insightful way to understand the organic unfolding of the kingdom in history and, through the kingdom's essential relationship with Jesus and the Spirit, the significant role human beings may play in its advancement as they allow themselves to be carried by the theologal dimension of reality—the "more" or grace of reality.

Humans do not control God's kingdom but rather recognize its fruits in all that nurtures and promotes life: justice, fraternity, hope, joy. God's kingdom establishes the minimum requirements for a basic and "just life," such as the availability of bread, respect for human dignity, and the creation of just social arrangements. "That life should be just," Sobrino explains, "expresses the aim that life should come to be real in opposition to the [forces] of the anti-kingdom. It expresses the ways of justice to build life . . . the relationship of solidarity and dignity in the kingdom. And . . . the basic conditions for the Kingdom."[112] At the same time, this kingdom in history, like life itself, is inherently open to a "more." It seeks to unfold dynamically toward greater realization in history and in its transcendent fulfillment.[113]

Because Jesus embodies the divine compassion that effectively confronts the demands of our conflicted existence and through his actions endeavors to concretize God's kingdom in history, his life is the criterion of justice and the way to it. While Jesus stressed that the kingdom is solely God's initiative and something God offers completely and freely, his ministry shows that the gratuitous character of the kingdom does not rule out human activity on its behalf. Indeed, the divine proposal places a claim on human cooperation with God's plan for humanity. In this sense, our pursuit of justice is constitutive of an ongoing process of personal, social, and spiritual liberation aimed at collaborating with the kingdom's initiative and guided by life's inherent orientation towards reconciliation with God. As the Christian discipleship outlined earlier sought to demonstrate, when the pursuit of justice is modeled after Jesus, then orthodoxy, orthopraxis, and orthopathy (right disposition or spirit in relation to reality) converge in our engagement of the world. Guided by Jesus's revelation and empowered by the Holy Spirit, our actions—limited as they may be—analogously correspond to God's initiative as they strive to respond to the demands of God's reality.[114]

Jesus's liberating actions on behalf of the kingdom express a love that is simultaneously universal and preferential. They demonstrate that in situations of enmity and conflict, where all too often life itself cannot be taken for granted, justice cannot be blind or neutral. Rather, one is first summoned to protect and defend those to whom the minimum requirements of life are being denied. Hence, it is important to insist that the kingdom is not exclusive but preferential. In this regard Sobrino observes, "As an eschatological reality, the Kingdom of God is universal and open to all, though not all in the same way."[115] In a conflicted history, the kingdom is first offered to the poor, and the poor manifest their reception of the kingdom through their appropriation of God's mercy and God's hope-giving plan for a reconciled humanity.[116] As liberated victims, they become primary agents in the process of healing and transforming the relationship that constitutes an oppressive reality, as they extend to their perpetrators a compassion similar to the one bestowed upon them. The perpetrators, on the other hand, evince their acceptance of the kingdom through their reception of God's forgiving mercy, which leads them to repentance, conversion, and the commitment to establish new relationships with their former victims.

In the case of the non-poor and the silent bystanders who wrongly assume that neutrality is a viable alternative in the face of suffering, the reception of the kingdom translates into drawing closer to the poor and establishing with them relationships of solidarity that can advance the cause for reconciliation. With the likes of Romero and Ellacuría in mind, Sobrino avers that "[the non-poor] can become prophetic figures who help the poor recover and maintain confidence in themselves, to develop

practices and to spread love. . . . The heart of the matter is our participating in some way, analogously, but truly in the world of the poor."[117]

The concept of God's kingdom proclaims Jesus's utopic vision for a renewed human community. To be sure, the form that such final communion will take is something reserved to God. Because of human finitude
and vulnerability to sin, our articulations of this Christian utopia and the
justice it bears remain incomplete and defective, but not entirely indefin-
able.[118] Today Jesus's proclamation continues to be a source of inspiration
that rouses us to imagine a more humane world, particularly if our imagination is allowed to be fashioned by the situation and hope of the poor.
And thus, as I argued previously, "there are [certain] formulations of the
utopia that draws history onward, that make history to be more than
itself . . . [and that] move human beings time and again to give their best
to make the Reign come true."[119]

The kingdom, however, is not only the articulation of something good
for humanity, but also a nascent historical reality infused with God's presence. Thus, the kingdom—inchoately but powerfully manifested in the
theologal dimension of reality—both steers and empowers Christians' efforts to anticipate and make present, even if in a provisional and imperfect manner, God's eschatological promises of a final reconciliation.

God's Victorious Forgiveness

Forgiveness is first and foremost God's acceptance, welcome, and embrace
of a sinful humanity. As an expression of God's gratuitous mercy, God's
forgiveness loses its full significance when its meaning is reduced to le-
galistic expressions that only convey exoneration from culpability or the
cancellation of debts. Rather, forgiveness evinces God's relationality and
the radical extent to which God will go to enter into communion with creation. The Old Testament offers ample examples of God's forgiveness (Isa
1:18, 43:25–26; Mic 7:18–19; Dan 9:9), but this is more clearly illustrated
through the narratives that depict God's repeated efforts to form a covenant with God's people (Gen 9:8–17, 12–17; Exod 19–24; Jer 31:30–33).
Hence, from a systematic approach to reconciliation, God's forgiveness is,
like justice, best understood when considered within the context of God's
plan for humanity—God's reconciling reign—and its inherent call to
conversion.

As we have seen, the kingdom establishes God's justice and expresses the efficacy and power of God's mercy on behalf of history's victims. But the kingdom's justice also unfolds dialectically over and against the forces that introduce enmity and perpetuate a conflicted world. God sides with the oppressed, which inevitably places God in conflict with the idols of death, their mediations, and their mediators (the oppressors). This conflict, however, has to be properly understood. While God rejects all that opposes life and humanity, God does not come into conflict with God's own creation.[120] God does not negate God's love for the oppressors but instead condemns their actions and the hostile relationships that constitute them—that is, God confronts them in their formal capacity as oppressors.[121] Such confrontation introduces a distinct modality into God's merciful love—forgiveness—and reveals a God bent on radically being a God-for-us. Forgiveness then finds its transcendent expression in a God whose power also manifests itself in terms of vulnerability and defenseless love.

If in the language of faith, the incarnation of God's Son, who empties himself to take up human nature, affirms the goodness of a creation in spite of its conflicted condition, Jesus's whole life manifests God's solidarity with a broken humanity and God's invitation to incorporate our lives into the new life of the kingdom. Because Jesus is the historical embodiment of God's forgiveness, that he draws closer to the sinners to offer them his acceptance—to welcome them—is a sign of the coming of the kingdom.[122] Indeed, Jesus underscores the kingdom as a source of forgiving grace and not judgment and thus as good news for all sinners. Nonetheless, the kingdom also presupposes a radical transformation in its recipients' form of existence.

For Sobrino, the distinction that Jesus makes between the conversion required from those who sin out of weakness—the poor, the publican, the prostitute—and those who sin as oppressors—the rich, the religious leaders—sheds light on the new type of relationships that configure the kingdom and human participation in its fulfillment. While those who sin out of weakness are called to trust in God's goodness and appropriate an active hope in the imminent coming of the kingdom, the oppressors are summoned to cease from wielding a power that directly opposes the kingdom.[123] As Sobrino notes, the only type of power that anticipates and advances the kingdom is "the power of love, of sacrifice, of truth. Every other kind of power, far from being neutral, is historically sinful. To the extent that it is not power dedicated to service, it is sin."[124] And yet, Jesus's proclamation of the kingdom not only confronts oppressors with the sinful nature of their power, it also assures them of their forgiveness and invites them to take their place in God's kingdom.[125] Indeed, Jesus's call to conversion is always preceded by the offer of God's love and acceptance.[126]

God's forgiving love is most radically captured in Jesus's cross, which is the culmination of Jesus's mission in a world seemingly ruled by the power of sin and injustice. His ministry shows that solidarity with the victims entails confronting their victimizer, which in Jesus's case led to his own victimization. Jesus went to his death bearing witness to the God of life and justice in a nonviolent manner. In spite of numerous and harsh confrontations, he never closed off the possibility of the oppressors' conversion, and even on the cross he prayed that they might be forgiven. While the cross certainly discloses God's judgment against sin and oppression, it reveals above all, in clearly historical terms, that forgiveness and the possibility of reconciliation come through self-sacrifice and the willingness to take upon oneself the consequence of the sins committed by others. Jesus's bearing of sin without retaliating, without dehumanizing the adversaries or giving up on the possibility of restoring his relationship with them, also demonstrates his profound solidarity with sinful humanity and his gratuitous love for the oppressors.

Speaking in more systematic terms, Sobrino explains that the cross expresses God's limitless and credible love for humanity. It reveals that "nothing was an obstacle to God's indicating his definitive, saving, welcoming, irrevocable yes to this world."[127] It is not only that, in the cross, God eschews retaliation on those who murdered God's Son, but that the crucified God becomes a defenseless victim in order to offer the oppressors the possibility of a future. The cross then reveals a God-for-us who freely gives up God's legitimate rights in order to liberate sinners from guilt and, above all, to offer them the gift of communion.

This same forgiveness is later extended by Christ, the risen victim, when he appears to his disciples. The resurrected Christ offers them his peace, bestows upon them (and us) his empowering spirit, and commissions his followers in the ministry of reconciliation. Sobrino explains that

Christ is the forgiving one, but he is also the offended one. . . . Today as well those who forgive open their eyes and know just what is being forgiven: responsibility in the continued crucifixion of entire peoples. To be able to see with new eyes the genuine reality of the world, to be able to stare it in the face despite its tragedy, to be able to perceive what it is to which God says a radical "no," is (logically) the first fruit of allowing oneself really to be pardoned.[128]

A God of Life: A Reconciling God

Sobrino describes a transcendent and deeply relational God who creates, restores, and sustains relationships through God's compassionate love. Such divine mercy grounds a relational and restorative justice that opposes a retributive understanding of God as well as soteriological theories that conceive Jesus's suffering as ensuing from a divine demand. Along with God's truth, the two converging modalities of God's compassion—justice and forgiveness—correspond to the two primary and complementary ways in which God reconciles the world. These two modalities of God's salvific activity also shed light on how a radically relational God stands simultaneously in continuity and discontinuity with a conflicted reality that calls for a liberating transformation. This God-in-relation becomes vulnerable and is affected by a suffering world, but God is not dependent upon the world or constituted by God's relationship with it. In other words, God's justice and forgiveness offer us a glimpse of the dialectical manner in which God relates to and manifests Godself in human history: God's otherness and affinity.[129]

God's justice underscores the efficacy of God's love. But divine justice also expresses God's power and alterity with respect to humanity. As illustrated by the resurrection, only God in God's absolute otherness has the capacity to overcome the death imposed by sin and bring to fulfillment the liberating justice that leads to reconciliation. On the other hand, God's forgiveness best captures the radical gratuity of God's merciful love and reveals the extent of God's solidarity with the human race. This solidarity is evident in the affinity established between God and humanity in the incarnation, and is even more clearly illuminated by the cross on which God reveals God's willingness to participate in the suffering of the victims, to share their fate, and also to forgive their victimizers. It should be noted that this closeness on God's part is especially significant for the victims of conflict, who often come to understand power as something dangerous and unreliable, as something that has been used against them.[130]

God's way of reconciling the world, in turn, points to a consistent trope in Sobrino's theology—namely that the *manner* in which God saves us is part and parcel of salvation itself. We could say that God is mindful of God's power and otherness, and thus takes much care not to impose God's reconciling justice upon humanity, as it were, from above. Instead, this God, who honors our freedom and wills to create a communion rooted in love, delicately tailors God's salvation to our human ways. Long before God establishes God's reign or reveals God's power by resurrecting the crucified victim, God has already drawn near to us. This means that victims and non-victims alike can trust in, collaborate with, and hope for the powerful justice of this God who is wholly other, because through the solidarity of the incarnation and the forgiving offering of God's own life, God has become explicitly and radically close to us. With this closeness, God has made God's love credible for us.[131]

Conclusion

The spirituality and theology of reconciliation put forth in these pages presumes a correspondence between God's gift of reconciliation through Christ and our appropriation of that gift through the creation of personal, social, and political relationships rooted in the values of God's kingdom. It also recognizes that while historical reality possesses an intrinsic dynamic tendency toward increasing degrees of reconciliation—toward the actualization of God's kingdom—this process is neither automatic nor mechanical. In fact, historical reality has been deformed by humanity's sinful choices, which are manifest in conditions of exclusion, injustice, and oppression.

This book does not explicitly endorse a particular political program or elaborate specific public policies, but rather articulates a discipleship capable of individually renewing and collectively empowering Christians to respond imaginatively to situations of socioeconomic conflict and to struggle for lasting peace therein. Although I present this spirituality as prescriptive, it is also versatile. It calls for a "creative" following of Jesus, underscoring the individuality of all subjects, the specificity of their situations, and the particularity of their personal vocations. While it is a specifically Christian theology, its insights carry a degree of universality and relevance to other worldviews.

Our examination suggests that because Jesus's incarnation, mission, cross, and resurrection are all deeply interrelated and maintain their significance only when taken together to express the whole of his life, no single event can sufficiently express the reconciling significance of Jesus's life. It further suggests that it is only by creatively following Jesus's example within our context and by appropriating the spirit with which he engaged reality that we can properly grasp the meaning of his life for the healing and transformation of our present reality, as well as for our reconciliation with God and among ourselves.

Compassion captures the fundamental manner in which God engages the world through the Holy Spirit and Jesus's reconciling mission. It is what originates and informs God, and in turn our own entire life and mission. As followers of Jesus, we are empowered to pursue the fullest realization of God's reconciling kingdom as the alternative to our violent world. The kingdom provides the reconciling vision that inspires a Christian utopia that is best understood as a provisional but viable historical project—that is, one that is not beyond the gifts and resources currently available to us.

Christian disciples, in their struggles to transform our conflicted society into one that reflects the values of God's reign, make their compassion practical through the pursuit of justice and forgiveness. These actions embody a spirit of fidelity to God's revelation and provide an honest response to a suffering world. Sobrino's profound understanding of the character of divine compassion allows us to appreciate how justice and forgiveness converge and complement one another. They are distinct but interrelated moments in any process of reconciliation that express the efficacy and gratuity of God's love. Because our expressions of justice and forgiveness are limited and imperfect, they ought to be understood as anticipatory signs whose fullness will be reached only through God and in God's future reign.

To be sure, all of the revolutionary processes that emerged in the 1970s failed to bring about the awaited change in socioeconomic structures that many Latin Americans hoped would rapidly and radically renovate the continent. In fact, in some Latin American countries, including El Salvador, the last thirty years have violently demonstrated the ambiguities, limitations, and overall human costs that accompany any serious attempt at social liberation and reconciliation, even when such efforts resulted in the reformation and democratization of the electoral process.

Despite the rampant problems that remain, honesty with reality demands that we also acknowledge that some significant changes have taken place within the political sphere in the region.[1] For the first time in their history, most Latin American nations have shed their military dictators and established their governments through electoral practices, initiating a process of political democratization that has, at least in principle, raised the possibility that concerns over human rights and economic democratization will be addressed by elected representatives of the people. While the transformation of socioeconomic structures in El Salvador and most Latin American nations lags far behind the recent progress made at the political level, this situation may hold unexpected opportunities for renewed steps toward reconciliation.

In this new context, our efforts to actualize Jesus's life and spirit call for the temperate appreciation of inchoate hopes such as the political one just highlighted. In the midst of adversity, it is important to bear in mind that engaging reality with honesty means not only exposing the evil and lies that surround us, but also identifying and cultivating sources of hope that affirm that the future will not be an endless continuation of the present, and that resignation or desperation are not the only available responses. The birth of new lives, the strengthening of communities, the elimination of unjust practices, minor political victories, the willingness to extend forgiveness, and the veneration of our martyrs are all sources of hope that are nurtured by and find their meaning in the subversive memory of Jesus's life, cross, and resurrection. They are also reasons to gather and celebrate that God continues to walk among us, and to remember that the future belongs only to God. Though often provisional and fragile, these hopes strengthen us as sacramental and anticipatory signs of Christ's final victory over injustice.

As we have seen, Jesus's resurrected spirit animates our hopes and inspires our Christian following. The spirit of honesty and faithfulness that enables us to address the demands of our conflicted reality converges with a spirit of trust that empowers us to surrender ourselves to a Father who is not only merciful but also mystery. We allow this grace to unfetter us from our fears and attachments and plunge us—incarnate us—among those who are largely excluded from the benefits of a globalized world. As we maintain this central commitment to solidarity with the victims and allow their "light" to illuminate our mission of compassion, our path toward reconciliation becomes concrete within the ambiguity and particularity of each situation.

Thus, we heed the pleas of the victims by remembering and honoring the lives of those who "died before their time" and by engaging in the daily struggles that seek to achieve the unimaginable as they point toward the possibility of reconciliation: humanizing our economic structures by improving wages and working conditions in order to guarantee the basic necessities of the great majorities; demanding a state that refuses premature amnesties, upholds the system of law, and strengthens our democratic

institutions; and enriching our civil society with cultural, labor, professional, civic, and religious organizations that bring together the different
voices of society, foster public participation, and promote cultural values
that reflect the dignity of the human person and our willingness to welcome all, even the former perpetrators. It is through such actions that we
encounter and make present the effectiveness and the gratuitousness of
God's love.

Each new situation challenges us to remain open to God's unexpected
grace and discern what the most appropriate or necessary steps might be
in light of the opportunities or resources reality offers at a particular time.
In engaging this reality, our efforts, like those of Ellacuría and Romero
before us, can only be provisional steps, and we do well to remain mindful of the limitations we face as we assess the opportunities (and dangers)
that each situation can realistically offer us—to paraphrase Sobrino, what
reality can currently give of itself.

As our martyrs evince with scandalous consistency, living as risen beings incarnated in the world of the victims with the mission of forgiving
reality and the oppressor may be the shortest way to the cross. Nonetheless, it remains the Christian way of engaging a conflicted reality: a spirituality that provides the foundation and sustenance to stand in resistance
to, and call for the transformation of, a culture of wealth that denies
human dignity.

In the final analysis, this journey can be undertaken only because we
are grounded in, sustained, and transformed by "a 'more' that touches us
and draws us despite ourselves."[2] This we do for no other reason than
the merciful and gratuitous love that compels us to communion.

Acknowledgments

In the last few years, I have received generous assistance and direction from a number of people and supporting communities that have enriched my life and without which this project would not have come to fruition. From my time at the University of Notre Dame, my friend and mentor J. Matthew Ashley provided invaluable insight and suggestions that were only matched by his tireless dedication to improving my efforts. I also owe a debt of gratitude to Margie Pfeil, Robert Krieg, and particularly Gustavo Gutiérrez, O.P., whose friendship and diaphanous life continue to inspire my work and illuminate my understanding of what it is to be human. I also want to thank Timothy Matovina for his steadfast support and encouragement, and Roger Haight, S.J., who accompanied me during my initial immersion into the world of theology and whose aggressive integrity and unquestionable fidelity stand as an example for all theologians.

My deep gratitude also goes to Boston College and my colleagues at the School of Theology and Ministry for their encouragement and unwavering support of my vocation as a theologian. I am truly blessed by their witness and friendship. I owe a special thanks to Richard Lennan who committed countless hours to this project. His sharp eyes, wise mentoring, and editorial expertise have guided me in this and other endeavors. I am also grateful to my colleagues who read significant parts of the manuscript and offered many helpful suggestions: Margaret Guider, Francine Cardman, and Nancy Pineda-Madrid.

Beyond BC, this project has benefited from the enthusiastic support of Kevin Burke, S.J., and the invaluable feedback of Robert Schreiter, C.P.P.S., who graciously identified ways to improve my argument. Gene McGarry provided careful editing that produced a tighter manuscript. I also wish to acknowledge the support of Fordham University Press and its director, Fredric Nachbaur, who brought it to completion.

This book would not be possible without the sustenance of my family, most especially my parents, Orfilio and Thaís, who showed me early on that compassion is the noblest of human qualities. Even though it will be a few more years before she can fully understand these words, I would like to thank my daughter, Hannah, for the many hours of play that she went without so I could complete this book. Finally, I would like to thank my compass, best friend, and wife, Kari. It is a wonderful gift and joy to continue to be in love with a person who has the mind of a poet and the heart of a pastor. Our long conversations as well as her insights, edits, and suggestions have vastly improved this project.

Notes

Introduction

1. Patrick J. Bracken and Celia Petty, *Rethinking the Trauma of War* (London: Free Association Books, 2001), 3, 9–20.

2. Jon Sobrino, *Christ the Liberator: A View from the Victims*, trans. Paul Burns (Maryknoll: Orbis Books, 2001), 7.

3. Priscilla B. Hayner, *Unspeakable Truths: Facing the Challenges of Truth Commissions* (New York: Routledge, 2010), xi–xii.

4. While in South Africa Desmond Tutu has stressed the notion of a common humanity (expressed in the idea of the "Rainbow people of God"), efforts in Northern Ireland have emphasized the nation's Christian (rather than Protestant or Catholic) tradition in order to foster unity within the country. See Maria Ericson, "Reconciliation and the Search for a Shared Moral Landscape: Insights and Challenges from Northern Ireland and South Africa," *Journal of Theology for Southern Africa* 115 (March 2003): 30.

1. Liberation and Reconciliation

1. Volf explains that the intrinsic character of the Christian faith is not to blame here. Rather, the fault lies in its adherents, who much too often shift their loyalty from the gospel to the interests of their culture, nation, or ethnic group. Miroslav Volf, "The Social Meaning of Reconciliation," *Interpretation* 54, no. 2 (April 2000): 158–60.

2. In an effort to grasp a working understanding of reconciliation, it has often been noted that the prefix "re-" itself can be problematic because it suggests, in a misleading manner, that the parties seeking to overcome enmity previously enjoyed a harmonious relationship. See Trudy Govier, *Taking Wrongs Seriously: Acknowledgment, Reconciliation, and the Politics of Sustainable Peace* (Amherst, N.Y.: Humanity Books, 2006), 11.

3. For example, the Norwegian sociologist and eminent peace scholar, Johan Galtung, has identified twelve distinct approaches to reconciliation. "After Violence, Reconstruction, Reconciliation, and Resolution: Coping with

Visible and Invisible Effects of War and Violence," in *Reconciliation, Justice, and Coexistence: Theory and Practice*, ed. Mohammed Abu-Nimeer (Lanham, Md.: Lexington Books, 2001), 3–23.

4. R. Scott Appleby, "Peacebuilding and Catholicism: Affinities, Convergences, and Possibilities," in *Peacebuilding: Catholic Theology, Ethics, and Praxis*, ed. Robert J. Schreiter, R. Scoot Appleby, and Gerard Powers (Maryknoll, N.Y.: Orbis, 2010), 3–22, at 16.

5. Daniel Philpott, "Beyond Politics as Usual: Is Reconciliation Compatible with Liberalism?," in *The Politics of Past Evil: Religion, Reconciliation, and the Dilemmas of Transitional Justice* (Notre Dame, Ind.: University of Notre Dame Press, 2006), 11–44, at 14. Italics in the original.

6. For a study on the terminology, rhetoric, and other factors that shape our perception of forgiveness/reconciliation see Rodney L. Petersen, "A Theology of Forgiveness: Terminology, Rhetoric & the Dialectic of Interfaith Relationships," in *Forgiveness and Reconciliation: Religion, Public Policy, and Conflict Transformation*, ed. Raymond G. Helmick and Rodney L. Petersen (Philadelphia: Templeton Foundation Press, [2001] 2002), 3–25.

7. Robert J. Schreiter, *Reconciliation: Mission & Ministry in a Changing Social Order* (Maryknoll, N.Y.: Orbis Books, 2001), 18–27.

8. Schreiter, *Reconciliation*, 34–36.

9. Cecil McCullough, "Bible and Reconciliation," in *Reconciliation in Religion and Society: Proceedings of a Conference Organized by the Irish School of Ecumenics and the University of Ulster*, ed. Michael Hurley (Belfast: Institute of Irish Studies, the Queen's University of Belfast in association with the University of Ulster, 1994), 28.

10. N. T. Wright, *Paul: In Fresh Perspective* (Minneapolis: Fortress Press, 2005), 21–25. While there is no specific term in the Hebrew Scriptures that is equivalent to the New Testament concept of reconciliation (*katallassein*), the underlying reality behind reconciliation is best captured in the Old Testament ideas of covenant and atonement. See Carmel McCarthy, "A Response [to Bible and Reconciliation]," in *Reconciliation in Religion and Society: Proceedings of a Conference Organised by the Irish School of Ecumenics and the University of Ulster*, 43. McCarthy also includes the notion of "shalom" with those of atonement and covenant.

11. God's covenant with the nation of Israel (Ex. 19–24; Deut; Josh 24) seems to follow the standard form of ancient Near Eastern suzerainty treaties, in which God, as suzerain, reminds Israel of God's salvific acts and invites the nation to enter into a covenant that mutually binds the parties to each other so long as the people accept God's claim on them and commit to obeying God's commandments. J. Arthur Thompson, "Covenant," in vol. 1 of *The International*

Standard Biblical Encyclopedia, ed. Geoffrey W. Bromiley (Grand Rapids, Mich.: Eerdmans, 1979), 791.

12. Gustavo Gutiérrez, *A Theology of Liberation: History, Politics, and Salvation*, 15th Anniversary Edition, trans. Caridad Inda, John Eagleson, and Matthew J. O'Connell (Maryknoll, N.Y.: Orbis Books, [1973], 1988), 89. Originally in Spanish, *Teología de la liberación, perspectivas* (Lima: Centro de Estudios y Publicaciones, 1971).

13. Stephen Westerholm, "Torah," in vol. 4 of *The International Standard Biblical Encyclopedia*, ed. Geoffrey W. Bromiley (Grand Rapids, Mich.: Eerdmans, 1979), 878.

14. The book of Deuteronomy, which at its core represents the application of the Law, is the major work of covenant theology and stands at the head of subsequent writings on the subject, including the prophetic literature. See N. T. Wright, *The New Testament and the People of God* (Minneapolis: Fortress Press, 1992), 260–64.

15. Jason J. Ripley, "Covenantal Concepts of Justice and Righteousness, and Catholic-Protestant Reconciliation: Theological Implications and Explorations," *Journal of Ecumenical Studies* 38, no. 1 (Winter 2001): 95–108, at 98.

16. The Hebrew word *kāphar [kpr]*, "to cover" or "to make atonement," which expresses the purpose of these offerings, is more prominently found in the books of Exodus, Leviticus, and Numbers. While *kāphar [kpr]* is used in different contexts, it has a key role in sacrificial rituals, where it is related to the removal of sin. See S. T. Kimbrough, Jr., "Reconciliation in the Old Testament," *Religion in Life* 41, no. 1 (Spring 1972): 41–42.

17. See Amos 5:21–24.

18. Hans Walter Wolff, "Prophecy from the Eighth through the Fifth Century," in *Interpreting the Prophets*, ed. James Luther Mays and Paul J. Achtemeier (Philadelphia: Fortress Press, 1987), 24.

19. N. T. Wright notes that common to both the major and the minor Prophets is the acknowledgment that Israel's exile is the result of her own sin, and "the problem will be solved by YHWH's dealing with the sin and thus restoring his people to their inheritance." *The New Testament and the People of God*, 273.

20. Wolff, "Prophecy," 20–21.

21. Guy P. Couturier notes that the essential aspects of the original covenant do not change: Both are theocentric, the people are the same, and their response is manifest in the same obedience to the law. See "Jeremiah," in *The New Jerome Biblical Commentary*, ed. Raymond E. Brown, Joseph A. Fitzmyer, and Roland E. Murphy (Upper Saddle River, N.J.: Prentice Hall, 1990), 290.

22. Wolff, "Prophecy," 21. See also Donald E. Gowan, *Theology of the Prophetic Books: The Death & Resurrection of Israel* (Louisville, Ky.: Westminster John Knox Press, 1998), 117.

23. John W. de Gruchy, *Reconciliation: Restoring Justice* (Minneapolis: Fortress Press, 2002), 45.

24. Ernst Kasemänn, "Some Thoughts on the Theme 'The Doctrine of Reconciliation in the New Testament,'" in *The Future of Our Religious Past: Essays in Honour of Rudolf Bultmann*, ed. James M. Robinson (New York: Harper & Row, 1971), 50. Seyoon Kim offers an excellent treatment of the origins of Paul's concept of reconciliation in "God Reconciled His Enemy to Himself: The Origin of Paul's Concept of Reconciliation," in *The Road from Damascus: The Impact of Paul's Conversion on His Life, Thought, and Ministry*, ed. Richard L. Longenecker (Grand Rapids, Mich.: Eerdmans, 1997), 102–24.

25. The main passages where the term *reconciliation* occurs are Rom 5:10–11; 2 Cor 5:18–20; Col 1:20; and Eph 2:16. Victor Paul Furnish notes, "In Eph. 2:16 and Col. 1:20 reconciliation is, respectively, of Jew and Gentile and of all things *within* the world (cosmos). In Romans and II Corinthians, however, it is a matter of the world itself—meaning humanity—being reconciled *with* God." "The Ministry of Reconciliation," *Currents in Theology and Mission* 4, no. 4, (August 4, 1977): 204–18, at 205. See also Graham Stanton, "Paul's Gospel," in *The Cambridge Companion to St. Paul*, ed. James D. G. Dunn (Cambridge: Cambridge University Press, 2003), 181.

26. For an excellent discussion on the contingent and "occasional" character of Paul's Epistle to the Romans, see J. Christiaan Beker, *Paul the Apostle: The Triumph of God in Life and Thought* (Philadelphia: Fortress Press, 1984), 59–93.

27. While in Romans 5:10, justification is attributed to Christ's death, in 4:29 it is attributed to his resurrection. As Joseph Fitzmyer explains, "It is not Pauline teaching that the Father willed the death of his Son to satisfy the debts owed to God or to the devil by human sinners. . . . Paul did not theorize about the Christ event, as did later theologians." See "Pauline Theology," in *The New Jerome Biblical Commentary*, 1399.

28. Fitzmyer, "The Letter to the Romans," in *The New Jerome Biblical Commentary*, 844.

29. A. Katherine Grieb, *The Story of Romans: A Narrative Defense of God's Righteousness* (Louisville, Ky.: Westminster John Knox Press, 2002), 63.

30. Furnish, "Ministry of Reconciliation," 207.

31. Jerome Murphy-O'Connor, "The Second Letter to the Corinthians," in *The New Jerome Biblical Commentary*, 822. See also Stanton, "Paul's Gospel," 181.

32. Beker, *Paul the Apostle*, 319.

33. Christoph Schwöbel, "Reconciliation: From Biblical Observations to Dogmatic Reconstruction," in *The Theology of Reconciliation*, ed. Colin E. Gunton (London: T & T Clark, 2003), 19.

34. Furnish, "Ministry of Reconciliation," 215.

35. Throughout this study, the terms *God's reign* and *God's kingdom* will be used interchangeably.

36. de Gruchy, *Reconciliation: Restoring Justice*, 20.

37. Daniel Philpott notes that the Abrahamic religions describe that ideal state as *shalom*. "Beyond Politics as Usual," 14.

38. Jon Sobrino, "Terrorism and Barbarity: New York and Afghanistan," in *Where is God?: Earthquake, Terrorism, Barbarity, and Hope*, trans. Margaret Wilde (Maryknoll, N.Y.: Orbis, 2006), 106–23, at 120.

39. Geiko Müller-Fahrenholz, *The Art of Forgiveness: Theological Reflections on Healing and Reconciliation* (Geneva: WCC Publications, 1996), 15.

40. Robert J. Schreiter, "Religion as Source and Resource for Reconciliation," in *Reconciliation in a World of Conflicts*, ed. Luiz Carlos Susin and María Pilar Aquino (London: SCM Press, 2003), 109. Schreiter notes a dramatic increase in possibilities for initiating processes of reconciliation beginning in the late 1980s as a consequence of the end of military dictatorships and civil wars in Latin America, the collapse of the Berlin Wall, and the resurgence of indigenous people with the United Nations' Year of the Indigenous in 1992.

41. Among others, here I have in mind the exemplary career of Raymond G. Helmick, S.J., and Robert Schreiter, C.C.P.S., whose expertise in conflict resolution has been enlisted in reconciliation processes all over the world, including those in Northern Ireland, Colombia, Lebanon, Israel and the Palestinian territories, the former Yugoslavia, the Kurdish territories in Iraq and Turkey, East Timor, and South Africa.

42. Thomas A. Lewis, "Actions as the Ties That Bind: Love, Praxis, and Community in the Thought of Gustavo Gutiérrez," *Journal of Religious Ethics* 33, no. 3 (2005): 539–67.

43. Hence the importance that Gutiérrez ascribes to utopian thinking as a rational way to mediate religious ideals in the political sphere. Gutiérrez, *A Theology of Liberation*, 138.

44. Miroslav Volf, for instance, focuses his work on the "*kind of selves we need to be in order to live in harmony with others.*" *Exclusion and Embrace: A Theological Exploration of Identity, Otherness, and Reconciliation* (Nashville: Abingdon Press, 1996), 21; italics in the original. In a similar vein, Robert J. Schreiter has proposed a spirituality of reconciliation that unfolds from Jesus's resurrection stories and offers a reflection on general strategies that are essential to a Christian process of reconciliation. See *The Ministry of Reconciliation: Spirituality and Strategies* (Maryknoll, N.Y.: Orbis Books, 2004), 13–19.

45. I am borrowing the framework of the different levels of reconciliation from John de Gruchy, *Reconciliation*, 26.

46. For a more detailed treatment of the actors involved in the process of reconciliation, see Govier, *Taking Wrongs Seriously*, 27–44. See also Mark Hay, O.M.I., "Ukubiyisana: Reconciliation in South Africa" (D. Min thesis, Catholic Theological Union, 1997), 158–84.

47. Ervin Staub, "Reconciliation after Genocide, Mass Killing, or Intractable Conflict: Understanding the Roots of Violence, Psychological Recovery, and Steps toward a General Theory," *Political Psychology* 27 (2006): 867–93, at 868.

48. Tristan Anne Borer, "A Taxonomy of Victims and Perpetrators: Human Rights and Reconciliation in South Africa," *Human Rights Quarterly* 25 (2003): 1088–116, at 1089.

49. In the United States, the type of "benefit" noted here can be illustrated by what some North American theologians refer to as "white privilege." Such benefit, however, can be equally derived from unjust socioeconomic, political, or gender structures that confer power on some and deny it to others. See M. Shawn Copeland, "Racism and the Vocation of the Christian Theologian," *Spiritus* 111 (2002): 15–29; and Charles E. Curran, "White Privilege," *Horizons* 32, no. 2 (2005): 361–67.

50. Sharon Lam, *The Trouble with Blame* (Cambridge, Mass.: Harvard University Press, 1996), 57. See also Scott Strauss, *The Order of Genocide: Race, Power, and War in Rwanda* (Ithaca, N.Y.: Cornell University Press, 2006).

51. South African Truth and Reconciliation Commission, Final Report, 5:259, http://www.justice.gov.za/trc/report/finalreport/Volume5.pdf (December 12, 2012).

52. Karl Rahner, *Foundations of Christian Faith*, trans. William Dych (New York: Crossroad, 1978), 110.

53. John de Gruchy makes a similar argument. *Reconciliation*, 191–92.

54. Volf, *Exclusion and Embrace*, 84.

55. Volf, *Exclusion and Embrace*, 85. Italics in the original.

56. Govier, *Taking Wrongs Seriously*, 21–22.

57. Govier, *Taking Wrongs Seriously*, 22.

58. The exception continues to be Cuba, under the leadership of Fidel Castro and his brother Raul Castro.

59. Jon Sobrino, "Conflicto y reconciliación: Camino cristiano hacia una utopía," *Estudios centroamericanos* 661–62 (2003): 1139–48, at 1147.

60. José Comblin and Jon Sobrino have written several insightful articles on forgiveness and reconciliation, but no systematic theology of reconciliation from a Latin American liberationist perspective has been published. See Sobrino's articles: "Christianity and Reconciliation: The Way to Utopia," in

Reconciliation in a World of Conflicts, 80–90; and "Latin America: Place of Sin and Place of Forgiveness" and "Personal Sin, Forgiveness, and Liberation," in *The Principle of Mercy: Taking the Crucified People from the Cross* (Maryknoll, N.Y.: Orbis, 1999), 58–68 and 83–101. See also José Comblin, *Reconciliación y Liberación* (San Isidro: Centro de Estudios Sociales [CESOC], 1989).

61. Explaining how the term "reconciliation" has been manipulated in the area of Christology, Jon Sobrino notes that although the "affirmation that Christ is the embodiment of universal reconciliation" is true, it has often been "ingeniously preached by some and defended by others out of self-interest. Such an emphasis is nothing else but an attempt to exempt Jesus from the conflict-ridden toils of history, to use Christianity as a support for some sort of ideology espousing peace and order and as a weapon against any kind of conflict subversion. It is an attempt to keep Christians strangers to the sinfulness and conflictual nature of history." In *Christology at the Crossroads: A Latin America Approach*, trans. John Drury (Maryknoll, N.Y.: Orbis Books, 1978), xvii.

62. Roy H. May, Jr., *Annual of the Society of Christian Ethics* 16 (1996): 41–58, at 54.

63. Juan Hernandez Pico, "Revolución, Violencia, Paz," in *Mysterium Liberationis: Conceptos fundamentales de la teología de liberación*, ed. Ignacio Ellacuría and Jon Sobrino (Madrid: Editorial Trota, 1990), 602.

64. Cardinal Alfonso López Trujillo, *Liberación y reconciliación: Breve recorrido histórico* (Lima: Editorial Latina, 1990), 71–72. My translation unless otherwise noted.

65. Gregory Baum, "A Theological Afterword," in *The Reconciliation of Peoples: Challenge to the Churches*, ed. Gregory Baum and Harold Wells (Maryknoll, N.Y.: Orbis, 1997), 184–92, at 188.

66. It should be noted that North American and European theologians have often praised the positive impact that liberation theology has had on the Christian understanding of reconciliation. See, for instance, Müller-Fahrenholz, *Art of Forgiveness*, 14. See also, Baum "A Theological Afterword," 185.

67. Joâo Batista Libânio, "Hope, Utopia, Resurrection," in *Mysterium Liberationis: Fundamental Concepts of Liberation Theology*, ed. Ignacio Ellacuría and Jon Sobrino (Maryknoll, N.Y.: Orbis, 1993), 716–28, at 721.

68. Gutiérrez, *A Theology of Liberation*, 96.

69. Gutiérrez, *A Theology of Liberation*, xxxviii and 24.

70. Ignacio Ellacuría, "Church of the Poor, Sacrament of Liberation," in *Mysterium Liberationis: Fundamental Concepts of Liberation Theology*, 543–64, at 556.

71. Joyce Murray makes a similar argument about Gustavo Gutiérrez's theology in "Liberation for Communion in the Soteriology of Gustavo Gutiérrez," *Theological Studies* 59 (1998): 51–59.

72. Gustavo Gutiérrez, *The Truth Shall Make You Free: Confrontations*, trans. Matthew J. O'Connell (Maryknoll, N.Y.: Orbis, 1990), 67.

73. Gutiérrez, *Truth Shall Make You Free*, 106.

74. Leonardo Boff, "Salvation in Jesus Christ and the Process of Liberation," trans. J. P. Donnelly, in *The Mystical and Political Dimension of the Christian Faith*, ed. Claude Gefíré and Gustavo Gutiérrez, *Concilium* 96 (Edinburgh: T. and T. Clark, 1974), 78.

75. Austin Flannery, ed., *Gaudium et Spes* 1, in *Vatican Council II: The Conciliar and Post Conciliar Documents*, vol. 1 (New York: Costello Publishing Company, 1996), 903.

76. Leonardo Boff, *When Theology Listens to the Poor* (San Francisco: Harper & Row, 1988), 10.

77. Gustavo Gutiérrez, "Option for the Poor," *Mysterium Liberationis: Fundamental Concepts of Liberation Theology*, 235–50, especially 239–44.

78. Paul Sigmund, *Liberation Theology at the Crossroads: Democracy or Revolution?* (New York: Oxford University Press, 1990), 188. See also the Vatican Congregation for the Doctrine of the Faith, "Instruction on Certain Aspects of the Theology of Liberation," *Origins* 14, no. 13 (September 13, 1984): IV.viii, 197; IX.vii, 201.

79. Stephen J. Pope, "Proper and Improper Partiality and the Preferential Option for the Poor," *Theological Studies* 54 (1993): 242–71.

80. Gutiérrez, "Option for the Poor," 235–50, at 239.

81. Indeed, according to Gutiérrez, the primary sin of the poor is often despair and fatalism. *On Job: God-Talk and the Suffering of the Innocent* (Maryknoll, N.Y.: Orbis, 1987), 97.

82. Gustavo Gutiérrez, *The Power of the Poor in History*, trans. Robert Barr (Maryknoll, N.Y.: Orbis, 1983), 95.

83. Puebla, *The Final Document*, no. 1142, in *Puebla and Beyond: Documentary and Commentary*, trans. John Drury, ed. John Eagleson and Philip Scharper (Maryknoll, N.Y.: Orbis, 1979), 265.

84. Ignacio Ellacuría, "Utopia and Prophecy in Latin America," in *Mysterium Liberationis: Fundamental Concepts of Liberation Theology*, 289–328, at 303.

85. Puebla, *The Final Document*, no. 1147.

86. As Gutiérrez succinctly notes, "the gratuitousness of God's love is the framework within which the requirement of practicing justice is to be located." *On Job*, 94.

87. Thomas L. Schubeck, S.J., *Liberation Ethics: Sources, Models, and Norms* (Minneapolis: Fortress, 1993), 37–60. See also Matthew L. Lamb, "The Theory-Praxis Relationship in Contemporary Christian Theologies," *CTS Proceedings* 31 (1976), 149–78.

88. This is not to deny that the church was in some ways an advocate for the poor, but the church did not identify itself with the great majority of the Christian faithful or recognize their concerns as her own.

89. Leonardo Boff and Clodovis Boff, *Introducing Liberation Theology*, trans. Paul Burns (Maryknoll, N.Y.: Orbis, 1987), 50.

90. Gutiérrez, *Theology of Liberation*, 25

91. David Tracy, *Christian Theology and the Culture of Pluralism* (New York: Crossroad, 1981), 390.

92. Boff and Boff, *Introducing Liberation Theology*, 24–32. See also Gutiérrez, *Truth Shall Make You Free*, 53–55 and 58–66.

93. Sobrino argues for the need to include these three dimensions in the Salvadoran process of reconciliation. He asserts, "In El Salvador, after the end of armed conflict, we insisted that the way to reconciliation needs three steps: truth, justice, and forgiveness." Sobrino, "Christianity and Reconciliation," 82.

94. Audrey R. Chapman, "Coming to Terms with the Past: Truth, Justice, and/or Reconciliation," *Annual of the Society of Christian Ethics* 19 (1999): 235–58.

95. See J. M. Vorster, "Truth, Reconciliation, Transformation and Human Rights," *The Ecumenical Review* 56, no. 4 (2004): 480–502.

96. *South African Truth and Reconciliation Commission, Final Report*, 1:111–114.

97. This is not to say that the achievements of the TRC were by any means insignificant. Even if the documentation recovered by the commission is limited and incomplete, it represents an important approximation of what happened in South Africa under apartheid, particularly in terms of the narrative of its victims.

98. See for instance, de Gruchy, *Reconciliation*, 159.

99. Volf, *Exclusion and Embrace*, 250–53; de Gruchy, *Reconciliation*, 159–60.

100. James H. Cone, *God of the Oppressed* (New York: Seabury Press, 1975), 102–3.

101. Dean Brackley, "Theology and Solidarity: Learning from Sobrino's Method," in *Hope and Solidarity: Jon Sobrino's Challenge to Christian Theology*, ed. Stephen J. Pope (Maryknoll, N.Y.: Orbis, 2008), 3–15, at 7. Italics in the original.

102. Schreiter, *Ministry of Reconciliation*, 75.

103. Johann Baptist Metz, *Faith in History and Society: Toward a Practical Fundamental Theology*, trans. Matthew Ashley (New York: The Crossroad Publishing Company, 2007), 71.

104. See Robert Schreiter, "Establishing a Shared Identity: The Role of the Healing of Memories and of Narrative" in *Peace and Reconciliation: In Search of*

a Shared Identity, ed. Sebastian Kim, Pauline Kollontai, and Greg Hoyland (Abingdon: Ashgate Publishing, 2008), 7–20.

105. Metz, *Faith in History and Society*, 75.

106. Schreiter, "Establishing a Shared Identity," 13.

107. Schreiter, "Establishing a Shared Identity," 14.

108. de Gruchy, *Reconciliation*, 178.

109. Schreiter, *Ministry of Reconciliation*, 18, 59.

110. Schreiter, "Establishing a Shared Identity," 14.

111. Schreiter, "Establishing a Shared Identity, 15. At the outset of the article, Schreiter is careful to note that establishing a shared identity between conflicting parties is "a complex undertaking in itself, involving an analysis of current identities—both as they are narrated within a community and to those outside the community—as well as adjudicating the different versions of history maintained by each party."

112. de Gruchy, *Reconciliation*, 164.

113. Dietrich Bonhoeffer, *The Cost of Discipleship*, trans. R. H. Fuller (New York: Macmillan, 1963), 45–47.

114. "The Kairos Document," Article 3.1, September 1985, http://www .sahistory.org.za/archive/challenge-church-theological-comment-political-crisis -south-africa-kairos-document-1985 (November 26, 2013).

115. de Gruchy, *Reconciliation*, 199.

116. Karen Lebacqz, *Six Theories of Justice: Perspectives from Philosophical and Theological Ethics* (Minneapolis: Augsburg, 1986), 9.

117. Volf, *Exclusion and Embrace*, 207.

118. Volf, *Exclusion and Embrace*, 213.

119. My gratitude to Robert Schreiter for pointing out the relevance of these approaches to the current discussion on reconciliation.

120. Daniel Philpott, *Just and Unjust Peace: An Ethic of Political Reconciliation* (New York: Oxford University Press, 2012), 75. Philpott makes the case that these scholars draw their stance either from the realist tradition that traces its roots back to Thucydides, Niccolo Machiavelli, Thomas Hobbes, and to the masters of suspicion (Marx, Nietzsche, and Freud), or from the liberal tradition that draws from Locke, Kant, and more recently John Rawls.

121. I draw these features from Philpott, *Just and Unjust Peace*, 74–93.

122. Daniel Philpott, "Peace After Genocide," *First Things*, no. 224 (June–July 2012): 39–46, at 40.

123. Aspects of restorative justice have been identified in Native American and New Zealand Maori communities, and many others. For a wider discussion on restorative justice, see Howard Zehr, *The Little Book of Restorative Justice* (Intercourse, Pa.: Good Books, 2002); Gerry Johnstone and Daniel Van Ness, ed., *Handbook of Restorative Justice* (Portland, Ore.: Willan Publishing,

2007); and Dennis Anderson, ed., *The Handbook of Restorative Justice: A Global Perspective* (New York: Routledge, 2006).

124. Daniel Philpott, "Reconciliation: A Catholic Ethic for Peacebuilding in the Political Order," 32.

125. Desmond Tutu, *No Future without Forgiveness* (New York: Doubleday, 2000), 54.

126. Robert Schreiter, "A Practical Theology of Healing, Forgiveness, and Reconciliation" and "Future Directions in Catholic Peacebuilding," in *Peacebuilding: Catholic Theology, Ethics, and Praxis*, 366–97, at 389; and 421–48, at 435.

127. Matthew J. Gaudet and William R. O'Neill, "Restoring Peace: Toward a Conversation between the Just War and Reconciliation Traditions," *Journal of the Society of Christian Ethics* 31.1 (2011): 37–66, at 50–51.

128. Philpott, *Just and Unjust Peace*, 99.

129. Govier, *Taking Wrongs Seriously*, 134.

130. Ismael García, *Justice in Latin American Theology of Liberation* (Atlanta, Ga.: John Knox Press, 1987), 1 and 11; Karen Lebacqz, *Six Theories of Justice: Perspectives from Philosophical and Theological Ethics*, 113–14.

131. Daniel M. Bell, Jr., "Sacrifice and Suffering: Beyond Human Rights and Capitalism," *Modern Theology* 18, no. 3 (2002): 333–59, at 335 and 339. See also Daniel M. Bell, Jr., *Liberation Theology after the End of History: The Refusal to Cease Suffering* (New York: Routledge, 2011).

132. Liberation theologians have often argued for the possibility of appropriating certain Marxist elements without also endorsing Marxism's atheistic philosophical framework. See Denys Turner, "Marxism, Liberation Theology and the Way of Negation," in *The Cambridge Companion to Liberation Theology*, ed. Christopher Rowland (New York: Cambridge University, 2007), 229–47, especially 231–33. See also Pedro Arrupe, "Marxist Analysis by Christians," in *Liberation Theology: A Documentary History*, ed. Alfred T. Hennelly (Maryknoll, N.Y.: Orbis, 1997), 307–13. The dependency theory was formulated by Latin American social scientists in the mid-1960s and its influence in liberation theology has, with time, dwindled. As the Brazilian economist Theotonio dos Santos summarizes, "Dependency is a situation in which certain groups of countries have their economies conditioned by the development and expansion of another country's economy." "La crisis de la teoría del desarrollo y las relaciones de dependencía en America Latina," quoted in Christian Smith, *The Emergence of Liberation Theology: Radical Religion and Social Movement Theory* (Chicago: University of Chicago Press, 1991), 145.

133. John R. Donahue, S.J., *What Does the Lord Require? A Bibliographical Essay on the Bible and Social Justice* (Saint Louis: Institute of Jesuit Resources, 2003), 23.

134. Gutiérrez, *A Theology of Liberation,* 135–40; and Ignacio Ellacuría, "Utopia and Prophecy," 289–328.

135. Here Gutiérrez is approvingly citing Dom Antonio Fragoso, *A Theology of Liberation,* 97.

136. Gutiérrez, *On Job,* 87.

137. Gutiérrez, *On Job,* 89.

138. In the conference at Medellin, Colombia, the bishops described the Latin American reality as a sinful situation rooted in "the oppressive structures that come from the abuse of ownership and of power and from exploitation of works or from unjust transactions." Second General Conference of Latin American Bishops, *The Church in the Present-Day Transformation of Latin America in the Light of the Council* (Washington: U.S. Catholic Conference, 1973), 78 and 49.

139. In his Second Pastoral Letter, written in 1977, Oscar Romero describes social sin as "the crystallization . . . of individuals' sins into permanent structures that keep sin in being, and make its force to be felt by the majority of the people." *Voice of the Voiceless: The Four Pastoral Letters and Other Statements,* trans. Michael J. Walsh (Maryknoll, N.Y.: Orbis Books, 2003), 64–84, at 68.

140. José Ignacio Gozález Faus, "Sin," in *Mysterium Liberationis: Fundamental Concepts of Liberation Theology,* 532–42, at 536.

141. Ignacio Ellacuría, "Human Rights in a Divided Society," in *Human Rights in the Americas: The Struggle for Consensus,* ed. Alfred T. Hennelly and John Langan (Washington: Georgetown University Press, 1982), 63.

142. Charles Taylor, "The Politics of Recognition," in *Multiculturalism: Examining the Politics of Recognition,* ed. Amy Gutmann (Princeton: Princeton University Press, 1994), 25–73, at 57.

143. Ignacio Ellacuría, "Fe y Justicia," *Escritos Teológicos,* vol. 3, ed. Aída Estela Sánchez (San Salvador: UCA Editores, 2001), 316, quoted in Michael Lee, *Bearing the Weight of Salvation: The Soteriology of Ignacio Ellacuría* (New York: Crossroad Publishing, 2008), 125.

144. John Paul II, "No Peace without Justice. No Justice without Forgiveness," Message for the World Day of Peace, no. 2 (January 1, 2002), http://www.vatican.va/holy_father/john_paul_ii/messages/peace/documents/hf_jp-ii_mes_20011211_xxxv-world-day-for-peace_en.html (March 11, 2007).

145. Stephen J. Pope, "The Convergence of Justice and Forgiveness: Lessons from El Salvador," *Theological Studies* 64 (2003): 812–35, at 812.

146. Ervin Staub and Laurie Anne Pearlman, "Healing, Reconciliation, and Forgiving after Genocide and Other Collective Violence," in *Forgiveness and Reconciliation: Religion, Public Policy and Reconciliation,* 205–27.

147. de Gruchy, *Reconciliation,* 167.

148. de Gruchy, *Reconciliation*, 169.

149. Volf, "Social Meaning of Reconciliation," 167.

150. Schreiter, *Ministry of Reconciliation*, 55.

151. Simon Wiesenthal, *The Sunflower: On the Possibilities and Limits of Forgiveness* (New York: Schocken Books, 1980).

152. Denny J. Weaver, *Mennonite Quarterly Review* 83, no. 2 (2009): 319–47, at 326.

153. Robert D. Enright, Suzanne Freedman, and Julio Rique, *Exploring Forgiveness* (Madison: University of Wisconsin Press, 1998), 2–4.

154. It should be noted that "emotions" here not only refer to feelings but also to embodied experiences that include thoughts, memories, and associations. Everett L. Worthington, "Unforgiveness, Forgiveness, and Reconciliation and Their Implications for Social Interventions," in *Forgiveness and Reconciliation: Religion, Public Policy and Reconciliation*, 171–92, at 173.

155. Worthington, "Unforgiveness, Forgiveness, and Reconciliation," 176–84.

156. Govier, *Taking Wrongs Seriously*, 96.

157. Schreiter, *Ministry of Reconciliation*, 80. Elsewhere Schreiter rightly warns us that while "[o]ne of the central ways of looking to the memory of the suffering of Jesus is to place the narrative of our own suffering in the narrative about Jesus . . . this can [also] be misused to legitimate unjust suffering." "Establishing a Shared Identity," 18.

158. Hannah Arendt, *The Human Condition*, 2nd ed. (Chicago: University of Chicago Press, 1998), 238.

159. Arendt, *Human Condition*, 237. She further explains that "Forgiving is the only reaction which does not merely re-act but acts anew and unexpectedly, unconditioned by the act which provoked it and therefore freeing from its consequences both the one who forgives and the one who is forgiven" (241).

160. Volf, *Exclusion and Embrace*, 123 and 224.

161. John Paul II, "No Peace without Justice. No Justice without Forgiveness," no. 3.

162. Leonardo Boff, *Way of the Cross: Way of Justice*, trans. John Drury (Maryknoll, N.Y.: Orbis Books, 1980), 54–55.

163. Segundo Galilea, "Liberation Theology and the New Task Facing Christians," in *Frontiers of Theology in Latin America*, ed. Rosino Gibellini (Maryknoll, N.Y.: Orbis Books, 1979), 176. Italics in the original.

164. Jon Sobrino, "Latin America: Place of Sin," 59–62.

165. Jon Sobrino, *Liberación con espíritu: Apuntes para una nueva espiritualidad* (San Salvador: UCA Editores, 1987), 63.

166. Jon Sobrino, "The Spirit of Liberation: Spirituality and the Following of Jesus," in *Mysterium Liberationis: Fundamental Concepts of Liberation Theology*, 677–701, at 686.

2. Confronting a Conflicted Reality

1. Stephen Bevans, "Models of Contextual Theology," *Missiology* 13, no. 2 (1985): 200.

2. Gustavo Gutiérrez, for instance, acknowledges that his efforts are self-consciously contextual when he introduces *A Theology of Liberation* by stating, "This book is an attempt at reflection, based on the Gospel and the experiences of men and women committed to the process of liberation in the oppressed and exploited land of Latin America." *A Theology of Liberation*, xiii.

3. Roger Haight, *Dynamics of Theology* (Maryknoll, N.Y.: Orbis Books, 2001), 3–5.

4. Although Sobrino acknowledges the importance that themes like cultural diversity and religious pluralism have for theology, he argues that these have lower priority for the theological task than the theme of suffering. See "Theology in a Suffering World: Theology as *Intellectus Amoris*," in *The Principle of Mercy: Taking the Crucified People from the Cross* (Maryknoll, N.Y.: Orbis Books, 1994), 27.

5. Bishop Gregorio Rosa Chávez, press conference, Salvadoran newspaper *La Prensa Gráfica*, January 7, 2007.

6. Christine Wade, "El Salvador: contradictions of neoliberalism and building sustainable peace," *International Journal of Peace Studies* 13, no. 2 (2008): 15–32, at 17.

7. Marigold Best and Pamela Hussey, "The Thorny Road to Reconciliation in El Salvador," in *Open Hands: Reconciliation, Justice, and Peace Work around the World*, ed. Barbara Butler (Rattlesden, UK: Kevin Mayhew LTD, 1998), 368.

8. Luis Armando González, "Estado, sociedad y economía en El Salvador (1880–1999)," in *El Salvador: La transición y sus problemas*, ed. Rodolfo Cardenal and Luis Armando González (San Salvador: UCA Editores, 2002), 30–35. See also José Armando Oliva and Héctor Samour, *Estudios Sociales y Cívica* (San Salvador: Ediciones Estudios Educativos, 1998), 150.

9. Two interrelated but distinct groups emerged within the Salvadoran elite: the more conservative and inflexible agro-financial faction, and the relatively more progressive agro-industrial faction. See, Italo López Vallecillos, "Fuerzas sociales y cambio social en El Salvador," *Estudios Centroamericanos* (referred to hereafter as *ECA*) 369–70 (1979): 558, quoted in Jeffery M. Paige, "Coffee and Power in El Salvador," *Latin American Research Review* 28, no. 3 (1993): 7–40.

10. The Farabundo Martí Front for National Liberation was first constituted in 1980 by five guerilla groups: the Popular Forces of Liberation (FPL), the National Resistance (RN), the Revolutionary Army of the People (ERP),

the Communist Party of El Salvador (PCS), and the Revolutionary Party of Central American Workers (PRTC). Their corresponding popular organizations were the Popular Revolutionary Bloc (BPR), the United Popular Action Front (FAPU), the 28th of February Popular Leagues (LP28), the National Democratic Union (UDN), and the Popular Liberation Movement (MLP). The FMLN broadened its coalition when it fashioned a political alliance with the Democratic Revolutionary Front (FDR), which was made up of a variety of progressive political parties, Christian and labor organizations, and university groups.

11. See Patrick Brogan, *World Conflicts: A Comprehensive Guide to World Strife since 1945* (Lanham, Md.: Scarecrow Press, 1998), 473. While some effects of the war can be assessed statistically, others are more difficult to quantify. The war's impact on the nation's psychosocial conditions and overall mental health, the tearing of the social fabric, and the deterioration of the environment are also significant and persist today as part of the tragic cost incurred by the Salvadoran civil war.

12. Scholars note that another important catalyst for the negotiations was the outrage at the killing of the Jesuit priests in 1989, a change in U.S. foreign policy, a softening in the FMLN ideological stance, and a shift of power from the agro-financial faction of the oligarchy to a more modern agro-industrial faction willing to enter into negotiations with the FMLN. See Sonja Wolf, "Subverting Democracy: Elite Rule and the Limits to Political Participation in Post-War El Salvador," *Journal of Latin American Studies* 41 (2009): 429–65, at 437–38. See also Angelika Rettberg, "The Private Sector and Peace in El Salvador, Guatemala, and Colombia," *Journal of Latin American Studies* 39 (2007): 463–94, at 469.

13. For a detailed account of the history of the peace accords by a participant, see Salvador Samayoa, *El Salvador: La reforma pactada* (San Salvador: UCA Editores, 2003). See also, *From Madness to Hope: The 12-Year War in El Salvador: Report of the Commission on the Truth for El Salvador*, Appendix to UN Doc. S/25500, April 1, 1993 (New York: United Nations Publications, 1993), 172.

14. Because of the government's past complicity in human rights violations and the overall malfunctioning of the Salvadoran legal system at the time, the commission did not recommend prosecuting the implicated perpetrators but rather providing monetary and moral compensation to the victims.

15. Jon Sobrino, "Theological Reflections on the Report of the Truth Commission," in *Impunity: An Ethical Perspective, Six Case Studies from Latin America*, ed. Charles Harper (Geneva: World Council of Churches Publications, 1996), 118.

16. Priscilla B. Hayner, *Unspeakable Truths: Facing the Challenge of Truth Commissions* (New York: Routledge, 2002), 40.

17. Juan Hernández Pico, S.J., "Una reconciliación frustrada y su superación," *Revista Latinoamericana de Teología* 85 (2012): 35–57, at 38–39.

18. Rettberg, "The Private Sector and Peace," 472. See also Wolf, "Subverting Democracy," 435–47.

19. The conservative Arena party, which led the government until 2008, implemented a series of neo-liberal policies that included the privatization of the banking and pension systems, as well as of the electrical and telecommunication services. It also enacted a regressive tax-reform, ratified the free trade agreement, and dollarized the Salvadoran economy.

20. In 2009, the poorest 20 percent of the population earned 4.2 percent of the GDP while the richest 20 percent accounted for 52.1 percent of the GDP. *Human Development Report 2010* (San Salvador: United Nations Development Program, 2010), http://hdr.undp.org/es/informes/nacional/americalatinacaribe/elsalvador/INDH_El_Salvador_2010.pdf (August 29, 2011), 239. For an excellent study on the impact of globalized economic groups and transnational corporations in the economic and political direction of Central America, see Alexander Segovia, "Integración real y grupos centroamericanos de poder económic," *ECA* 691–92 (2006): 517–82, http://library.fes.de/pdf-files/bueros/fesamcentral/07598.pdf.

21. While the world average rate for crime is the equivalent of 8.8 homicides for every 100,000 inhabitants, El Salvador's rate in 2009 was almost eight times greater (71 homicides per 100,000 inhabitants), and more than one-third of the population claimed at the time to have been victims of a crime in the last twelve months. *Human Development Report 2010*, 275.

22. Two excellent articles on this subject are Mauricio Gaborit, "Los círculos de la violencia," *ECA* 685–86 (2005): 1145–54; and José Miguel Cruz, "Los factores asociados a las pandillas juveniles en Centroamérica," *ECA* 685–86 (2005): 1155–82.

23. Roland Paris, "Peacebuilding in Central America: Reproducing the Sources of Conflict?" *International Peacekeeping* 9, no. 4 (2002): 39–68, at 55. Even though the national level of poverty has decreased from 65 percent in 1992 (the last year of the war) to 43 percent in 2008, this poverty reduction is largely tied to foreign aid, an unprecedented national exodus that has relieved domestic social pressures (more than 2.5 million Salvadorans live outside the country), and particularly to the ever-increasing level of remittances sent by Salvadorans living abroad to their families in El Salvador, which in 2006 represented almost 20 percent of the gross national product. *Human Development Report 2010*, 193.

24. According to this poll, more than 50 percent of those interviewed attested that the peace accords have been fulfilled only in a small measure and 60 percent believe that the situation of the country is equally bad or worse than it was during the time of the conflict. Public Opinion Poll conducted November 20–26, 2011 by the Instituto Universitario de Opinión Pública (IUDOP), Universidad Centroamericana "José Simeón Cañas" (UCA).

25. The FMLN party, which assumed the presidency in 2009, advanced some limited social reforms directed at improving education and health, but has been unable to implement the structural economic changes it promised during the electoral campaign. So far, it has also left the controversial amnesty law intact.

26. Jon Sobrino, "Teología desde la realidad," in *Panorama de la teología latinoamericana: Cuando vida y pensamiento son inseparable*, ed. Juan Tamayo and Juan Bosch (Estella: Editorial Verbo Divino, 2001), 611–28, at 611. My translation.

27. While Sobrino insists on the need for an integral liberation that stresses the transformation of economic and social structures, he also recognizes that theology must pay more attention to the significant role that cultural, racial, gender, and environmental issues play in the process of liberation. See "La teología y el 'principio de liberación,'" *Revista Latinoamericana de Teología* 35 (1995): 115.

28. Jon Sobrino was born into a Basque family in Barcelona, Spain in 1938. After attending a Jesuit secondary school, he entered the Society of Jesus. In 1957, he was sent to El Salvador to join what at that time was known as the Central American Vice-Province of the Society of Jesus.

29. Jon Sobrino, "Introduction: Awakening from the Sleep of Inhumanity," in *The Principle of Mercy*, 2.

30. See the Spanish version, "Despertar del sueño de la cruel inhumanidad," in *El Principio Misericordia: Bajar de la cruz a los pueblos crucificado* (San Salvador, UCA Editores, 1992), 12.

31. In addition to "Introduction: Awakening from the Sleep of Inhumanity," see "Teología desde la realidad," 611–628.

32. Sobrino, "Teología desde la realidad," 613.

33. Sobrino, "Awakening from the Sleep of Inhumanity," 2.

34. Sobrino, however, was unsatisfied with Karl Rahner's formulation of Christ as the "absolute bearer of salvation." See his short summary of Rahner's Christological development in *Christology at the Crossroads*, 22–25.

35. Sobrino, "Teología desde la realidad," 613–14. My translation.

36. Jon Sobrino, "Reflexiones sobre Karl Rahner desde América Latina. En el XX aniversario de su Muerte," *Revista Latinoamericana de Teología* 61 (2004): 3–18, at 10.

37. Karl Rahner, *Foundations of Christian Faith: An Introduction to the Idea of Christianity* (New York: Crossroad Publishing, 2000), 126–33.

38. Rahner, *Foundations of Christian Faith*, 140.

39. Jon Sobrino, "Karl Rahner and Liberation Theology," *The Way* 43, no. 4 (2004): 53–66.

40. Sobrino, "Karl Rahner and Liberation Theology," 53–66, at 57. Italics in the original.

41. Sobrino, "Reflexiones sobre Karl Rahner desde América Latina," 13.

42. *Gaudium et Spes* 11. In *Vatican Council II*, 912, quoted in Sobrino, "Reflexiones sobre Karl Rahner desde América Latina," *Revista Latinoamericana de Teología* 61 (2004): 15.

43. Sobrino, "Awakening from the Sleep of Inhumanity," 3.

44. Sobrino, "Teología desde la realidad," 616. My translation.

45. See Enrique Dussel, *A History of the Church in Latin America: Colonialism to Liberation (1492–1979)* (Grand Rapids, Mich.: Eerdmans, 1981), 101–24; and Smith, *The Emergence of Liberation Theology*, 71–121.

46. See Dussel, *History of the Church in Latin America*, 101–24.

47. The terms "base ecclesial community," "Christian base community," and *comunidad ecclesial de base* (CEB) are used interchangeably. On the origins of these communities, see Marcello de C. Azevedo, *Basic Ecclesial Communities in Brazil: The Challenge of a New Way of Being Church*, trans. John Drury (Washington: Georgetown University Press, 1987).

48. Sobrino, "Awakening from the Sleep of Inhumanity," 3.

49. Gutiérrez, "Introduction to the Revised Edition: Expanding the View," in *A Theology of Liberation*, xxviii.

50. Gutiérrez, *Theology of Liberation*, 29.

51. Ignacio Ellacuría, "Salvation History and Salvation in History," in *Freedom Made Flesh: The Mission of Christ and His Church* (Maryknoll, N.Y.: Orbis Books, 1975), 3–19, at 3. Italics in the original.

52. Rahner, *Foundations of Christian Faith*, 39–41 and 117–37; see also Gutiérrez, *Theology of Liberation*, 43–44.

53. Gutiérrez, *Theology of Liberation*, 85; see also Ignacio Ellacuría, "The Historicity of Christian Salvation," in *Mysterium Liberationis: Fundamental Concepts of Liberation Theology*, 251–89.

54. Gutiérrez, *Theology of Liberation*, xxxviii.

55. It is difficult to pinpoint the exact "birthday" of Latin America liberation theology. While the General Conferences of the Council of Latin American Bishops in Medellín had a tremendous impact on the renewal of the church throughout the 1970s, important theological reflections preceded Medellín. José Comblin, for instance, identifies the years between 1966 and 1973 as the first phase of liberation theology's development. See "Treinta

años de teología latinoamericana," in *El mar se abrió*, ed. Luiz Carlos Susin (Santander: Editorial Sal Terrae, 2001), 163. See also Juan Luis Segundo, "The Future of Christianity in Latin America," and Roberto Oliveros Maqueo, "Meeting of Theologians at Petrópolis," in *Liberation Theology: A Documentary History*, 29–47.

56. Christian Smith, *Emergence of Liberation Theology*, 13.

57. Pablo Richard, *Death of Christendoms, Birth of the Church: Historical Analysis and Theological Interpretation of the Church in Latin America* (Maryknoll, N.Y.: Orbis Books, 1987), quoted in *Liberation Theology: A Documentary History*, 40. See also O. Ernesto Valiente, "The Reception of Vatican II in Latin America," *Theological Studies* 73 (2012): 795–823.

58. *Humanae salutis*, Apostolic Constitution, December 25, 1961, http://www.vatican.va/holy_father/john_xxiii/apost_constitutions/1961/documents/hf_j-xxiii_apc_19611225_humanae-salutis_sp.html.

59. Giuseppe Ruggiere, "Faith and History," in *The Reception of Vatican II*, ed. Giuseppe Alberigo, Jean-Pierre Jossua, and Joseph A. Komonchak (Washington: Catholic University of America, 1987), 91–114, at 98.

60. Medellín, "Poverty," 1, 2. These and all direct references to the text of the Medellín Conference are taken from the Second General Conference of Latin American Bishops, *The Church in the Present-Day Transformation of Latin America*, vol. 2 (Bogotá: General Secretariat of CELAM, 1970).

61. Medellín, "Youth," 15.

62. Medellín, "Poverty," 4, 6, and 7.

63. "Document on Peace," 14, Second General Conference of Latin American Bishops, quoted in *Liberation Theology: A Documentary History*, 109.

64. Ignacio Martín-Baró, "Oscar Romero: Voice of the Downtrodden," in Oscar Romero, *Voice of the Voiceless: The Four Pastoral Letters and Other Statements*, 1–21, at 4.

65. In the next few years, nineteen priests, five religious women, and hundreds of catechists would join their lives to those of 75,000 Salvadorans, victims of a violent civil war.

66. Teresa Whitfield, *Paying the Price: Ignacio Ellacuría and the Murdered Jesuits of El Salvador* (Philadelphia: Temple University Press, 1994), 52–55.

67. Sobrino describes the event and quotes Monsignor Romero in *Witnesses to the Kingdom: The Martyrs of El Salvador and the Crucified Peoples* (Maryknoll, N.Y.: Orbis Books, 2003), 13.

68. Rutilio Grande, S.J. was murdered on March 12, 1977, with two lay companions. Many of Romero's biographers, including Sobrino, believe that this event sealed the transformation of the archbishop.

69. Sobrino, *Witnesses to the Kingdom*, 31–32.

70. Jon Sobrino, "Good News to the Poor," homily delivered in the Church of the University of Louvain on February 2, 1985, in *Archbishop Romero: Memories and Reflections*, trans. Robert R. Barr (Maryknoll, N.Y.: Orbis Books, 1990), 203.

71. Jon Sobrino, *Christ the Liberator: A View from the Victims* (Maryknoll, N.Y.: Orbis Books, 2001), 216.

72. Sobrino, *Witnesses to the Kingdom*, 31.

73. Sobrino tells us that "[Romero] taught theology to speak of God and the poor in one breath . . . to speak of the God of the poor, and he taught it *how* to speak of God and the poor." *Archbishop Romero: Memories and Reflections*, 175.

74. Here I am paraphrasing Gustavo Gutiérrez in an article honoring Ignacio Ellacuría, "No One Takes My Life from Me; I Give It Freely," in *Love That Produces Hope: The Thought of Ignacio Ellacuría*, ed. Kevin F. Burke and Robert Lassalle-Klein (Collegeville, Minn.: Liturgical Press, 2006), 70.

75. Ignacio Ellacuría was born in the Basque city of Portugalete, Spain, on November 9, 1930. He entered the Society of Jesus in 1947 at the age of sixteen, and first came to El Salvador the following year as a Jesuit novice.

76. Whitfield, *Paying the Price*, 44–45. For an excellent discussion of Ellacuría's appropriation of the Ignatian Spiritual Exercises, see J. Matthew Ashley, "Ignacio Ellacuría and the Spiritual Exercises of Ignatius Loyola," *Theological Studies* 61, no. 1 (2000): 16–39; and "Contemplation in the Action of Justice: Ignacio Ellacuría and Ignatian Spirituality," in *Love That Produces Hope*, 144–65.

77. Commenting on the General Congregation's decree, Sobrino writes, "The issue is not simply the service of faith and the promotion of justice but the pursuit of these goals in a world ruled by unbelief and injustice. . . . In their mission, then, Jesuits must keep clearly before them the fact that the faith they are trying to serve is not something evident, something already possessed socially and culturally, but rather a faith that must win its way." Jon Sobrino, *The True Church and the Poor*, trans. Matthew J. O'Connell (Maryknoll, N.Y.: Orbis Books, 1984), 65.

78. Ellacuría's writings on the role of the university in the public sphere are collected in *Escritos Universitarios* (San Salvador: UCA Editores, 1999).

79. Jon Sobrino's reflection on this massacre can be found in both *Witnesses to the Kingdom* and *The Principle of Mercy*. Sobrino narrowly escaped death because he was lecturing in Thailand at the time.

80. Jon Sobrino, "Ignacio Ellacuría, the Human Being and the Christian: 'Taking the Crucified People Down from the Cross,'" in *Love That Produces Hope*, 4–5.

81. Sobrino, "Ignacio Ellacuría," 56.

82. Jon Sobrino, "Letter to Ignacio Ellacuría," in "Ignacio Ellacuría, the Human Being and the Christian," 59.

83. While we do not have enough evidence to allow us to assess the influence that Sobrino's work may have had on Ellacuría's, it is likely that the influence was mutual. On this, Kevin Burke has rightly noted that it is easier to trace the influence of Ellacuría on Sobrino not only because of the latter's copious reflections on the former's life and death, but also because as a philosopher and theologian Ellacuría concentrated his work in the areas of foundation and method—disciplines upon which a systematic theologian, like Sobrino, tends to rely heavily. See Kevin F. Burke, *The Ground Beneath the Cross: The Theology of Ignacio Ellacuría* (Washington: Georgetown University Press, 2000), 23.

84. Héctor Samour, "Zubiri y la filosofía de la liberación," *Realidad* 87 (2002), 371–92, at 372. Also available online at http://academia.edu/1641033/Zubiri_y_la_filosofia_de_la_liberacion.

85. Ignacio Ellacuría, "Superación del reduccionismo idealista," *ECA* no. 477 (1988): 636–37. For a detailed commentary on Zubiri's treatment of the reductionist idealism of Western philosophy, see Robert Lassalle-Klein, "Ignacio Ellacuría's Debt to Xavier Zubiri: Critical Principles for a Latin American Philosophy and Theology of Liberation," in *Love That Produces Hope*, 88–98.

86. Zubiri points out that Western thought has consistently assumed that sensory perception precedes the intellect and that the intellect alone organizes the manifold data provided by the senses to capture the essence of the things perceived. Hence, our understanding of the powers of human intelligence has been largely circumscribed by what this intelligence can logically predicate, conceive, or judge about reality in its attempt to grasp the essence of things. Zubiri calls this distortion the "logification of intelligence" because it primarily stresses what the mind—as the logos—can tell us about the perceived reality. Simultaneously, the separation of the function of the senses from those of the intellect has led us to equate our conceptualization of reality with reality itself, and thus reduce our understanding of reality to the sum total of essences or entities lacking openness and dynamism. This process is what Zubiri calls the "entification of reality." See Ignacio Ellacuría, "La superación del reduccionismo idealista en Zubiri," *ECA* 477 (1988): 633–50. See also Héctor Samour, *Voluntad de liberación: El pensamiento filosófico de Ignacio Ellacuría* (San Salvador: UCA Editores, 2002), 47; and Burke, *Ground Beneath the Cross*, 45.

87. Sobrino, *Where Is God?: Earthquake, Terrorism, Barbarity, and Hope*, trans. Margaret Wilde (Maryknoll, N.Y.: Orbis Books, 2004), 29–48.

88. Michael E. Lee, *Bearing the Weight of Salvation*, 44.

89. Xavier Zubiri, *Inteligencia sentiente: inteligencia y realidad*, 10, quoted in Burke, *Ground Beneath the Cross*, 46.

90. In Zubiri's own words, "It is not only that human sensing and intellection are not in opposition. Rather their intrinsic and formal unity constitutes a single and distinct act of apprehension." Zubiri, *Inteligencia sentiente: inteligencia sentiente*, 23, quoted in Lassalle-Klein, "Ignacio Ellacuría's Debt to Xavier Zubiri," 99. Hence, the distortions of intelligence and reality ensue from not properly recognizing that through their unitary faculty of "sentient intelligence," human persons apprehend reality not as a concept or idea but as that which is real. Zubiri explains that knowing has a three-part structure. The primary apprehension of reality is complemented by two other modes of intellection: logos and reason. Grounded in the apprehension of the senses, logos contributes to a fuller understanding of reality by assessing how this apprehension of reality is real in relation to other things. Then, through further examination of the reality at hand, reason explains how this reality relates to and actualizes itself in worldly reality such as science, art, or theology. See Lassalle-Klein, "Ignacio Ellacuría's Debt to Xavier Zubiri," 99–102.

91. Ignacio Ellacuría, "La nueva obra de Zubiri: 'Inteligencia Sentiente,'" *Razón y Fe* 995 (1981): 135, quoted in Burke, *Ground Beneath the Cross*, 47.

92. Ellacuría, "La nueva obra de Zubiri," 135.

93. Ignacio Ellacuría, *Escritos Teológicos* (San Salvador: UCA Editores, 2000), 270, quoted in Michael E. Lee, *Bearing the Weight of Salvation: The Soteriology of Ignacio Ellacuría*, 47.

94. Diego Gracia, "Zubiri, Xavier," in *Dictionary of Fundamental Theology*, ed. René Latourelle and Rino Fisichella (New York: Crossroad Publishing, 1995), 1166, quoted in Lassalle-Klein, "Ignacio Ellacuría's Debt to Xavier Zubiri," 122 n. 107.

95. Ignacio Ellacuría, "La superación del reduccionismo idealista en Zubiri," 648, quoted in Lassalle-Klein, "Ignacio Ellacuría's Debt to Xavier Zubiri," 103.

96. Xavier Zubiri, *Nature, History, God*, trans. Thomas B. Fowler, Jr. (Washington: University Press of America, 1981), 323. *Theologal* is a technical term in Ignacio Ellacuría's and Jon Sobrino's theology that finds its origins in Xavier Zubiri's work, and should not be confused with *theological*. While the term *theological* refers to the study of God, *theologal* seeks to express the grounding of all reality in God. A theologal dimension of reality refers to the "God dimension" or "graced" dimension of reality, and a theologal spirituality refers to the spirit with which the human person encounters God and makes God present in historical reality. See Burke, *Ground Beneath the Cross*, 40 n. 48.

97. Xavier Zubiri, *Sobre el sentimiento y la volición* (Madrid: Alianza Editorial/Fundación Xavier Zubiri, 1992), 112.

98. Jon Sobrino, *Christ the Liberator*, 309. The relationship of the human person with reality will be discussed in terms of Sobrino's theologal spirituality in the following chapter. See Sobrino, "Spirit of Liberation," 677–701, especially 680–85.

99. Sobrino, "Spirit of Liberation," 685.

100. Xavier Zubiri, "El problema teologal del hombre," in *Teología y mundo contemporáneo: Homenaje a Karl Rahner* (Madrid: Ediciones Cristianidad, 1975), http://www.zubiri.org/works/spanishworks/problemateologal.htm.

101. Zubiri, "El problema teologal del hombre," 58. My translation.

102. Burke, *Ground Beneath the Cross*, 46. See also María Lucrecia Rovaletti, "Man, Experience of God: The problem of God in Xavier Zubiri," *Xavier Zubiri Review* 2 (1999): 65–66.

103. Zubiri, "El problema teologal del hombre," 59.

104. Zubiri, "El Problema teologal del hombre," 59.

105. Zubiri, "El problema teologal del hombre," 61. Ellacuría notes that "creation can be seen as the grafting [*plasmación*] *ad extra* of the Trinitarian life itself, a freely desired grafting [*plasmación*]. It would not be an abstract causality, but an act of communication and self-giving by the divine life itself. This grafting [*plasmación*] and self-communication has degrees and limits; each thing, with its own limits, is a limited way of being God. This limited way is precisely the nature of each thing." "The Historicity of Christian Salvation," 276. Italics in the original.

106. Zubiri, *Nature, History, God*, 333.

107. As Zubiri explains, "Rather than 'infinite,' 'necessary,' 'perfect,' etc., which just yet are excessively complicated ontological attributes, I believe I can dare to call God, as He is patent to man in his constitutive religation, *ens fundamentale* or *fundamentante*. . . . That which religates us does so under this special form which consists in grounding us through making us to be. Hence, our existence has a fundament, in all of the many senses of this word. The primary attribute *quo ad nos* of divinity is fundamentality." *Nature, History, God*, 329–30.

108. Ignacio Ellacuría, "Zubiri, filósofo teologal," in *Vida Nueva* no. 1249 (1980): 45, quoted in Burke, *Ground Beneath the Cross*, 31. Amended translation.

109. Michael E. Lee, "Liberation Theology's Transcendent Moment: The Work of Xavier Zubiri and Ignacio Ellacuría as Noncontrastive Discourse," *Journal of Religion* 83, no. 2 (April 2003): 226–43.

110. For an excellent assessment of Rahner's influence on Ellacuría, see Martin Maier, S.J., "Karl Rahner: The Teacher of Ignacio Ellacuría," in *Love*

that Produces Hope, 128–43. Ellacuría approvingly mentions Rahner's treatment of the supernatural existential in "Historia de la salvación," 604.

111. Rahner, *Foundations of Christian Faith*, 116–33. According to Rahner, there are two ways in which God's self-communication to every human being should be understood: first, as an offer that God makes to every human person from the moment of his or her creation, even prior to the person's freedom. The second mode of self-communication is that of an acceptance or rejection of God's offer. This means that for God's self-communication to take place, the person must accept it. Hence, God's self-communication can be understood in two (or three) ways: as an offer, and then as an offer accepted or rejected.

112. Karl Rahner, "The Theology of Symbol," in *Theological Investigations*, vol. 4 (Baltimore: Helicon Press, 1966), 221–52.

113. See Karl Rahner, "History of Salvation and Salvation-History," in *Theological Investigations*, vol. 5 (Baltimore: Helicon Press, 1966), 98–114.

114. Ignacio Ellacuría, "El objeto de la filosofía," *ECA* 396–97 (1981): 963–80, quoted in Burke, *Ground Beneath the Cross*, 57.

115. Jon Sobrino, *Jesus the Liberator: A Historical-Theological Reading of Jesus of Nazareth* (Maryknoll, N.Y.: Orbis Books, 1993), 132.

116. Ignacio Ellacuría, "El objeto de la filosofía," quoted in Antonio González, "Assessing the Philosophical Achievement of Ignacio Ellacuría," in *Love that Produces Hope*, 80.

117. Martin Maier insightfully notes that, in Ellacuría's work, "The framework inherent in the nature/supernatural dualism is superseded by the framework inherent in the distinction between history-of-salvation/salvation history." See "Karl Rahner: The Teacher of Ignacio Ellacuría," 138.

118. Ellacuría, "Historia de la salvación," 597–628.

119. Ellacuría, "Historia de la salvación," 520.

120. Ellacuría, "Historicidad de la salvación cristiana," in *Escritos Teológicos*, vol. 1, 541.

121. Ellacuría, "Historia de la salvación," 605. Like Zubiri, Ellacuría's notion of "transcendence" must also be properly understood since this is not a transcendence that takes place as a separation away from reality, but rather within reality itself.

122. As Ellacuría warns us, "History, which is the place par excellence of God's revelation and glorification, is also the place of obfuscation and perdition." In "Historia de la salvación," 609. My translation.

123. Ignacio Ellacuría, "Fundamentación biológica de la ética," *ECA* 368 (1979): 419–28.

124. Héctor Samour, *Voluntad de liberación*, 119. Samour explains that the human tie (*religación*) to the power of the real serves as the point of support and fundament for the realization of the person.

125. While this biological nature is among the "structures of possibility" that generate the capacity to mediate salvation, it is important to keep in mind that human apprehension is initially and fundamentally a biological activity. In fact Zubiri and Ellacuría describe the human person as the "reality animal" to stress the person's biological constitution, which enables him or her to grasp reality in real things. For a concise and clear explanation of Zubiri's use of the term "reality animal," see Burke, *Ground Beneath the Cross*, 74–85.

126. Ellacuría, "Fundamentación biológica de la ética," 423.

127. Ellacuría, "Fundamentación biológica de la ética," 422. Ellacuría then underscores the collaborative role of the human person in the historical fulfillment of reality.

128. Ellacuría, "Fundamentación biológica de la ética," 422, quoted in Burke, *Ground Beneath the Cross*, 107. For the sake of clarity, I have replaced the term "reality animal" with "human person."

129. See Samour, *Voluntad de liberación*, 115–18; and Lassalle-Klein, "Ignacio Ellacuría's Debt to Xavier Zubiri," 113–16.

130. Sobrino, *Jesus the Liberator*, 279, n. 40.

131. See, for instance, Sobrino, *Jesus the Liberator*, 34; *Christ the Liberator*, 327; *No Salvation Outside the Poor: Prophetic-Utopian Essays* (Maryknoll, N.Y.: Orbis Books, 2008), 2; "Ignacio Ellacuría, the Human Being and the Christian," 18–19.

132. Ellacuría, "Hacia una fundamentación del método teológico latino-americano," 208; quoted in Burke, *Ground Beneath the Cross*, 100.

133. Ellacuría, "Hacia una fundamentación del método teológico latino-americano," 208. Here the translation of Ellacuría's terminology is borrowed from Burke, *Ground Beneath the Cross*, 100–8.

134. Sobrino, "Ignacio Ellacuría," 18–19.

135. Burke, *Ground Beneath the Cross*, 101.

136. Ellacuría, "Fundamentación biológica de la ética," 422; quoted in Burke, *Ground Beneath the Cross*, 106.

137. Héctor Samour, "Filosofía y libertad," in *Ignacio Ellacuría: Aquella libertad esclarecida*, ed. Jon Sobrino and Rolando Alvarado (San Salvador: UCA Editores, 1999), 116.

138. Ellacuría, "Hacia una fundamentación del método teológico latino-americano," 211.

139. Ignacio Ellacuría, "La teología como momento ideológico de la praxis eclesial," *Estudios Eclesiásticos* 207 (1978): 457–76; quoted in Sobrino, "Theology in a Suffering World," 38.

140. Ellacuría, "Hacia una fundamentación del método teológico latino-americano," 108.

141. See, for instance, Sobrino's approach to God's Kingdom in *Jesus the Liberator*, 69–70.

3. Theology as a Task Guided by the Spirit

1. Sandra Schneiders identifies four different referents for "spirituality" as it is commonly used by contemporary practicing Christians: one's prayer life; "an intensified faith life which embraces the whole of one's daily experience"; "the whole of personal experience"; and (d) "the implication of Christian commitment for social and political life." "Theology and Spirituality: Strangers, Rivals or Partners?" *Horizons* 13, no. 2 (1986): 253–74, at 254.

2. Sandra M. Schneiders, I.H.M., "The Study of Christian Spirituality: Contours and Dynamics of a Discipline," in *Minding the Spirit: The Study of Christian Spirituality*, ed. Elizabeth A. Dreyer and Mark S. Burrows (Baltimore, Md.: Johns Hopkins University Press, 2005), 7.

3. Annice Callahan, R.C.S.J., "The Relationship between Spirituality and Theology," *Horizons* 16, no. 2 (1989): 266–74, at 266.

4. Contemporary theologians often lament the separation between theology and spirituality that began in the High Middle Ages as theology started to identify itself as a science distinct from the spiritual life. This distinction led to a separation that was intensified by the modernist chasm between theory and practice. Efforts to overcome this separation are evident in the work of theologians such as Karl Rahner, Hans von Balthasar, Marie-Dominique Chenu, and Yves Congar. This same concern to bring theology and spirituality closer together is one of the identifying features of contemporary liberation theologies. See Gutiérrez, *A Theology of Liberation*, 3–5.

5. This is Annice Callahan's assessment of the influence that Rahner's spirituality has on his theology. I argue that such is the case with other theologies, including that of Jon Sobrino. See Callahan, "The Relationship between Spirituality and Theology," 266.

6. A similar point is made by J. Matthew Ashley and Jon Sobrino, who reference both Hans Urs von Baltahasar and Karl Rahner. See J. Matthew Ashley, "The Mystery of God and Compassion for the Poor: The Spiritual Basis of Theology," in *Hope and Solidarity*; Sobrino, "Spirituality and the Following of Jesus," 678.

7. From M.-D. Chenu, *Une ecole de téologie: Le Saulchoir* (Paris: Cerf, 1985), quoted in Gustavo Gutiérrez, *We Drink from Our Own Wells: The Spiritual Journey of a People* (Maryknoll, N.Y.: Orbis Books, 1984), 147 n. 2.

8. Walter Principe has noted three interrelated levels of spirituality: a real or existential level, the formulation of the teaching about lived reality, and the study of scholars of the first and second level of spirituality. "Christian

Spirituality," in *The New Dictionary of Catholic Spirituality*, ed. M. Downey (Collegeville, Minn.: Liturgical Press, 1993), 931–38. For an excellent study on the definitions of and approaches to Christian spirituality, see *Minding the Spirit: The Study of Christian Spirituality*, ed. Elizabeth A. Dreyer and Mark S. Burrows (Baltimore, Md.: Johns Hopkins University Press, 2005).

9. Bernard McGinn, "The Letter and the Spirit: Spirituality as an Academic Discipline," in *Minding the Spirit: The Study of Christian Spirituality*, 29. In a similar vein, Sobrino, writing in 1985, notes that "we are witnessing today a new concern for, and a rebirth of, the 'spiritual' element in the life of Christians and religious." "The Importance of the Spiritual Life Today," in *Spirituality of Liberation: Toward Political Holiness*, 7.

10. Sandra M. Schneiders, "Spirituality in the Academy," *Theological Studies* 50 (1989): 676–77. Schneiders also notes that theologians like Mary Collins, Charles Curran, Margaret Farley, Gustavo Gutiérrez, Monika Hellwig, Hans Küng, Bernard Lonergan, Rosemary Radford Ruther, Edward Schillebeeckx, and Dorothee Soelle all share Karl Rahner's conviction that "only a theology that is rooted in the spiritual commitment of the theologian and oriented toward praxis will be meaningful in the Church of the future" (677).

11. See for instance, Gutiérrez, *Theology of Liberation*, xxxii–xxxiii, 5, and 116–20; and *We Drink from Our Own Well: The Spiritual Journey of a People*, 35–38. Jon Sobrino's explicit book on a spirituality of liberation was published in its Spanish version in 1985: *Liberación con Espíritu: Apuntes para una Nueva Espiritualidad* (Santander: Sal Terrae, 1985). This was later published in English as *Spirituality of Liberation: Toward Political Holiness*.

12. Gutiérrez, *Theology of Liberation*, 117. Originally published as *Teología de la Liberación, Perspectivas* (Lima: CEP, 1971). For works that outline the development of a Latin American liberationist spirituality, see Leonardo Boff, "The Need for Political Saints: From a Spirituality of Liberation to the Practice of Liberation," *Cross-current* 30, no. 4 (1980–81): 369–84; Segundo Galilea, "La liberación como encuentro de la política y de la contemplación," *Concilium* 96 (1974): 313–27; Segundo Galilea, *The Way of Living Faith: A Spirituality of Liberation* (San Francisco: Harper and Row, 1988); Gustavo Gutiérrez, *We Drink From Our Own Wells: The Spiritual Journey of a People*; and Pedro Casaldáliga and José María Vigil, *Political Holiness: The Spirituality of Liberation* (Maryknoll, N.Y.: Orbis Books, 1994).

13. Sobrino, "Spirituality and the Following of Jesus," 679.

14. Jon Sobrino, "Espiritualidad y Teología," in *Liberación con Espíritu: Apuntes para una nueva Espiritualidad* (San Salvador: UCA Editores, 1985), 63. My translation. See also "Spirituality and Theology," in *Spirituality of Liberation: Toward Political Holiness*, 46–79, at 49.

15. My interpretation of the integrating dimension that spirituality may offer to theology draws on Matthew Ashley's lucid analysis of the subject in "The Mystery of God and Compassion for the Poor," 63–75.

16. Jon Sobrino, "Spirituality and Liberation," in *Spirituality of Liberation: Toward Political Holiness*, 27.

17. Sobrino, "Spirituality and the Following of Jesus," 691–92.

18. Sobrino, "Spirituality and Liberation," 28.

19. Sobrino, *Christ the Liberator*, 328.

20. See Sandra M. Schneiders, "Approaches to the Study of Christian Spirituality," in *The Blackwell Companion to Christian Spirituality*, ed. Arthur Holder (Malden, Mass.: Blackwell Publishing, 2005), 19–29; and Bernard McGinn, "The Letter and the Spirit: Spirituality as an Academic Discipline," 29–35.

21. Schneiders, "Approaches," 26–27.

22. Sobrino, "Spirituality and the Following of Jesus," 680.

23. While the Second Vatican Council distinguishes between the "temporal" and the "transcendental," it rejects the view that stressed a radical separation between grace and nature and relegated the former to a supernatural plane inaccessible to our experience. Our human efforts contribute to the realization of God's will and are associated with Christ's redemptive action. See, for instance, Flannery, ed., *Gaudium et Spes* 1, 11, 24, 34, 38, 41, 43, 45, 56, 64, 91, and so on, in *Vatican Council II*.

24. Jon Sobrino, "Presuppositions and Foundations of Spirituality," in *Spirituality of Liberation: Toward Political Holiness*, 4 (italics in original). See also Jon Sobrino, *Liberación con Espíritu: Apuntes para una nueva espiritualidad*, 12.

25. Sobrino, "Presuppositions and Foundations, 13.

26. Sobrino, "Spirituality and Theology," 46–79, at 67.

27. Sobrino, "Spirituality and Theology," 68.

28. Sobrino, "Spirituality and Theology," 69.

29. Sobrino, "Presuppositions and Foundations," 13.

30. Sobrino, "Spirituality and the Following of Jesus," 678. Translation amended.

31. Ashley, "The Mystery of God and Compassion for the Poor," 65–66.

32. While Ellacuría's threefold dimension of engaging reality implicitly assumes the presence of the transcendent in each one of these dimensions, Sobrino, building on his colleague's work and rooted in his own personal experience, explicitly adds a human disposition or spirit that actualizes our encounter with the transcendent—the willingness to be carried by the grace in reality.

33. Sobrino, "Spirituality and the Following of Jesus," 681.

34. Sobrino, "Presuppositions and Foundations of Spirituality," 14.

35. Sobrino, "Presuppositions and Foundations of Spirituality," 16.

36. Sobrino, "Spirituality and the Following of Jesus," 682.

37. Sobrino, "Presuppositions and Foundations of Spirituality," 18.

38. Sobrino, "Spirituality and the Following of Jesus," 685.

39. Sobrino, "Spirituality and the Following of Jesus," 684.

40. Sobrino, "Spirituality and the Following of Jesus," 684.

41. Sobrino, "Presuppositions and Foundations of Spirituality," 19.

42. Sobrino, "Spirituality and the Following of Jesus," 685.

43. Sobrino, *Jesus the Liberator*, 7.

44. Sobrino, "Spirituality and the Following of Jesus," 685.

45. Sobrino, "Spirituality and the Following of Jesus," 685.

46. Sobrino, "Presuppositions and Foundations of Spirituality," 19.

47. Sobrino, "Spirituality and the Following of Jesus," 686. Italics in the original. Translation amended.

48. Sobrino, "Spirituality and the Following of Jesus," 686.

49. Sobrino, "Following Jesus as Discernment," in *Discernment of the Spirit and of Spirits*, ed. Casiano Floristán and Christian Duquoc (New York: The Seabury Press, 1979), 14–27, at 18.

50. Here it is important to keep in mind that our following of Jesus does not replicate Jesus's actions. For instance, there is a proper way to think of grace being incarnate in us, but this is not "incarnation" in the way that applies only to Jesus.

51. Sobrino, "Following Jesus as Discernment," 21.

52. Sobrino, "Following Jesus as Discernment," 18.

53. Sobrino, "Spirituality and the Following of Jesus," 687. See also Sobrino, "Following Jesus as Discernment," 21–23.

54. Sobrino, "Spirituality and the Following of Jesus," 687.

55. For an excellent treatment of the scriptural foundations for the preferential option for the poor, see Gustavo Gutiérrez, "Option for the Poor," 235–50.

56. For an excellent treatment of Sobrino's "principle of mercy" from the perspective of moral theology, see James F. Keenan, S.J., "Radicalizing the Comprehensiveness of Mercy: Christian Identity in Theological Ethics," in *Hope and Solidarity*, 187–200.

57. Sobrino's usage of the term "principle" is analogous to Ernst Bloch's usage in his three-volume work *The Principle of Hope* (Cambridge, Mass.: MIT Press, 1995).

58. Jon Sobrino, "The Samaritan Church and the Principle of Mercy," in *The Principle of Mercy*, 16.

59. Sobrino, "Samaritan Church and the Principle of Mercy," 17.

60. Sobrino, "Spirituality and the Following of Jesus," 687.

61. Jon Sobrino, "Systematic Christology: Jesus Christ, the Absolute Mediator," in *Mysterium Liberationis*, 440–61, at 447.

62. Jon Sobrino, "Theological Understanding in European and Latin American Theology," in *The True Church and the Poor*, 8.

63. Jon Sobrino, "Theological Understanding," 15–16.

64. Jon Sobrino, "Theology in a Suffering World," 29.

65. Jon Sobrino, "Evil and Hope: A Reflection from the Victims," *CTSA Proceedings* 50 (1995): 71–84, at 80.

66. Sobrino contends that to properly understand the sacred scriptures and God's revelation in the present, the human person must actualize certain existential pre-dispositions that are necessary to overcome the historical and cultural distance that exists between the sacred texts and the present time. See Jon Sobrino, "Teología en un Mundo Sufriente: La Teología de la Liberación como 'Intellectus Amoris,'" *Revista Latinoamericana de Teología* 15 (1988): 243–65, at 249–50.

67. Brackley, "Theology and Solidarity," 8.

68. Sobrino, *The Principle of Mercy*, 33. See also Sobrino, "Spirituality and the Following of Jesus," 683.

69. Jon Sobrino, "¿Cómo hacer teología? La teología como *Intellectus Amoris*," *Sal Terrae* 5 (May 1989): 412–13. My translation.

70. Sobrino, *Jesus the Liberator*, 43. In a more recent article Sobrino adds that "the sources must be read in a *context*, a *location*, the *ubi* of the Aristotelian categories, to which must be added the *epoch*, the *quando*. This spatio-temporal context can make the text give something or other of itself, so that the fundamental question will be, What is the best context from which to read the texts about Jesus of Nazareth?" See "Jesus of Galilee from the Salvadoran Context: Compassion, Hope, and Following the Light of the Cross," *Theological Studies* 70 (2009): 439. Italics in the original.

71. Sobrino, *Jesus the Liberator*, 27; translation amended. See Jon Sobrino, *Jesucristo Liberador: Lectura Historica-Teológica de Jesús de Nazaret* (San Salvador: UCA Editores, 1991), 58. See also Sobrino, *The Principle of Mercy*, 31. Although the original text reads "theological sense," this may be a mistranslation or a misprint because Sobrino's expression "theologal" seems more appropriate in this context.

72. In examining the characteristics of an apt theological place, Sobrino distinguishes between place as a concrete geographical location (categorical *ubi*)—for example, a university, a seminary, or an ecclesial base community—and the location understood as a substantial reality (substantial *quid*)—e.g., the world of the poor. Indeed, for him, the world of the poor is the reality or situation that should primarily inform and guide a theologian's reflection. "¿Cómo hacer teología? La teología como *Intellectus Amoris*," 414–15.

73. Sobrino, *Jesus The Liberator*, 31–35.

74. Sobrino, *Jesus The Liberator*, 28. Sobrino makes a distinction between the theologal and theological place: the world of the poor as a social-theologal location, and the church of the poor—located therein—as the most fitting place to live the Christian faith and reflect upon it. While the ecclesial reality preserves the contents of theology, the social reality influences our theological approach by promoting its conversion and the transformation of reality. See *Jesus The Liberator*, 30.

75. In fact, our attempts to uncritically harmonize our understanding of God with the world of the oppressed can easily lead to the manipulation of the truth and to averting a necessary process of conversion in our personal lives and in our theological frames of interpretation. Thus, despite the sacramental character of reality, God cannot always be conceived only analogically, merely as the transcendent continuation of historical reality. See, Sobrino, *The True Church and the Poor*, 25.

76. This prompt to conversion is threefold: It first calls for an interpretation of the whole of reality from the perspective of the victims of history. Second, it demands a de-centered praxis on behalf of the victims and against their situation. Third, it is rooted in the hope that such praxis gives to the processes of historical and transcendent salvation. Sobrino, "¿Cómo hacer teología? La teología como *Intellectus Amoris*," 411–12.

77. Sobrino, *Spirituality of Liberation: Toward Political Holiness*, 15.

78. *Gaudium et Spes* 4. In *Vatican Council II*, 905.

79. *Gaudium et Spes* 11. In *Vatican Council II*, 912.

80. Sobrino, *Jesus the Liberator*, 25.

81. Sobrino, "¿Cómo hacer teología? La teología como *Intellectus Amoris*," 399.

82. Sobrino, "La Teología y El 'Principio Liberación,' " in *Revista Latinoamericana de Teología* 35 (1995): 124. Although it may seem obvious, it is good to remember that the sacred scriptures are rooted in historical events that have been interpreted and elevated to theological concepts.

83. Sobrino, "La Teología y el 'Principio Liberación,' " 119. The emphasis and hyphenation are Sobrino's.

84. Gutiérrez, *A Theology of Liberation*, xxxiv.

85. Leonardo Boff, *When Theology Listens to the Poor*, 10.

86. Sobrino, *The Principle of Mercy*, vii. It is somewhat paradoxical that while in Latin America the modes and mechanisms of oppression have changed throughout the centuries, the foremost sign of the times has remained the same. Five hundred years ago, the Dominican priest Bartolomé de las Casas had already written, "In the Indies I leave Jesus Christ, our God, being whipped and afflicted, and buffeted and crucified, not once, but a thousand

times, as often as the Spaniards assault and destroy those people." Gustavo Gutiérrez, *Dios y el Oro de las Indians*, (Salamanca, 2d ed., 1990), 157, quoted in Sobrino, *Jesus the Liberator*, 11.

87. Sobrino appeals to the declarations of the Second General Conference of Latin American Bishops in Medellin and to the "sensus fidelium" to argue that the "crucified people" embody the signs of the times. See "¿Cómo hacer teología? La teología como *Intellectus Amoris*," 400–1.

88. Jorge Costadoat, S.J., "Los signos de los tiempos en la teología de liberación," in *Signos de Estos Tiempos: Interpretación teológica de nuestra época*, ed. Fernando Berrios, Jorge Costadoat, and Diego García (Santiago de Chile: Ediciones Universidad Alberto Hurtado, 2008), 131–48, at 132–33. Sobrino suggests that just as the sacred scriptures illuminate our understanding of historical reality, our experience of reality sheds light on and enhances our understanding of revelation. See Sobrino, "La Teología y el 'Principio Liber-ación,'" 123–24.

89. Brackley, "Theology and Solidarity," 12.

90. Sobrino, "¿Cómo hacer teología? La teología como *Intellectus Amoris*," 402.

91. As Robert Lassalle-Klein has noted, Ellacuría uses the term *historiciza-tion* in two different ways. First, it refers to the transformative effect that human praxis exerts over the historical and natural dimensions of reality. Secondly, and more relevant to Sobrino's methodology, to historicize a concept is to understand its relationship to and impact on historical reality. "Ignacio Ellacuría's Debt to Xavier Zubiri," 108–10.

92. Sobrino notes that "there are two important lessons that Latin Ameri-can Christology learns from the Gospels . . . we cannot turn the figure of Jesus into theology without turning him into history and telling the story of his life and fate . . . we cannot turn Jesus into history without turning him into theology as good news and so an essential reference for the communities." *Jesus the Liberator*, 63.

93. Sobrino, *Jesus the Liberator*, 17. Sobrino identifies three alienating Christological distortions: an abstract Christ whose title is disassociated from the historical Jesus to whom the title was given and thus assumes different meanings (i.e., Christ the powerful, but manifesting the power of the oppres-sors, not the power of service); a reconciling Christ conceived of as a peaceful Jesus stripped of his prophetic voice; and an absolutely Absolute Christ who is put forward as something ultimate and distant that is disassociated from historical reality. In his absoluteness, such a Christ loses his relational character both with the Trinity and with the human community. *Jesus the Liberator*, 14–17.

94. Sobrino, "Theological Understanding," 13–14.

95. Sobrino, "Theological Understanding," 15.

96. Jon Sobrino, "Doing Theology From Amidst the Victims," in *The Future of Theology: Essays in Honor of Jürgen Moltmann*, ed. Miroslav Volf, Carmen Kreig, and Thomas Kurcharz (Grand Rapids, Mich.: Eerdmans, 1996), 164–75, at 171.

97. Sobrino often underscores that the scriptures illustrate that God's distinctive response to human suffering is mercy, which the texts depict as ultimate in the reality of God. "This means," he says, "that mercy is the necessary and correct response to a suffering world. . . . [W]ithout accepting this there will be no understanding of God, Jesus, or the human person." "¿Cómo hacer teología? La teología como *Intellectus Amoris*," 405. My translation.

98. See Avery Dulles, "The Symbolic Structure of Revelation," *Theological Studies* 41 (1980): 51–73.

99. Sobrino, "Teología en un Mundo Sufriente," 260.

100. Sobrino, "¿Cómo hacer teología? La teología como *Intellectus Amoris*," 405. My translation.

101. Sobrino, "Theology in a Suffering World," 42.

102. Sobrino, *Jesus the Liberator*, 35.

103. Sobrino, *Jesus the Liberator*, 189. This insight again evinces that an honest and appropriate apprehension of reality not only entails a noetic but also ethical and praxical dimensions.

104. Sobrino, "Spirituality and the Following of Jesus," 682. Translation amended. See the article's Spanish version, "Espiritualidad y Seguimiento de Jesús, in *Mysterium liberationis: Conceptos fundamentales de la teología de liberación*, vol. 2 (Madrid: Editorial Trota, S.A., 1994), 454.

105. Sobrino, "La Teología y El 'Principio Liberación,'" 127.

106. Ignacio Ellacuría, "La Teología como Momento Ideológico de la Praxis Eclesial," *Estudios Eclesiásticos* 207 (1978): 457–76, quoted in Sobrino, "Theology in a Suffering World," 38.

107. See Jürgen Moltmann, *Theology of Hope: On the Ground and the Implications of a Christian Eschatology*, trans. James Leitch (New York: Harper & Row, 1974). Sobrino further suggests that theology can be conceived on the whole as faith, hope, and love seeking understanding, since each one of these dimensions offers us important theological content that captures the fitting response to God's self-revelation and provides the means for theological intelligence to approach the reality of God, as well as the human possibility to grasp it.

108. Sobrino, "From a Theology of Liberation to a Theology of Martyrdom," in *Witnesses to the Kingdom*, 107.

109. Sobrino, "Theology in a Suffering World," 38.

110. Sobrino contends that in liberation theology, "the concrete way of doing theology already expresses in *actu* how the *theos* of theology is understood and how one responds and corresponds to this *theos*." "Theology in a Suffering World," 40.

111. Sobrino, "Theology in a Suffering World," 42.

112. Sobrino, "Theology in a Suffering World," 39.

113. Sobrino notes that when theology is solely understood as *intellectus fidei*, it offers the necessary task of proclaiming, explaining, and communicating theological truth, but it "is also exposed to the danger of refraining from changing reality and of abandoning reality to itself." See "Theology in a Suffering World," 42.

114. Sobrino, "Theology in a Suffering World," 44.

115. Two examples might help to make this clearer. In the struggle for justice, our individualist and self-serving hopes often become reconfigured in a Christian decentered hope (i.e., hope for a community forged by the values of God's kingdom) that includes far more than our limited personal visions and needs. In a similar manner, through our praxis of justice our doctrines and understanding of God are invariably challenged by the powerful negativity encountered in reality. And because those who practice justice will often be persecuted, it is also through this praxis that our faith in the crucified and yet liberating God takes root and becomes concretized. As such, this praxis of justice calls for a deep questioning and understanding of our faith, even as it becomes a way of concretizing, sustaining, and Christianizing it. Sobrino, "Theology in a Suffering World," 44–45.

116. Sobrino, "Teología en un Mundo Sufriente," 263.

117. Sobrino, *No Salvation Outside the Poor*, 12.

118. Sobrino, "Teología en un Mundo Sufriente," 264.

119. Sobrino, *No Salvation Outside the Poor*, 12.

120. Sobrino, "La Teología y El 'Principio Liberación,'" 139.

121. Sobrino, "¿Cómo hacer teología? La teología como *Intellectus Amoris*," 410. My translation.

122. Sobrino, "La Teología y El 'Principio Liberación,'" 139. My translation.

123. Sobrino, "La Teología y El 'Principio Liberación,'" 140.

124. Sobrino, "Teología en un Mundo Sufriente," 264. My translation.

125. Sobrino, "Teología en un Mundo Sufriente," 264.

4. Life and Spirit of the True Human Being

1. Sobrino, "Spirituality and the Following of Jesus," 682.

2. As indicated in the previous chapter, I use the capitalized term "Spirit" to refer to the third person of the Trinity—the Holy Spirit—and the term

"spirit" to refer to how the Holy Spirit becomes actualized in the life of Jesus and other human persons.

3. Sobrino, *Christ the Liberator*, 323.

4. Jorge Costadoat, S.J., "Seguimiento de Cristo en América Latina," *Gregorianum* 93, no. 3 (2012): 573–92, at 580.

5. Sobrino, *Jesus the Liberator*, 11–17, especially at 15–16. Although Sobrino does not identify any specific expressions of this Christological image, I suggest that Cardenal Alfonso López Trujillo's short reflection, "El Cristo Reconciliador," evinces some of the theological elements that Sobrino argues against. See *Vida y espiritualidad* 24, no. 69 (2008): 83–87.

6. Sobrino, *Jesus the Liberator*, 16.

7. Sobrino, *Jesus the Liberator*, 7.

8. Sobrino, *Jesus the Liberator*, 36–40.

9. Sobrino notes that the historical Jesus "is objectively, the best *mystagogia* toward the Christ of faith, and the affinity we obtain in the practice of discipleship is, subjectively, the best *mystagogia* for gaining access to Jesus and so to Christ." *Jesus the Liberator*, 55. Italics in the original.

10. Sobrino, *Jesus the Liberator*, 39.

11. Sobrino, *Jesus the Liberator*, 50. As Robert Lassalle-Klein has rightly noted, "This inclusion of both the 'spirit' and the resurrection of Jesus in what Sobrino calls his 'historical' reality helps us see that his understanding of the historical reality of Jesus transcends the positivism of historical facts." "Jesus of Galilee and the Crucified People: The Contextual Christology of Jon Sobrino and Ignacio Ellacuría," *Theological Studies* 70 (2009): 347–76, at 359.

12. Sobrino, *Jesus the Liberator*, 52.

13. Sobrino, *Jesus the Liberator*, 37–40. Scripture scholar Dan Harrington has praised Sobrino's approach to Christology, noting that "it involves taking seriously the historical data about Jesus and trying to do theology on the basis of and in the light of these data. "What Got Jesus Killed," in *Hope and Solidarity: Jon Sobrino's Challenge to Christian Theology*, ed. Stephen J. Pope (Maryknoll, N.Y.: Orbis, 2008), 79–89, at 81.

14. See Congregation for the Doctrine of the Faith, "Notification on the Works of Father Jon Sobrino: Jesucristo liberador. Lectura histórico-teológica de Jesús de Nazaret (Madrid, 1991) [1] and La fe en Jeucristo. Ensayo desde las Víctimas (San Salvador, 1999) [2]," in *Hope and Solidarity: Jon Sobrino's Challange to Christian Theology*, 255–66.

15. Sobrino, *Jesus the Liberator*, 55.

16. Jorge Costadoat, S.J., "La liberación en la cristología de Jon Sobrino," *Teología y Vida* 44 (2003): 62–84.

17. Jon Sobrino, "Systematic Christology: Jesus Christ, the Absolute Mediator of the Reign of God," 440–61, at 451.

18. Sobrino also acknowledges other manifestations of the Spirit in Jesus. These include the Spirit of *newness*, the Spirit of *truth and life*, the Spirit of *ecstasy* to the Father, and the Spirit of *gratuitousness*. See *Christ the Liberator*, 328–30.

19. Jon Sobrino, *Christ the Liberator*, 327.

20. For instance, even as Jesus's cross underscores the importance of his faithfulness to God's mission, the passion assumes Jesus's perseverance in his original and honest assessment of reality and his willingness to let himself be led by the "more"—that is, the grace—of reality. While Sobrino does not explicitly correlate the structure of Jesus's life with the fundamental theologal dispositions, he does correlate them with Ellacuría's threefold structure of confronting reality. See *Christ the Liberator*, 327.

21. Although it may seems strange that we begin our examination with the incarnation after having insisted on stressing the historical Jesus, there is no question that this is the first element in the structure of Jesus's life and the central belief in a disciple's life.

22. Sobrino thus asserts, "God's self-revelation is, then, reaction to the suffering some human beings inflict on others—the suffering victims." *Christ the Liberator*, 82.

23. Jon Sobrino, "The Kingdom of God and the Theologal Dimension of the Poor: The Jesuanic Principle," in *Who Do You Say That I Am? Confessing the Mystery of Christ*, ed. John C. Cavadini and Laura Holt (Notre Dame, Ind.: University of Notre Dame Press, 2004), 126.

24. Sobrino, "The Kingdom of God," 127

25. Sobrino, "The Kingdom of God," 126.

26. Sobrino, *Christ the Liberator*, 83. Italics in the original.

27. Jon Sobrino, "Extra Pauperes Nulla Salus," in *No Salvation Outside the Poor*, 55. Italics in the original.

28. Sobrino, "Spirituality and the Following of Jesus," 688.

29. Sobrino, "Spirituality and the Following of Jesus," 688.

30. Sobrino, *Jesus the Liberator*, 80. Sobrino further explains that these two groups can only be separated conceptually and that the New Testament often refers to the *economically sociologically* poor as a single group or class: They are the crowds, the multitude. *Jesus the Liberator*, 81.

31. Sobrino, *Jesus the Liberator*, 80. Addressing the world of the poor from a more systematic perspective, Sobrino writes, "[W]e have poverty in both the absolute and the relative sense, expressed in different ways and different degrees, depending on whether the poor are peasants, women, indigenous, and so on. In an effort to synthesize, perhaps we can say that the poor are *the deprived and oppressed, with respect to the material basics of human life*; they are *those who have no voice, no freedom, no dignity*; they are *those who have no name,*

no existence." "Depth and Urgency of the Option for the Poor," in *No Salvation Outside the Poor,* 26. Italics in the original.

32. Sobrino, *Witnesses to the Kingdom,* 138.

33. Sobrino, "Depth and Urgency of the Option for the Poor," 21. Elsewhere Sobrino notes that "In virtue of their historical reality, the poor are 'other' in a privileged fashion. They mediate the 'otherness' of God, and especially the 'utter otherness' of God." "Jesus' Proclamation of the Reign of God: Importance for Today," in *Spirituality of Liberation: Toward Political Holiness,* 127.

34. From the perspective of the transcendent, Jesus's mission mediates God's definite will for humanity and underscores God's commitment to persevere in his merciful response to the demands of reality initiated in the incarnation.

35. Sobrino, *Jesus the Liberator,* 67.

36. Sobrino, *Jesus the Liberator,* 69.

37. Sobrino, *Jesus the Liberator,* 67.

38. Commenting on the theological implications of understanding the kingdom of God as a unified duality, Sobrino writes, "The totality can be formulated generically as 'transcendence in history,' and the 'Kingdom of God' facilitates this, since 'Kingdom' is history and the 'of God' is transcendence." *Jesus the Liberator,* 123.

39. Sobrino, *Jesus the Liberator,* 69.

40. The terms "kingdom" and "reign" of God are used interchangeably. In order to determine its content and what God's kingdom meant for Jesus, Sobrino examines how Jesus engaged this historic-transcendent reality by enlisting a three-pronged approach that he organizes under the rubrics of: the notional way, the way of the addressee, and the way of practice. See *Jesus the Liberator,* 69–70.

41. Sobrino, *Jesus the Liberator,* 71. Sobrino notes that the gospel narratives interpret the kingdom against different traditions—prophetic, apocalyptic, wisdom—but "one key datum emerges again and again as the crucial one: Jesus appears on the scene with a utopia for human beings, and a utopia bestowed directly on the poor majorities." "Jesus' Proclamation of the Reign of God," 120.

42. Sobrino, *Jesus the Liberator,* 71.

43. Sobrino, *Jesus the Liberator,* 72.

44. This *metanoia,* Sobrino tells us, "is a task for the listener: the hope the poor must come to feel, the radical change required of the oppressors, the demands made on all to live a life worthy of the Kingdom." *Jesus the Liberator,* 76–77.

45. For Sobrino, this is the vital core of Jesus's message. See *Jesus the Liberator,* 77.

46. Here Sobrino cites the scripture scholar Joachim Jeremias, who explains that an essential feature of Jesus's preaching is "the offer of salvation Jesus makes to the poor. . . . The Kingdom belongs *uniquely to the poor*." Joachim Jeremias, *Teología del Nuevo Testamento*, 5th ed. (Salamanca: Ediciones Sígueme, 1986), 137, quoted in *Jesus the Liberator*, 79. Italics in the original.

47. Sobrino, *Spirituality of Liberation: Toward Political Holiness*, 127 and 36–37.

48. Sobrino, *Spirituality of Liberation: Toward Political Holiness*, 5 and 37.

49. Sobrino notes, "For hermeneutics this means that the *kingdom* is not only a 'meaning' concept—meaning hope—but also a 'praxic' one, implying putting its meaning into practice: that is, the need for a practice to initiate it, and thereby generating a better understanding of what the Kingdom is." *Jesus the Liberator*, 87–88. Italics in the original.

50. Sobrino explains that these terms are used in a systematic rather than a biblical sense. *Jesus the Liberator*, 161.

51. Sobrino, *Christ the Liberator*, 213. This same point is stressed by J. Matthew Ashley in "The Mystery of God and Compassion for the Poor," 72.

52. Sobrino, *Jesus the Liberator*, 88–89.

53. Sobrino, *Jesus the Liberator*, 90.

54. Sobrino, *Jesus the Liberator*, 90.

55. I am borrowing the insight that Jesus "gave spirit" from J. Matthew Ashley. See "The Mystery of God and Compassion for the Poor," 68.

56. Sobrino, *Christ the Liberator*, 209–18.

57. Sobrino, *Christ the Liberator*, 211.

58. Sobrino, *Jesus the Liberator*, 93.

59. Sobrino, *Jesus the Liberator*, 93. Sobrino explains that this faith, which does not depend upon doctrinal truths, transforms the human person from within in such a way that subject is enabled to actively collaborates in his or her own salvation.

60. Jon Sobrino, "Personal Sin, Forgiveness, and Liberation," 90. Italics in the original.

61. Sobrino, *Jesus the Liberator*, 96; see also "Personal Sin, Forgiveness, and Liberation," 92.

62. Sobrino, "Personal Sin, Forgiveness, and Liberation," 92.

63. Sobrino, "Personal Sin, Forgiveness, and Liberation," 92.

64. Sobrino, *Jesus the Liberator*, 96.

65. Sobrino, *Jesus the Liberator*, 97.

66. Sobrino, "Personal Sin, Forgiveness, and Liberation," 96. Italics in the original.

67. Sobrino, *Jesus the Liberator*, 101. Jesus's parables not only convey the kingdom's imminence, gratuitousness, and partiality toward the poor, but they are also designed to lead Jesus's adversaries into a moment of personal crisis,

discernment, and ultimate decision so that they may realize that they must convert and put their talents to work on behalf of the kingdom (Luke 19:12–27; Matt 24:45–51, 25:14–30; Mark 13:33–37).

68. Sobrino, *Jesus the Liberator*, 102.

69. As we noted regarding Jesus's practice of casting out devils, historical reality unfolds in a state of conflict where Jesus must struggle against the Evil One in order to mediate God's kingdom.

70. Sobrino, *Jesus the Liberator*, 162. As we will see in the next chapter, this theologal-idolatric interpretation also has its limitations because it does not account for the fluidity that characterizes the functioning of social structures and the ambiguity of the human condition and our often inconsistent behavior.

71. Sobrino, *Jesus the Liberator*, 161.

72. Sobrino, *Jesus the Liberator*, 170–74.

73. Sobrino, *Jesus the Liberator*, 169.

74. Sobrino, *Jesus the Liberator*, 170.

75. According to Sobrino, Jesus is particularly concerned with how these groups misuse their power: Instead of using it to bring people to God, they wield it in order to oppress them. Hence, Jesus warns people against their teachings and example, and harshly denounces their oppressive behavior (Luke 11:42–45; Matt 23:15, 17, 19, 26). See *Jesus the Liberator*, 174.

76. Sobrino, *Jesus the Liberator*, 178.

77. Sobrino, *Jesus the Liberator*, 177. For Sobrino, that Jesus threatened to destroy the temple (Mark 14:58, 15:29; Acts 6:1) also indicates that he is proclaiming a new setting for our encounter with God (Matt 18:20, 25:31–49; John 4:21, 23).

78. Sobrino, *Jesus the Liberator*, 178.

79. Sobrino, *Jesus the Liberator*, 161.

80. Sobrino, "Jesus' Proclamation of the Reign of God," 124.

81. Sobrino, *Jesus the Liberator*, 138.

82. Sobrino, *Jesus the Liberator*, 142.

83. Sobrino, *Jesus the Liberator*, 146.

84. Sobrino, *Jesus the Liberator*, 147.

85. For Jesus, these meals are both anticipatory celebrations, "signs of the coming of the Kingdom and of the realization of his ideals," as well as honest and joyful recognitions of God's ultimate goodness and of all that is good in reality. Sobrino, *Jesus the Liberator*, 103.

86. Sobrino, *Jesus the Liberator*, 149.

87. Sobrino, *Jesus the Liberator*, 153–54.

88. Sobrino, *Jesus the Liberator*, 149–50. We need to consider that Jesus may have been attracted by less dangerous and even by flawed notions of how to engage reality and conduct his mission.

89. Sobrino, *Jesus the Liberator*, 149. According to Sobrino, this is indicated by the place the temptations occupy in the synoptics: after Jesus's baptism, when he comes to realize his mission, and before the beginning of his public life.

90. Sobrino, *Jesus the Liberator*, 154.

91. Sobrino, *Jesus the Liberator*, 156.

92. Sobrino, *Jesus the Liberator*, 154.

93. Sobrino, *Jesus the Liberator*, 138.

94. Sobrino, "Toward a Determination of the Nature of Priesthood," in *The Principle of Mercy*, 133.

95. Sobrino, "The Samaritan Church and the Principle of Mercy," 17.

96. Jesus's free self-surrender to God is particularly evident in his prayer in the garden on the night before his crucifixion in Mark 14:35–36 (cf. Matt 26:39; Luke 22:41–42). For Sobrino, "What this prayer reveals of God is not the scandal of being good news . . . but the scandal of total obscurity." *Jesus the Liberator*, 141.

97. Sobrino, "Spirituality and the Following of Jesus," 694.

98. Sobrino, *Jesus the Liberator*, 150–52.

99. Sobrino, *Jesus the Liberator*, 151.

100. Sobrino, *Jesus the Liberator*, 151.

101. Sobrino, *Jesus the Liberator*, 148.

102. Sobrino notes that the gospels do not provide enough information to develop a systematic doctrine on violence rooted in Jesus's words and actions. He quotes Ellacuría at length to articulate a nuanced approach to Christians' relationship to violence: "it would seem that from a more Christian point of view, that of the perfection of discipleship of the historical Jesus, Christians who are doubly Christian in their lives and actions, the first and most audacious in combating all forms of injustice, should not use violence. It is not that violence is always and in all cases to be rejected by a Christian, but Christians as such do not normally give their specific witness through violence." Ellacuría, "Violence and Non-Violence in the Struggle for Peace and Liberation," *Concilium* 215 (1988): 69–97, quoted in *Jesus the Liberator*, 218.

103. Sobrino, *Jesus the Liberator*, 148.

104. Sobrino, *Jesus the Liberator*, 201.

105. Sobrino, *Jesus the Liberator*, 201.

106. Sobrino, *Jesus the Liberator*, 202.

107. Sobrino, *Jesus the Liberator*, 202–3.

108. Sobrino, *Jesus the Liberator*, 203.

109. On this point, Sobrino notes that Jesus's two key gestures during the meal—partaking of the bread and sharing the cup—should be interpreted respectively as an offering of salvation and as an invitation to his disciples to

participate in the death that is inherent to, and often the consequence of, a life of service. See *Jesus the Liberator*, 203.

110. Sobrino writes, "The gesture of offering them the cup—though the words were heavily theologized—is an invitation to his disciples to participate in his death." *Jesus the Liberator*, 203.

111. Sobrino, *Jesus the Liberator*, 203.

112. In a few lapidarian statements, Sobrino writes, "God becomes temptation for Jesus when he has to discern true saving power. God becomes enigma for him by absolutely holding back the day of the coming of the Kingdom, which Jesus had thought close at hand. God becomes mystery for him when God's will goes beyond the logic of the Kingdom and demands an undreamt-of suffering at the end of which lies the cross." *Jesus the Liberator*, 157–58.

113. Sobrino, *Jesus the Liberator*, 239.

114. Sobrino, who prefers to use the Ignatian terminology of "desolation" (i.e., that what Jesus heard from God was much more God's silence than God's closeness), finds in this experience "the most wounding element of Jesus' death." *Jesus the Liberator*, 239.

115. Sobrino, *Jesus the Liberator*, 244.

116. Sobrino, *Jesus the Liberator*, 244. Sobrino acknowledges that the mystery of the cross cannot be articulated or explained away but insists that the cross must be borne, and that this bearing manifests a love that surpasses any human logic

117. Sobrino underscores that what is pleasing to God is not a single occurrence in Jesus's life but all of it because all the elements of his life are deeply interrelated and maintain their significance only when taken together to express the whole.

118. Sobrino, *Jesus the Liberator*, 229.

119. Sobrino, *Jesus the Liberator*, 229. Sobrino notes that the culmination of Jesus's life on the cross is salvific. He writes, "Jesus's cross as the culmination of his whole life can be understood as bringing salvation. This saving efficacy is shown more in the form of an exemplary cause than of an efficient cause. But this does not mean that it is not effective: there stands Jesus, faithful and merciful to the end, inviting and inspiring human beings to reproduce in their turn the *homo verus*, true humanity." *Jesus the Liberator*, 230.

120. Sobrino, *Jesus the Liberator*, 230.

121. Sobrino, *Christ the Liberator*, 13. He adds, "the following of Jesus can contain a sort of historical reverberation of his resurrection with two essential elements: what there is of *fullness* in the resurrection, even in the midst of the limitations of history, and what there is of *victory* in the resurrection against the enslavement of history." Italics in the original.

122. Sobrino borrows this term from a homily given more than thirty years ago by Ignacio Ellacuría. See *Christ the Liberator*, 12.

123. Sobrino, *Christ the Liberator*, 13.

124. Sobrino, *Christ the Liberator*, 17.

125. Sobrino, *Christ the Liberator*, 20–21.

126. Sobrino, *Christ the Liberator*, 59. Italics in the original.

127. Sobrino, *Christ the Liberator*, 17–18.

128. Sobrino, *Christ the Liberator*, 63.

129. Sobrino, *Christ the Liberator*, 102.

130. Sobrino argues that the incorporation of the Cross into the disciples' faith prevents them from controlling who Jesus was and what they may have expected him to accomplish. *Christ the Liberator*, 98–104.

131. Sobrino, *Christ the Liberator*, 105.

132. Sobrino, *Christ the Liberator*, 105–6.

133. Sobrino, *Christ the Liberator*, 60. This explains, Sobrino tells us, why the delay of the parousia brought about a deep crisis in the early Church, and why the notion of the universal resurrection and the recreation of reality was pushed into the background. Hence, the early church concentrated its faith on the personal resurrection of Jesus, which gradually led to the theological neglect of God's kingdom. See *Christ the Liberator*, 221–38.

134. Sobrino, *Christ the Liberator*, 35.

135. Sobrino observes that the writings of Luke and Paul clearly attest to the fact that through the resurrection of Jesus the "Spirit *already* molds history in the present" and adds that it would be paradoxical and even absurd if the resurrection could remain as something extrinsic to the human condition since "this would suppose that the eschatological had come about in history but that it had no effect in our present life—except in hope." *Christ the Liberator*, 13.

136. Sobrino, *Christ the Liberator*, 67.

137. Sobrino acknowledges the difference between the Easter experience and those experiences that we may have of the Easter event today. He notes, "The essential difference between them is that the Easter experience, besides being the first, has fullness as its content, in the sense of anticipated fulfillment of the end of history, while experiences throughout history clearly depend on that first one for being understood as analogous Easter experiences; their content would make them experiences of finality, but without the distinction of referring to the finality of the end time." *Christ the Liberator*, 66.

138. Sobrino, *Christ the Liberator*, 21.

139. Sobrino, *Christ the Liberator*, 22.

140. Sobrino, *Christ the Liberator*, 22.

141. Sobrino, *Christ the Liberator*, 36.

142. Sobrino builds this argument in conversation with Rudolf Bultmann, Willi Marxsen, Wolfhart Pannenberg, Karl Rahner, and Leonardo Boff. He underscores three insights from these theologians: First, we cannot speak of the resurrection by assuming, in advance, that we fully know what we are speaking about. Second, the New Testament texts assume certain anthropological presuppositions in those who were granted the experience of the resurrection. Third, hope is to be understood in its communal, partial, and practical sense—that is, "a hope of justice for the weak and a life lived for justice" are hermeneutical principles necessary to grasp the resurrection. See *Christ the Liberator*, 22–34.

143. Sobrino, *Christ the Liberator*, 35–36.

144. Sobrino, *Christ the Liberator*, 42. Italics in the original.

145. Sobrino, *Christ the Liberator*, 37–41.

146. Sobrino, *Christ the Liberator*, 44.

147. Sobrino, *Christ the Liberator*, 47.

148. Sobrino, *Christ the Liberator*, 47–48.

149. Sobrino, *Christ the Liberator*, 49.

150. Sobrino, *Christ the Liberator*, 48. Italics in the original.

151. Sobrino, *Christ the Liberator*, 53.

152. Sobrino, *Christ the Liberator*, 52. Sobrino acknowledges that the resurrection can be understood either as a promise that points to the future, or as a future reality that seeks its becoming in the present, but he prefers to see the resurrection as a promise. Key to both of these approaches is the notion that something has already happened in the present that now points to the definitive future. See also, Jürgen Moltmann, *Theology of Hope* (New York: Harper and Row, 1977); and Wolfhart Pannenberg, *Theology and the Kingdom of God* (Philadelphia: Westminster Press, 1969).

153. Moltmann, *Theology of Hope*, quoted in Sobrino, *Christ the Liberator*, 52.

154. Sobrino, *Christ the Liberator*, 53.

155. Sobrino, *Christ the Liberator*, 13.

156. Sobrino, *Christ the Liberator*, 72.

157. Sobrino, *Christ the Liberator*, 76.

158. Sobrino, *Witnesses to the Kingdom*, 117–18.

159. Sobrino, *Christ the Liberator*, 77.

5. Reconciling Reality

1. Walter Benjamin, "Theses on the Philosophy of History," in *Illuminations*, ed. Hannah Arendt, trans. Harry Zohn (New York: Schocken, 1968), 253–64, at 256.

2. Eduardo Galeano, *Open Veins of Latin America: Five Centuries of the Pillage of a Continent*, trans. Cedric Belfrage, 25th anniversary edition (New York: Monthly Review Press, 1997), 3.

3. Karl Rahner, "The Theology of Symbol," *Theological Investigations*, IV (Baltimore, Md.: Helicon Press, 1966), 221–52. See also Sobrino, *Where Is God? Earthquake, Terrorism, Barbarity, and Hope*, 43.

4. *Gaudium et Spes* 11. In *Vatican Council II*, 912.

5. "Poverty" 1, 2. The Second General Conference of Latin American Bishops, *Church in the Present-Day Transformation of Latin America*, vol. 2.

6. "Justice," 1. The Second General Conference of Latin American Bishops, *Church in the Present-Day Transformation of Latin America*, vol. 2.

7. Sobrino, *Jesus the Liberator*, 162.

8. Sobrino, *Jesus the Liberator*, 162.

9. Volf, *Exclusion and Embrace*, 99–105.

10. Volf, *Exclusion and Embrace*, 103.

11. This is evident, for instance, in his description of the hope that the resurrection generates in the life of both the victims and the non-victims. See Sobrino, *No Salvation Outside the Poor*, 102–4.

12. Sobrino, *Where Is God?* 127, 129–30.

13. Jon Sobrino, "Evil and Hope: A Reflection from the Victims," *Catholic Theological Society Proceedings* 50 (1995): 71–84, at 72.

14. Lisa Cahill, "A Theology of Peacebuilding," in *Peacebuilding: Catholic Theology, Ethics, and Praxis*, 300–31, at 303.

15. Cahill, "A Theology of Peacebuilding," 304. To explain the sinner's lack of empathy, Cahill draws from William Sloane Coffin, who defines the root of evil as "the absence of imaginative empathy for others." Such a definition is consistent with Sobrino's interpretation of sin. Cahill cites Coffin's radio interview with Tom Ashbrook, "On Point," WBUR, NPR Boston, September 11, 2002 (http://onpoint.wbur.org/2002/09/11/the-soul-of-a-nation), rebroadcast on Good Friday, April 14, 2006, during the week of Coffin's death.

16. Jon Sobrino, "Being Honest Toward Reality," in *Where Is God? Earthquake, Terrorism, Barbarity, and Hope*, 29–48, at 38.

17. Sobrino, "Being Honest Toward Reality," 41.

18. Sobrino, "Personal Sin, Forgiveness and Liberation," in *The Principle of Mercy*, 83–101, at 86.

19. For a more detailed treatment of idolatry from the perspective of Latin American liberation theology, see Juan Luis Segundo, *Our Idea of God* (Maryknoll, N.Y.: Orbis, 1974), and Pablo Richard et al., *The Battle of the Gods* (Maryknoll, N.Y.: Orbis Books, 1984).

20. Sobrino, *Jesus the Liberator*, 185–86.

21. Oscar Romero identifies three idolatries in the Salvadoran society: the absolutization of wealth and private property, the absolutization of national security, and the absolutization of organizations. For Sobrino, however, the absolutization of wealth is the most significant. "The Church's Mission amid National Crisis," in *Voice of the Voiceless: The Four Pastoral Letters and Other Statements* (Maryknoll, N.Y.: Orbis, 2003), 114–61, at 133–36.

22. Sobrino writes that "the idol by definition, originator all of the others, is the economic configuration of society, which is unjust, structural, lasting, with many other organs at its service: military, political, cultural, juridical, intellectuals and often religious, which partake analogously of the being of the idol." *Jesus the Liberator*, 186.

23. William T. Cavanaugh has rightly noted that in our contemporary consumer-driven economy, consumption is often falsely portrayed as the solution for the suffering of others, since the increase of consumption promotes the development of the economy and additional jobs. He adds that in the end such consumerism blocks the in-breaking of God's kingdom and only fosters "endless superficial novelty." *Being Consumed: Economics and Christian Desire* (Grand Rapids, Mich.: Eerdmans, 2008), 93.

24. Sobrino, *Jesus the Liberator*, 186.

25. Jon Sobrino, "Christianity and Reconciliation," 81–90, at 81.

26. This section expands on material previously developed in O. Ernesto Valiente, "From Conflict to Reconciliation: Discipleship in the Theology of Jon Sobrino," *Theological Studies* 74 (2013): 655–82.

27. Sobrino, *The True Church and the Poor*, 309.

28. Sobrino argues for the need to include these three dimensions in the Salvadoran process of reconciliation. "Christianity and Reconciliation," 82.

29. Here I am drawing on Sobrino's insight that there are negative by-products proper to the practice of liberation. See "Spirituality and Liberation," in *Spirituality of Liberation: Toward Political Holiness* (Maryknoll, N.Y.: Orbis, 1988), 23–45, at 27–28.

30. Sobrino's spirituality has a profoundly Trinitarian character: by following the structure of Jesus's life empowered by his same Spirit one finds, collaborates with, and makes God present in history.

31. Sobrino claims that "this decentering of God in favor of human beings, poor, weak, and victimized, is the fundamental thesis of the Christian religion." *Where Is God? Earthquake, Terrorism, Barbarity, and Hope*, trans. Margaret Wilde (Maryknoll, N.Y.: Orbis, 2004), 134.

32. Sobrino, *Where Is God?* 33, emphases original.

33. Sobrino borrows the term *civilization of wealth* from Ellacuría; see Sobrino, "Utopia and Prophecy in Latin America," in *Fundamental Concepts of Liberation Theology*, 289–328.

34. On the effects of globalization in Latin America, see Franz J. Hinkelammert, "Globalization as Cover-Up: An Ideology to Disguise and Justify Current Wrongs," in *Globalization and Its Victims*, ed. Jon Sobrino and Felix Wilfred (London: SCM, 2001), 25–34; and Luis de Sebastian, *Problemas de la globalización* (Barcelona: Cuadernos Cristianisme i Justicia, 2005).

35. Sobrino, *"Extra Pauperes Nulla Salus,"* in *No Salvation Outside the Poor: Prophetic-Utopian Essays* (Maryknoll, N.Y.: Orbis, 2008), 35–76, esp. 35–48. The United Nations Economic Commission for Latin American and the Caribbean (ELCLAC), for instance, notes that "globalization has not only engendered growing interdependence; it has also given rise to marked international inequalities. Expressed in terms of a metaphor widely employed in recent debates, the world economy is essentially an 'uneven playing field,' whose distinctive characteristics are a concentration of capital and technology generation in developed countries and the strong influence of those countries on trade in goods and services. These asymmetries in the global order are at the root of profound international inequalities in income distribution." Jon Sobrino, "Inequalities and Asymmetries in the Global Order," in *Globalization and Development* (New York: United Nations, 2002), 75; also at http://www .eclac.cl/publicaciones/xml/0/10030/Globalization-Chap3.pdf (accessed January 12, 2013).

36. Sobrino, "Place of Sin and Place of Forgiveness," 62.

37. Puebla, *The Final Document*, no. 1147, in *Puebla and Beyond: Documentation and Commentary*, 265–66.

38. Sobrino, *"Extra Pauperes Nulla Salus,"* 63.

39. Jon Sobrino, "Bearing with One Another in Faith: A Theological Analysis of Christian Solidarity," in *Principle of Mercy*, 144–72, at 151.

40. Sobrino describes this solidarity as "poor people and nonpoor people mutually bearing one another, giving to 'each other' and receiving 'from each other' the best that they have, in order to arrive at being 'with one another.'" *"Extra pauperes nulla salus,"* 63. See also, Sobrino, "Bearing with One Another in Faith," 144–72.

41. Sobrino, "Personal Sin, Forgiveness, and Liberation," 96–97.

42. Sobrino, "Place of Sin and Place of Forgiveness," 58–68.

43. Sobrino, "Place of Sin and Place of Forgiveness," 59–62.

44. Sobrino, "Christianity and Reconciliation" 88. Sobrino also notes that while the definitive *mediator* (Jesus) of the kingdom has arrived, the *mediation* (God's reign) is not yet fully present in history. See Sobrino, "Central Position of the Reign of God in Liberation Theology," in *Mysterium Liberationis*, 372.

45. Sobrino uses the term "forgiving reality" to indicate the need to transform those aspects of reality that represent a denial of God's will for humanity. See his "Place of Sin and Place of Forgiveness," 60–61.

46. "Utopia," Sobrino tells us, "establishes the content of humanness: that which human beings must reach for and by which all progress will be judged human or inhuman . . . and establishes the hope that humanness is possible." *Where Is God?* 120.

47. This discussion raises the question of the relationship between our efforts on behalf of the kingdom—our utopic vision and projects—and the kingdom itself. Here, the words of *Gaudium et Spes* (no. 39) are helpful: " . . . although we must be careful to distinguish earthly progress clearly from the increase of the Kingdom of Christ, such progress is of vital concern to the Kingdom of God, insofar as it can contribute to the better ordering of human society. "In *Vatican Council II*, 938.

48. See, for instance, Sobrino, "The Crucified People and the Civilization of Poverty," in *No Salvation Outside the Poor*, 1–18; and "The Kingdom of God and the Theologal Dimension of the Poor," in *Who Do You Say That I Am: Confessing the Mystery of Christ*, ed. John C. Cavadini and Laura Holt (Notre Dame, Ind.: University of Notre Dame, 2004), 109–45. For Ellacuría's treatment of the "culture of wealth" and the "culture of poverty," see especially his "Utopia and Prophecy in Latin America," in *Mysterium Liberationis*, 289–328.

49. Ignacio Ellacuría, "Utopia y profetismo desde América latina," *Revista latinoamericana de teología* 17 (1989): 141–84, at 170; quoted in "Crucified People and the Civilization of Poverty," 14.

50. Sobrino, "Crucified People," 16.

51. Sobrino, "Place of Sin and Place of Forgiveness," 61.

52. Sobrino, "*Extra pauperes nulla salus*," 61. For a description of the privileged role of the poor in helping us discern the content of God's kingdom, see *Jesus the Liberator*, 79–87.

53. Ellacuría, "Utopia y profetismo," 170; quoted in "Crucified People and the Civilization of Poverty," 15. Treating the specific social arrangements that might best foster the common good or the appropriate relationship between the state and civil society in Latin America are beyond the scope of this paper. Nonetheless, justice should not be understood only as a matter of redistributing economic resources or promoting democratic electoral processes. Justice, in its core biblical meaning, refers to one's right relationship with God and others, with special concern for the powerless or marginalized. See John R. Donahue, S.J., *What Does the Lord Require: A Bibliographical Essay on the Bible and Social Justice* (Saint Louis: Institute of Jesuit Resources, 2003), 23.

54. Sobrino, "Crucified People," 16.

55. Sobrino also defines the oppressors as the "*analogatum princeps* of personal wrongdoing in sin." "Place of Sin and Place of Forgiveness," 62.

56. Sobrino, "Christianity and Reconciliation," 82.

57. Sobrino, "Christianity and Reconciliation," 84.

58. Sobrino, *Jesus the Liberator*, 104.

59. Sobrino, Place of Sin and Place of Forgiveness," 64.

60. Sobrino, "*Extra Pauperes Nulla Salus*," 67.

61. Sobrino, "Place of Sin and Place of Forgiveness," 64.

62. Sobrino, "Place of Sin and Place of Forgiveness," 64.

63. Sobrino adds: "Those who forgive open their eyes and know just what is being forgiven: responsibility in the continued crucifixion of entire peoples. To be able to see with new eyes the genuine reality of the world, to be able to stare it in the face despite its tragedy, to be able to perceive what it is to which God says a radical 'no,' is (logically) the first fruit of allowing oneself really to be pardoned." "Personal Sin, Forgiveness, and Liberation," in *Principle of Mercy*, 95–96.

64. Thus, we may say that, for Sobrino, Jesus's cross was a historical and not a theological necessity.

65. Jon Sobrino, "La teología y el 'principio de liberación,'" *Revista latino-americana de teología* 35 (1995): 115–40, at 135; see also "*Extra Pauperes Nulla Salus*," 64.

66. Jon Sobrino, "Apuntes para una espiritualidad en tiempos de violencia: Reflexiones desde la perspectiva salvadoreña," *Revista latinoamericana de teología* 29 (1993): 189–208, at 202. In this same article, Sobrino upholds the logic of the "just war"; thus he acknowledges that in some extreme circumstances the limited use of violence may be necessary to protect the lives of innocent victims and avoid greater evils.

67. Sobrino writes: "The victims' suffering, by its nature ['disarms'] the power of evil, not magically but historically. This is a way of trying to explain conceptually the saving element of Christ's suffering on the cross: sin has discharged all its force against him, but in doing so sin itself has been left without force." "*Extra Pauperes Nulla Salus*," 65.

68. Sobrino, "Place of Sin and Place of Forgiveness," 63.

69. Sobrino, *Christ the Liberator: A View from the Victims*, trans. Paul Burns (Maryknoll, N.Y.: Orbis, 2001), 17.

70. Sobrino, *Christ the Liberator*, 36.

71. Sobrino, *Christ the Liberator*, 13.

72. Sobrino, "The Resurrection of One Crucified," in *No Salvation Outside the Poor*, 99–108, at 102.

73. For Sobrino, Jesus's resurrection "implies communion with others, a logical presupposition in cultures in which individualism has not taken root: speaking of the 'fullness' of an isolated individual makes little sense." "Resurrection of One Crucified," 106.

74. Sobrino, "Conflicto y reconciliación," 1147.

75. Sobrino, "The Hope of the Poor in Latin America," in *Spirituality of Liberation*, 157–68, at 162–63.

76. Sobrino, "The Hope of the Poor in Latin America," 163.

77. Sobrino, "Spirituality and Liberation," 33.

78. Sobrino, *Christ the Liberator*, 45.

79. Sobrino, "Resurrection of One Crucified," 103.

80. Sobrino, "Spirituality and the Following of Jesus," 693.

81. Sobrino writes: "The logic of the forgiven and grateful one—with all due caution when it comes to the enthusiasm of converts—is what opens the heart to a limitless salvific, historical practice." "Personal Sin, Forgiveness, and Liberation," 91.

82. The hope of the resurrection understood as one that stresses the victory of God's justice over injustice does not imply that this hope becomes de-universalized. Rather, it demands certain conditions and a particular setting—the world of the victims—from which it embraces all, victims and non-victims. See *Christ the Liberator*, 43.

83. Sobrino, *Christ the Liberator*, 47.

84. Sobrino, *Christ the Liberator*, 47–48.

85. Sobrino, "Conflicto y reconciliación," 1147. The "shared table" is an eschatological metaphor that Sobrino borrows from one of Rutilio Grande's last homilies, preached on February 13, 1977, a month before he was murdered. That day, Grande proclaimed, "We come to share at this table which is a symbol of our brotherhood, a table with a stool and a big napkin for each human being. We have a common Father, and therefore all of us are brothers" (quoted by William J. O'Malley, S.J., "El Salvador: Rutilio Grande, S.J.," in *The Voice of Blood: Five Christian Martyrs of Our Time* (Maryknoll, N.Y.: Orbis, 1995), 1–63, at 43.

86. Sobrino, *Christ the Liberator*, 53.

87. Sobrino, "Resurrection of One Crucified," 105–6.

88. On the relationship between grief and the construction of meaning, see Melissa M. Kelley, *Grief: Contemporary Theory and the Practice of Ministry* (Minneapolis: Fortress, 2010). See also Robert Schreiter, *The Ministry of Reconciliation*, 40–82.

89. Sobrino, *Jesus the Liberator*, 69

90. Sobrino, *Jesus in Latin America*, 52.

91. Sobrino, *Christ the Liberator*, 81.

92. Sobrino, "Christianity and Reconciliation," 81–90, at 82.

93. Drawing on the Old Testament, Sobrino notes that "God is a God-*of*, a God-*for*, a God-*in*, never a God-in-himself." *Jesus the Liberator*, 69.

94. Sobrino, *Spirituality of Liberation*, 56.

95. This scripture passage is quoted in Sobrino, "Christianity and Reconciliation," 82. See also "Spirituality and the Following of Jesus," 681.

96. Sobrino, "Christianity and Reconciliation: The Way to Utopia," 82.

97. Sobrino, *Jesus in Latin America*, 101.

98. Sobrino, *Christ the Liberator*, 198.

99. Sobrino, *Jesus in Latin America*, 46. Sobrino further explains that he does not use "the relational category of filiation in order to weaken the ontological reality of the divine nature in Christ . . . [but rather] to afford the *intellectus fidei* some access to how Jesus can be God by explaining *what* there is in human nature that would entail the likelihood of its being able to be assumed by God in such wise that what would be assumed could actually be God." Italics in the original.

100. Sobrino, "Christianity and Reconciliation: The Way to Utopia," 82.

101. Sobrino, *Christ the Liberator*, 199.

102. Sobrino, "Systematic Christology: Jesus Christ, The Absolute Mediator," 440–61, at 455.

103. "To put the reality of Jesus into words," Sobrino avers, ". . . We have to mention his manner of being. . . . This—with which his human, divine, and saving being is shot through—is what produces courage, inspiration, and joy. This is what makes him good news." *Christ the Liberator*, 214.

104. Sobrino, "Systematic Christology: Jesus Christ, The Absolute Mediator," 456.

105. Sobrino, *Principle of Mercy*, 17.

106. Sobrino, *Christ the Liberator*, 82. Although God is affected by his relationships with humanity, it must be insisted that God transcends them and is not constituted by them.

107. Sobrino, *Jesus in Latin America*, 136.

108. Jon Sobrino, "The Centrality of the Kingdom of God Announced by Jesus," in *No Salvation Outside the Poor*, 77–98, at 78.

109. Sobrino, *Christ the Liberator*, 316.

110. Sobrino, *Christ the Liberator*, 314. See also "Central Position of the Reign of God in Liberation Theology," 372.

111. Speaking in systematic terms, Sobrino describes God's kingdom as the "reign of life . . . a historical reality (a just life for the poor) and a reality with an intrinsic tendency to be 'more' (ultimately, utopia)." "Central Position of the Reign of God," 380.

112. Sobrino, *Jesus the Liberator*, 131.

113. Sobrino, "Central Position of the Reign of God," 380.

114. Sobrino, *Jesus the Liberator*, 190. See also *Christ the Liberator*, 209–10.

115. Sobrino, *Jesus the Liberator*, 82. In other words, the addressees of the kingdom—all of humanity—whether they accept or reject God's offer, take an

active stand vis-à-vis God's offer, and the acceptance of the kingdom elicits from each one of us different responses.

116. As noted before, this preference that God manifests for the poor is not rooted in the poor themselves (i.e., their moral attributes), but in God's gratuitous and merciful response to "their threatened, negated life." Sobrino, *Where Is God?* 83.

117. Sobrino, *"Extra Pauperes Nulla Salus,"* in *No Salvation Outside the Poor*, 77–98, at 69–70.

118. Although Christian utopian visions cannot claim to be identical to the kingdom of God, the proclamation of God's kingdom provides the foundation for a Christian understanding of salvation that begins in history and points to an eschatological future. It establishes "that which humans are to reach for and by which all progress will be judged human or inhuman. . . . [It also] establishes the hope that humanness is possible." Sobrino, *Where Is God?* 120.

119. Sobrino, "Central Position of the Reign of God," 382.

120. Sobrino, *Where Is God?* 135.

121. Sobrino, "Latin America: Place of Sin and Forgiveness," 65.

122. Sobrino, *Jesus the Liberator*, 96.

123. As Sobrino notes, this misuse of power "produces a clear-cut division between those who hold power (the oppressors) and those who suffer from it use (the oppressed)." *Christology at the Crossroads*, 53.

124. Sobrino, *Christology at the Crossroads*, 55.

125. Sobrino explains that Jesus enlists different methods to help oppressors recognize their sinfulness. "[Jesus] uses a sapiential *mystagogia* (wealth serves no purpose at the moment of death), and he uses an eschatological *mystagogia* (it is better to enter the Reign of God minus a hand or an eye than to go to eternal fire). But his basic *mystagogia* is strictly theo-logal: God is essentially inclined to forgiveness." "Personal Sin, Forgiveness, and Liberation," 89–90.

126. Sobrino, "Personal Sin, Forgiveness, and Liberation," 90.

127. Sobrino, *Jesus the Liberator*, 231.

128. Sobrino, "Personal Sin, Forgiveness, and Liberation," 95–96.

129. Sobrino, *Jesus the Liberator*, 247–49. See also *Christ the Liberator*, 87–88.

130. Sobrino, *Christ the Liberator*, 86.

131. Sobrino, *Christ the Liberator*, 87.

Conclusion

1. To put these changes in a larger historical context, it may be helpful to remember how, following the work of Latin American economists and social

scientists in the 1950s and 60s, most liberation theologians enlisted the dependency theory. With all its limitations, dependency theory made possible a structural analysis of the causes of poverty in Latin America and unveiled the flaws in the models for development offered by First World nations. Hence, most liberation theologians rejected the self-serving programs for social and economic reform that capitalistic nations were pushing on Latin America and insisted instead on the need for radical socioeconomic transformation. They looked to some of the revolutionary processes that emerged in the 1970s with the hope that these would rapidly and radically renovate the continent. While these efforts, carried out at a great human cost, did not bring about the expected change in socioeconomic structures, in some places such as El Salvador they nonetheless achieved significant steps toward social transformation through the reformation and democratization of the electoral process. Later, the fall of the Berlin Wall and the collapse of the socialist states in Eastern Europe left the Western nations at the center of world economic power, with the United States the sole political and military superpower in the world. In the last thirty years, this change in the global political order has largely led to the rapid expansion of powerful multinational corporations, along with capitalism and its "culture of wealth," in most of the world.

2. Sobrino, *Christ the Liberator*, 78.

Selected Bibliography

Works by Jon Sobrino

BOOKS AND COLLECTED ESSAYS

Archbishop Romero: Memories and Reflections. Translated by Robert R. Barr. Maryknoll, N.Y.: Orbis Books, 1990.

Cartas a Ellacuría: 1989–200. Madrid: Trotta, 2004.

Christology at the Crossroads: A Latin American Approach. Translated by John Drury. Maryknoll, N.Y.: Orbis Books, 1978.

Christ the Liberator: A View from the Victims. Translated by Paul Burns. Maryknoll, N.Y.: Orbis Books, 2001. In Spanish, *La fe en Jesucristo: Ensayo desde las víctimas.* Madrid: Editorial Trotta, 1999.

Companions of Jesus: The Murder and Martyrdom of the Salvadoran Jesuits. Glasgow: Catholic Institute for International Relations, 1990.

"Good News to the Poor." Homily delivered in the Church of the University of Louvain on February 2, 1985. In *Archbishop Romero: Memories and Reflections,* translated by Robert R. Barr. Maryknoll, N.Y.: Orbis Books, 1990.

Ignacio Ellacuría: Aquella libertad esclarecida. Edited by Jon Sobrino and Rolando Alvarado. San Salvador: UCA Editores, 1999.

Ignacio Ellacuría: El Hombre, El Pensador, El Cristianismo. Edited by Jon Sobrino, Ignacio Ellacuría, and Rodolfo Cardenal. Bilbao, Spain: Ega, 1994.

Jesus in Latin America. Maryknoll, N.Y.: Orbis Books, 1987. In Spanish, *Jesús en América Latina: su significado para la fe y la cristología.* San Salvador: UCA Editores, 1982.

Jesus the Liberator: A Historical-Theological Reading of Jesus of Nazareth. Maryknoll, N.Y.: Orbis Books, 1993. In Spanish, *Jesucristo liberador: Lectura historico-teológica de Jesús de-Nazaret.* San Salvador: UCA Editores, 1991.

Mysterium Liberationis: Fundamental Concepts of Liberation Theology. Edited by Ignacio Ellacuría and Jon Sobrino. Maryknoll, N.Y.: Orbis Books, 1993. In Spanish, *Mysterium liberationis: Conceptos fundamentales de la teología de la liberación.* 2 volumes. Madrid: Editorial Trotta, 1990.

No Salvation Outside the Poor: Prophetic-Utopian Essays. Maryknoll, N.Y.: Orbis Books, 2008. In Spanish, *Fuera de los pobres no hay salvacíon: Pequeños ensayos utópico-proféticos.* Madrid: Editorial Trotta, 2007.

The Principle of Mercy: Taking the Crucified People from the Cross.
   Maryknoll, N.Y.: Orbis Books, 1994. In Spanish, *El Principio Misericorida:*
   bajar de la cruz a los pueblos crucificado. San Salvador, UCA Editores, 1992.

Reality and Hope. Edited by Virgilio P. Elizondo and Jon Sobrino. *Concilium*
   1999/5. Maryknoll, N.Y.: Orbis Books, 1999.

Resurrección de la verdadera Iglesia: los pobres, lugar teológico de la eclesiologia.
   Colección Teológica Latinoamericana. Vol. 8. San Salvador: UCA Editores,
   1986.

"The Resurrection of One Crucified." In *No Salvation Outside the Poor:*
   Prophetic-Utopian Essays, 99–108. Maryknoll, N.Y.: Orbis Books, 2008.

Rethinking Martyrdom. Edited by Teresa Okure, Jon Sobrino, and Felix Wilfred.
   Concilium 2003/1. London: SCM Press, 2003.

Spirituality of Liberation: Toward Political Holiness. Translated Robert Barr.
   Maryknoll, N.Y.: Orbis Books, 1988. In Spanish, *Liberación con espíritu:*
   Apuntes para una nueva espiritualidad. Santander: Sal Terrae, 1985; San
   Salvador: UCA Editores (1987), 1994.

Systematic Theology: Perspectives from Liberation Theology. Edited by Jon
   Sobrino and Ignacio Ellacuría. Maryknoll, N.Y.: Orbis Books, 1996.

Terremoto, terrorismo, varbarie y utopía: El Salvador, Nueva York, Afganistán.
   Colección Teología Latinoamericana v. 29. San Salvador: UCA Editores,
   2003.

Theology of Christian Solidarity. Translated by Phillip Berryman. Edited by Jon
   Sobrino, and Juan Hernández Pico. Maryknoll, N.Y.: Orbis Books, 1985.

The True Church and the Poor. Translated by Matthew J. O'Connell. Maryknoll, N.Y.: Orbis Books, 1984.

Where Is God? Earthquake, Terrorism, Barbarity, and Hope. Translated by
   Margaret Wilde. Maryknoll, N.Y.: Orbis Books, 2004.

Witnesses to the Kingdom: The Martyrs of El Salvador and the Crucified Peoples.
   Maryknoll, N.Y.: Orbis Books, 2003.

ARTICLES

"La aparición del Dios de la vida en Jesús de Nazaret." In *La Lucha de los dioses:*
   trabajo colectivo de biblistas, teólogos y científicos sociales. San Jose: Departa-
   mento Ecuménico De Investigaciones, Centro Antonio Valdivieso, 1980,
   79–121. In English, "The Epiphany of the God of Life in Jesus of Nazareth."
   In *Idols of Death and the God of Life: a Theology,* translated by Barbara E.
   Campbell and Bonnie Shephard, 66–102. Maryknoll, N.Y.: Orbis Books,
   1983.

"Apuntes para una espiritualidad en tiempos de violencia. Reflexiones desde la
   experiencia salvadoreña." *Revista Latinoamericana de Teología* 29 (1993):
   189–208.

"Awakening from the Sleep of Inhumanity." *Christian Century* 108 (1991): 364–70.

"Bearing with One Another in Faith: A Theological Analysis of Christian Solidarity." In *The Principle of Mercy: Taking the Crucified People from the Cross*, 144–72. Maryknoll, N.Y.: Orbis Books, 1994.

"The Centrality of the Kingdom of God Announced by Jesus." In *No Salvation Outside the Poor: Prophetic-Utopian Essays*, 77–98. Maryknoll, N.Y.: Orbis Books, 2008.

"Central Position of the Reign of God in Liberation Theology." In *Mysterium Liberationis: Fundamental Concepts of Liberation Theology*, edited by Ignacio Ellacuría and Jon Sobrino, 372. Maryknoll, N.Y.: Orbis Books, 1993.

"Christianity and Reconciliation: The Way to a Utopia." In *Reconciliation in a World of Conflicts. Concilium* 2003/5, edited by Luiz Carlos Susin and María Pilar Aquino, 80–90. London: SCM Press, 2003.

"Christian Prayer and New Testament Theology: A Basis for Social Justice and Spirituality." In *Western Spirituality: Historical Roots, Ecumenical Routes*, edited by Matthew Fox, 76–114. Notre Dame: Fides/Claretian, 1979.

"Church as Advocate: Who Are the Poor—Those Who Die." *Witness* 64 (1981): 14–16.

"¿Cómo hacer teología? La teología como *Intellectus Amoris*." *Revista de Teologia Pastoral* 77, no. 5 (1989): 397–417.

"Conflicto y reconciliación: Camino cristiano hacia una utopía." *Estudios Centroamericanos* (cited hereafter as *ECA*) 661–62 (2003): 1139–48.

"El conocimiento teológico en la teología Europea." *ECA* 30 (1975): 426–45.

"Crisis en la Iglesia?" *ECA* 231 (1967): 647–56.

"The Crucified People and the Civilization of Poverty." In *No Salvation Outside the Poor: Prophetic-Utopian Essays*, 1–18. Maryknoll, N.Y.: Orbis Books, 2008.

"A Crucified People's Faith in the Son of God." In *Jesus, Son of God?* Vol. 153 of *Concilium*, edited by E. Schillebeeckx and Johannes Baptist Metz, 23–28. New York: Seabury Press, 1982.

"Current Problems in Christology in Latin American Theology." In *Theology and Discovery: Essays in Honor of Karl Rahner, S.J.*, edited by William J. Kelly, 189–221. Milwaukee: Marquette University Press, 1980.

"Death and the Hope for Life." In *Theology in the Americas*, edited by Cornel West, Caridad Guidote, and Margaret Coakley, 62–70. Maryknoll, N.Y.: Orbis Books, 1982.

"Depth and Urgency of the Option for the Poor." In *No Salvation Outside the Poor: Prophetic-Utopian Essays*. Maryknoll, N.Y.: Orbis Books, 2008.

"De una teología solo de liberación a una teología del martirio." *Revista Latinoamericana de Teología* 28 (1993): 27–48.

"Los derechos humanos y los pueblos oprimidos. Reflexiones histórico-teológicas." *Revista Latinoamericana de Teología* 43 (1988): 79–102.

"Despertar del sueño de la cruel inhumanidad." In *El Principio Misericordia: Bajar de la cruz a los pueblos crucificado.* San Salvador, UCA Editores, 1992.

"Doing Theology from Amidst the Victims" In *The Future of Theology: Essays in Honor of Jürgen Moltmann*, edited by Miroslav Volf, Carmen Kreig, and Thomas Kurcharz, 164–75. Grand Rapids, Mich.: Eerdmans, 1996.

"Eastern Religions and Liberation." *Horizons* 18/1 (1991): 78–92.

"Epilogue: 'Turning Back History.'" In *A Different World Is Possible. Concilium* 2004/5, edited by Luiz Carlos Susin, Jon Sobrino, and Felix Wilfred, 125–33. London: SCM Press, 2004.

"Espiritualidad y Teología." In *Liberación con Espíritu: Apuntes para una nueva Espiritualidad.* San Salvador: UCA Editores, 1985.

"Evil and Hope: A Reflection from the Victims." *Catholic Theological Society Proceedings* 50 (1995): 71–84.

"Extra Pauperes Nulla Salus." In *No Salvation Outside the Poor: Prophetic-Utopian Essays*, 35–76. Maryknoll, N.Y.: Orbis Books, 2008.

"La fe en el Dios crucificado. Reflexiones desde El Salvador." *Revista Latinoamericana de Teología* 31 (1994): 49–75.

"Fenomenologia de la esperanza en Gabriel Marcel I." *ECA* 209 (1965): 257–61.

"Fenomenologia de la esperanza en Gabriel Marcel II." *ECA* 209 (1965): 283–89.

"Following Jesus as Discernment." In *Discernment of the Spirit and of Spirits. Concilium* 119, edited by Casiano Floristán and Christian Duquoc, 14–27. New York: The Seabury Press, 1979.

"The Following of Jesus and Faith in Christ." In *The Myth/Truth of God Incarnate*, edited by Durstan R. McDonald, 105–22. Wilton, Conn: Morehouse Barlow Co., 1979.

"From a Theology of Liberation to a Theology of Martyrdom." In *Witnesses to the Kingdom: The Martyrs of El Salvador and the Crucified Peoples.* Maryknoll, N.Y.: Orbis Books, 2003.

"The Hope of the Poor in Latin America" In *Spirituality of Liberation: Toward Political Holiness*, translated by Robert Barr, 157–68. Maryknoll, N.Y.: Orbis Books, 1988.

"Ignacio Ellacuría, el hombre y el cristiano. 'Bajar de la cruz al pueblo crucificado (I).'" *Revista Latinoamericana de Teología* 11 (12), (1994): 131–61.

"Ignacio Ellacuría, el hombre y el cristiano. 'Bajar de la cruz al pueblo crucificado (II).'" *Revista Latinoamericana de Teología* 11 (33), (1994): 215–44.

"Ignacio Ellacuría, the Human Being and the Christian: 'Taking the Crucified People Down from the Cross.'" In *Love That Produces Hope: The Thought of*

Ignacio Ellacuría, edited by Kevin F. Burke and Robert Lassalle-Klein. Collegeville, Minn.: Liturgical Press, 2006.

"The Importance of the Spiritual Life Today." In *Spirituality of Liberation: Toward Political Holiness*, translated by Robert Barr. Maryknoll, N.Y.: Orbis Books, 1988.

"Introduction: Awakening from the Sleep of Inhumanity." In *The Principle of Mercy: Taking the Crucified People from the Cross*. Maryknoll, N.Y.: Orbis Books, 1994. "Jesus of Galilee from the Salvadoran Context: Compassion, Hope, and Following the Light of the Cross." *Theological Studies* 70 (2009): 437–60.

"Jesus' Proclamation of the Reign of God: Importance for Today." In *Spirituality of Liberation: Toward Political Holiness*, translated by Robert Barr, 127. Maryknoll, N.Y.: Orbis Books, 1988.

"Jesus' Relationship with the Poor and Outcasts: Its Importance for Fundamental Moral Theology." In *Dignity of the Despised of the Earth. Concilium* 130, edited by Jacques Pohier and Dietmar Mieth, 12–20. New York: Seabury Press, 1979.

"Jesus, Theology, and Good News." In *Future of Liberation Theology: Essays in Honor of Gustavo Gutiérrez*, edited by Marc H. Ellis and Otto Maduro, 189–202. Maryknoll, N.Y.: Orbis, 1989.

"¿Es Jesús una Buena noticia?" *Revista Latinoamericana de Teología* 30 (1993): 293–304.

"Karl Rahner and Liberation Theology." *The Way* 43, no. 4 (2004): 53–66.

"The Kingdom of God and the Theologal Dimension of the Poor: The Jesuanic Principle." In *Who Do You Say That I Am? Confessing the Mystery of Christ*, edited by John C. Cavadini and Laura Holt, 109–45. Notre Dame, Ind.: University of Notre Dame Press, 2004.

"Latin America: Guatemala/El Salvador." In *Religion as a Source of Violence. Concilium* 1997/4, edited by Wim Beuken and Karl-Josef Kuschel, 38–54. Maryknoll, N.Y.: Orbis Books, 1997.

"Latin America: Place of Sin and Place of Forgiveness." In *The Principle of Mercy: Taking the Crucified People from the Cross*, 58–69. Maryknoll, N.Y.: Orbis Books, 1994.

"Letter to Ignacio Ellacuría." In "Ignacio Ellacuría, the Human Being and the Christian: 'Taking the Crucified People Down from the Cross.'" In *Love That Produces Hope: The Thought of Ignacio Ellacuría*, edited by Kevin F. Burke and Robert Lassalle-Klein. Collegeville, Minn.: Liturgical Press, 2006.

"Los mártires de la UCA. Exigencia y gracia." *Revista Latinoamericana de Teología* 78 (2009): 227–39.

"Los mártires latinoamericanos. Interpeleación y gracia para la Iglesia." *Revista Latinoamericana de Teología* 48 (1999): 307–30."Martyrs: An Appeal to the Church." In *Rethinking Martyrdom. Concilium* 2003/1, edited by Teresa Okure, Jon Sobrino, and Felix Wilfred, 139–48. London: SCM Press, 2003.

"Mito, antropología e historia en el pensamiento bíblico." *ECA* 305 (1974): 171–88.

"La muerte de Jesús y la liberación en la historia." *ECA* 322/323 (1975): 483–511.

"La opción por los pobres: dar y recibir 'Humanizar la humanidad.'" *Revista Latinoamericana de Teología* 60 (2003): 283–307.

"Our World: Cruelty and Compassion." In *Rethinking Martyrdom. Concilium* 2003/1, edited by Teresa Okure, Jon Sobrino, and Felix Wilfred, 15–23. London: SCM Press, 2003.

"La pascua de Jesús y la revelación de Dios desde la perspectiva de las victimas." *Revista Latinoamericana de Teología* 34 (1995): 79–91.

"Personal Sin, Forgiveness, and Liberation." In *The Principle of Mercy: Taking the Crucified People from the Cross*, 83–101. Maryknoll, N.Y.: Orbis Books, 1994.

"Political Holiness: A Profile." In *Martyrdom Today. Concilium* 1983/3, edited by Johann Baptist Metz and Edward Schillebeeckx, 18–23. New York: Seabury Press, 1983.

"Poverty Means Death to the Poor." *Cross Currents* 36, no. 3 (1986): 267–76.

"Presuppositions and Foundations of Spirituality." In *Spirituality of Liberation: Toward Political Holiness*, translated by Robert Barr. Maryknoll, N.Y.: Orbis Books, 1988.

"'El pueblo crucificado' y 'la civilización de la pobreza.' 'El hacerse cargo de la realidad' de Ignacio Ellacuría." *Revista Latinoamericana de Teología* 66 (2005): 209–28.

"Redeeming Globalization Through Its Victims." In *Globalization and Its Victims. Concilium* 2001/5, edited by Jon Sobrino and Felix Wilfred, 105–14. London: SCM Press, 2001.

"Reflexiones sobre Karl Rahner desde América Latina. En el XX aniversario de su Muerte." *Revista Latinoamericana de Teología* 61 (2004): 3–18.

"Resurreccion de una Iglesia popular." In *Cruz Y Resurreccion*, 83–159. Mexico City: Centro de Reflexion Teológica, 1978.

"Rutilio Grande. El nacimiento de una Iglesia nueva, salvadoreña y evangélica." *Revista Latinoamericana de Teología* 70 (2007): 3–12.

"The Samaritan Church and the Principle of Mercy." In *The Principle of Mercy: Taking the Crucified People from the Cross*, 16. Maryknoll, N.Y.: Orbis Books, 1994.

"Sanctuary: A Theological Analysis." Coauthored with Walter Petry. *Cross Currents* 38, no. 2 (1988): 164–172.

"The Significance of Puebla for the Catholic Church in Latin America." In *Puebla and Beyond: Documentation and Commentary*, edited by John Eagleson and Philip J. Scharper, 289–309. Maryknoll, N.Y.: Orbis Books, 1979.

"Los 'signos de los tiempos' en la teología de la liberación." *Estudios Eclesiasticos* 64 (1989): 249–69.

"The Spirit of Liberation: Spirituality and the Following of Jesus." In *Mysterium Liberationis: Fundamental Concepts of Liberation Theology*, edited by Ignacio Ellacuría and Jon Sobrino, 677–701. Maryknoll, N.Y.: Orbis Books, 1993. In Spanish, "Espiritualidad y Seguimiento de Jesús." In vol. 2 of *Mysterium liberationis: Conceptos fundamentales de la teología de liberación*. Madrid: Editorial Trota, S.A., 1994.

"Spirituality and Liberation." In *Spirituality of Liberation: Toward Political Holiness*, translated by Robert Barr. Maryknoll, N.Y.: Orbis Books, 1988.

"Spirituality and Theology." In *Spirituality of Liberation: Toward Political Holiness*, translated by Robert Barr, 46–79. Maryknoll, N.Y.: Orbis Books, 1988.

"Spirituality of Liberation: Toward Political Holiness." *Horizons* 16 (1989): 140–50.

"Systematic Christology: Jesus Christ, the Absolute Mediator." In *Mysterium Liberationis: Fundamental Concepts of Liberation Theology*, edited by Ignacio Ellacuría and Jon Sobrino, 440–61. Maryknoll, N.Y.: Orbis Books, 1993.

"Teología desde la realidad." In *El mar se abrió: treinta años de teología en América Latina*, edited by Luiz Carlos Susin, 140–56. Santander: Editorial Sal Terrae, 2001.

"Teología desde la realidad." In *Panorama de la teología latinoamericana: Cuando vida y pensamiento son inseparable*, edited by Juan Tamayo and Juan Bosch, 611–28. Estella: Editorial Verbo Divino, 2001. My translation.

"Teología en un mundo sufriente. La teología de la liberación como 'intellectus amoris.'" *Revista Latinoamericana de Teología* 15 (1988): 243–66.

"La teología y el Principio de Liberación." *Revista Latinoamericana de Teología* 35 (1995): 115–40.

"Theological Reflections on the Report of the Truth Commission." In *Impunity: an Ethical Perspective, Six Case Studies from Latin America*, edited by Charles Harper. Geneva: World Council of Churches Publications, 1996.

"Theological Understanding in European and Latin American Theology." In *The True Church and the Poor*, translated by Matthew J. O'Connell. Maryknoll, N.Y.: Orbis Books, 1984.

"Theology in a Suffering World: Theology as *Intellectus Amoris*." In *The Principle of Mercy: Taking the Crucified People from the Cross*. Maryknoll, N.Y.: Orbis Books, 1994. Originally published in *Pluralism and Oppression: Theology in World Perspective*, edited by Paul Knitter, 153–87. Annual Publication of the College Theological Society 34. Lanham, Md.: University Press of America, 1988.

"Theology of the Poor." In *500 Years: Domination or Liberation? Theological Alternatives for the Americas in the 1990's*, edited by Philip E. Wheaton, 101–14. Ocean City: Skipjack Press, 1992.

"Toward a Determination of the Nature of Priesthood." In *The Principle of Mercy: Taking the Crucified People from the Cross*, 133. Maryknoll, N.Y.: Orbis Books, 1994.

"El *Theos* de la *teo-logía* ante el Foro Social Mundial." *Revista Latinoamericana de Teología* 71 (2007): 211–24.

"La unidad y el conflicto dentro de la Iglesia." In *Capitalismo*, 183–213. San Jose, Costa Rica: Editorial Universitaria Centroamericana, 1978.

"The Universalization of Solidarity and Hope: 'the March for Peace,' Butembo, Democratic Republic of Congo, February 24–March 4, 2001." In *Globalization and Its Victims. Concilium* 2001/5, edited by Jon Sobrino and Felix Wilfred Ed, 115–21. London: SCM Press, 2001.

"La utopía de los pobres y el reino de Dios." *Revista Latinoamericana de Teología* 56 (2002): 145–70.

"The Winds in Santo Domingo and the Evangelization of Culture." In *Santo Domingo and Beyond: Documents and Commentaries from the Fourth General Conference of Latin American Bishops*, edited by Alfred T. Hennelly, 167–83. Maryknoll, N.Y.: Orbis Books, 1993.

Secondary Literature

Anderson, Bernhard W. *Understanding the Old Testament.* Upper Saddle River: Prentice Hall, 1998.

Anderson, Dennis, ed. *The Handbook of Restorative Justice: A Global Perspective.* New York: Routledge, 2006.

Anderson, Thomas P. *Matanza: El Salvador's Communist Revolt of 1932.* Lincoln: University of Nebraska Press, 1971.

Appleby, R. Scott. "Peacebuilding and Catholicism: Affinities, Convergences, and Possibilities." In *Peacebuilding: Catholic Theology, Ethics, and Praxis*, edited by Robert J. Schreiter, R. Scott Appleby, and Gerard Powers, 3–22. Maryknoll, N.Y.: Orbis, 2010.

Aquino, María Pilar. "Evil and Hope: A Response to Jon Sobrino." *The Catholic Society of America Proceedings* 50 (1995): 85–92.

Arendt, Hannah. *The Human Condition.* 2nd ed. Chicago: University of Chicago Press, 1998.

Arrupe, Pedro. "Marxist Analysis by Christians." In *Liberation Theology: A Documentary History*, edited by Alfred T. Hennelly, 307–13. Maryknoll, N.Y.: Orbis, 1997.

Ashley, J. Matthew. "Apocalypticism in Political and Liberation Theology: Toward an Historical Docta Ignorantia." *Horizons* 27, no. 1 (2000): 22–43.

———. "Contemplation in the Action of Justice: Ignacio Ellacuría and Ignatian Spirituality." In *Love That Produces Hope: The Thought of Ignacio Ellacuría*, edited by Kevin F. Burke and Robert Lassalle-Klein, 144–65. Collegeville, Minn.: Liturgical Press, 2006.

———. "Ignacio Ellacuría and the Spiritual Exercises of Ignatius Loyola." *Theological Studies* 61, no. 1 (March 2000): 16–39.

———. "The Mystery of God and Compassion for the Poor: The Spiritual Basis of Theology." In *Hope and Solidarity: Jon Sobrino's Challenge to Christian Theology*, edited by Stephen Pope. Maryknoll, N.Y.: Orbis Books, 2008.

———. "The Resurrection of Jesus and the Resurrection Discipleship in the Systematic Theology of Jon Sobrino." Paper presented at the Catholic Theological Society of America, June 9, 2005.

Azevedo, Marcello de Carvalho. *Basic Ecclesial Communities in Brazil: The Challenge of a New Way of Being Church*. Translated by John Drury. Washington: Georgetown University Press, 1987.

Baum, Gregory. "Liberating Victims and Victimizers." *Christian Century*, February 4–11, 1998: 117–20.

Baum, Gregory, and Harold Wells, eds. "A Theological Afterword." In *The Reconciliation of Peoples: Challenge to the Churches*, 184–92. Maryknoll, N.Y.: Orbis Books, 1997.

Beker, Johan Christiaan. *Paul the Apostle: The Triumph of God in Life and Thought*. Philadelphia: Fortress Press, 1984.

Bell, Daniel M., Jr. *Liberation Theology after the End of History: The Refusal to Cease Suffering*. New York: Routledge, 2011.

———. "Sacrifice and Suffering: Beyond Human Rights and Capitalism." *Modern Theology* 18, no. 3 (2002): 333–59.

Benjamin, Walter. *Illuminations*, edited with an introduction by Hannah Arendt, translated by Harry Zohn, 253–64. New York: Schocken, 1968.

Best, Marigold, and Pamela Hussey. "The Thorny Road to Reconciliation in El Salvador." In *Open Hands: Reconciliation, Justice, and Peace Work around the World*, edited by Barbara Butler. Rattlesden, UK: Kevin Mayhew LTD, 1998.

Bevans, Stephen. "Models of Contextual Theology." *Missiology* 13, no. 2 (April 1985): 185–202.

Bloch, Ernst. *The Principle of Hope*. Cambridge: MIT Press, 1995.

Boff, Leonardo. "The Need for Political Saints: From a Spirituality of Liberation to the Practice of Liberation." *Cross-current* 30, no. 4 (1980–1981): 369–84.

———. "Salvation in Jesus Christ and the Process of Liberation," translated by J. P. Donnelly. In *The Mystical and Political Dimension of the Christian*

Faith, edited by Claude Gefíré and Gustavo Gutiérrez. *Concilium* 96. Edinburgh: T. and T. Clark, 1974.

———. *Way of the Cross: Way of Justice*. Translated by John Drury. Maryknoll, N.Y.: Orbis Books, 1980.

———. *When Theology Listens to the Poor*. San Francisco: Harper & Row, 1988.

Boff, Leonardo, and Clodovis Boff. *Introducing Liberation Theology*, translated by Paul Burns. Maryknoll, N.Y.: Orbis, 1987.

Bonhoeffer, Dietrich. *The Cost of Discipleship*. Translated by R. H. Fuller. New York: Macmillan, 1963.

Borer, Tristan Anne. "A Taxonomy of Victims and Perpetrators: Human Rights and Reconciliation in South Africa," *Human Rights Quarterly* 25 (2003): 1088–116.

Bracken, Patrick J., and Celia Petty. *Rethinking the Trauma of War*. London: Free Association Books, 2001.

Brackley, Dean. "Theology and Solidarity: Learning from Sobrino's Method." In *Hope and Solidarity: Jon Sobrino's Challenge to Christian Theology*, edited by Stephen J. Pope, 3–15. Maryknoll, N.Y.: Orbis, 2008.

Brogan, Patrick. *World Conflicts: A Comprehensive Guide to World Strife Since 1945*. Lanham: Scarecrow Press, 1998.

Burke, Kevin F. *The Ground Beneath the Cross: The Theology of Ignacio Ellacuría*. Washington: Georgetown University Press, 2000.

Burke, Kevin F., and Robert Lassalle-Klein, eds. *Love That Produces Hope: The Thought of Ignacio Ellacuría*. Collegeville, Minn.: Liturgical Press, 2006.

Cahill, Lisa. "A Theology of Peacebuilding." In *Peacebuilding: Catholic Theology, Ethics, and Praxis*, edited by Robert J. Schreiter, R. Scott Appleby, and Gerard Powers, 300–31. Maryknoll, N.Y.: Orbis Books, 2010.

Callahan, Annice, R.C.S.J. "The Relationship between Spirituality and Theology." *Horizons* 16, no. 2 (1989): 266–74.

Casaldáliga, Pedro, and José María Vigil. *Political Holiness: The Spirituality of Liberation*. Maryknoll, N.Y.: Orbis Books, 1994.

Cavanaugh, William T. *Being Consumed: Economics and Christian Desire*. Grand Rapids, Mich.: Eerdmans, 2008.

Chapman, Audrey R. "Coming to Terms with the Past: Truth, Justice, and/ or Reconciliation." *Annual of the Society of Christian Ethics* 19 (1999): 235–58.

Chávez, Gregorio Rosa. Press conference. In the Salvadoran newspaper *La Prensa Grafica*, January 7, 2007.

Chenu, Marie-Dominique. *Une ecole de téologie: Le Saulchoir*. Paris: Cerf, 1985. Quoted in Gustavo Gutiérrez, *We Drink from Our Own Wells: The Spiritual Journey of a People* (Maryknoll, N.Y.: Orbis Books, 1984), 147 n. 2.

Coffin, William Sloane. Interview by Tom Ashbrook. *On Point*. WBUR, NPR Boston, September 11, 2002, rebroadcast April 14, 2006. Quoted in Lisa Cahill, "A Theology of Peacebuilding," in *Peacebuilding: Catholic Theology, Ethics, and Praxis*, ed. Robert J. Schreiter, R. Scott Appleby, and Gerard Powers (Maryknoll, N.Y.: Orbis, 2010), 304.

Comblin, José. *Reconciliación y Liberación*. San Isidro, Chile: Centro de Estudios Sociales (CESOC), 1987.

———. "Treinta años de teología latinoamericana." In *El mar se abrió: treinta años de teología en América Latina*, edited by Luiz Carlos Susin, 164–76. Santander: Editorial Sal Terrae, 2001.

Comision Economica para América Latina y el Caribe (CEPAL). "El Salvador." In *Estudio economico de America Latina y el Caribe: 2004–2005*. New York: CEPAL, 2005.

Cone, James H. *God of the Oppressed*. New York: Seabury Press, 1975.

Copeland, Shawn M. "Racism and the Vocation of the Christian Theologian." *Spiritus* 111 (2002): 15–29.

Costadoat, Jorge, S.J. "La liberación en la cristología de Jon Sobrino." *Teología y Vida* 44 (2003): 62–84.

———. "Seguimiento de Cristo en América Latina." *Gregorianum* 93, no. 3 (2012): 573–92.

———. "Los signos de los tiempos en la teología de liberación." In *Signos de Estos Tiempos: Interpretación teológica de nuestra época*, edited by Fernando Berrios, Jorge Costadoat, and Diego García, 131–48. Santiago de Chile: Ediciones Universidad Alberto Hurtado, 2008.

Couturier, Guy P. "Jeremiah." In *The New Jerome Biblical Commentary*, edited by Raymond E. Brown, Joseph A. Fitzmyer, and Roland E. Murphy, 290. Upper Saddle River, N.J.: Prentice Hall, 1990.

Crowley, Paul. *Unwanted Wisdom: Suffering, the Cross, and Hope*. New York: Continuum, 2005.

Cruz, José Miguel. "Los factores asociados a las pandillas juveniles en Centro-américa." *ECA* 685–686 (November–December 2005): 1155–82.

Curran, Charles E. "White Privilege." *Horizons* 32, no. 2 (2005): 361–67.

Danner, Mark. *The Massacre at El Mozote: a Parable of the Cold War*. New York: Vintage Books, 1994.

Dawson, Andrew. "The Origins and Character of the Base Ecclesial Community: A Brazilian Perspective." In *The Cambridge Companion to Liberation Theology*, edited by Christopher Rowland, 139–58. New York: Cambridge University Press, 2007.

de Gruchy, John W. *Christianity and Democracy: A Theology for a Just World Order*. New York: Cambridge University Press, 1995.

———. *Reconciliation: Restoring Justice.* Minneapolis: Fortress Press, 2002.

Dellaferrera, Nelso, Lucio Gera, Miguel Angel Nadur Dalla, Luis Hector Rivas, and Pablo Sudar. *Evangelización, liberación y reconciliación: Hacia una nueva evangelización.* Buenos Aires: Ediciones Paulinas, 1987.

DeLugan, Robin Maria. Reimagining *National Belonging: Post-Civil War El Salvador in a Global Context.* Tucson: The University of Arizona Press, 2012.

Donahue, John R., S.J. *What Does the Lord Require? A Bibliographical Essay on the Bible and Social Justice.* Saint Louis: Institute of Jesuit Resources, 2003.

dos Santos, Theotonio. "La crisis de la teoría del desarrolloy la relaciones de dependencía en America Latina." Quoted in Christian Smith, *The Emergence of Liberation Theology: Radical Religion and Social Movement Theory* (Chicago: University of Chicago Press, 1991), 145.

Dreyer, Elizabeth A., and Mark S. Burrows, eds. *Minding the Spirit: The Study of Christian Spirituality.* Baltimore: Johns Hopkins University Press, 2005.

Duffy, Stephen. *The Graced Horizon: Nature and Grace in Modern Catholic Thought.* Collegeville, Minn.: Liturgical Press, 1992.

Dulles, Avery. "The Symbolic Structure of Revelation." *Theological Studies* 41 (1980): 51–73.

Dussel, Enrique. *A History of the Church in Latin America: Colonialism to Liberation (1492–1979),* 101–24. Grand Rapids, Mich.: Eerdmans, 1981.

Eagleson, John, and Philip Scharper, eds. *Puebla and Beyond: Documentation and Commentary.* Maryknoll, N.Y.: Orbis Books, 1980.

Ellacuría, Ignacio. "Church of the Poor, Sacrament of Liberation." In *Mysterium Liberationis: Fundamental Concepts of Liberation Theology,* edited by Ignacio Ellacuría and Jon Sobrino, 543–64. Maryknoll, N.Y.: Orbis Books, 1993.

———. *Conversión de la Iglesia al reino de Dios,* 207–8. San Salvador: UCA Editores: 1985. Quoted in Jon Sobrino, *Jesus the Liberator: A Historical-Theological Reading of Jesus of Nazareth* (Maryknoll, N.Y.: Orbis Books, 1993), 278 n. 24.

———. *Escritos Teológicos.* Vol. 1–2. San Salvador: UCA Editores, 2000.

———. *Escritos Universitarios.* San Salvador: UCA Editores, 1999.

———. "Fe y Justicia." Vol. 3 of *Escritos Teológicos,* edited by Aída Estela Sánchez, 316. San Salvador: UCA Editores, 2001. Quoted in Michael Lee, *Bearing the Weight of Salvation: The Soteriology of Ignacio Ellacuría* (New York: Crossroad Publishing, 2008), 125.

———. "Fundamentación biológica de la ética." *ECA* 368 (1979): 419–28.

———. "Fundamentación biológica de la ética." *ECA* 368 (1979): 422. Quoted in Kevin F. Burke, ed., *The Ground Beneath the Cross: The Theology of Ignacio Ellacuría* (Washington: Georgetown University Press, 2000), 106–7.

———. "Hacia una fundamentación del método teológico latinoamericano," 208. Quoted in Kevin F. Burke, ed., *The Ground Beneath the Cross: The Theology of Ignacio Ellacuría* (Washington: Georgetown University Press, 2000), 100.

———. "Historia de la salvación." In vol. 1 of *Escritos Teológicos*. San Salvador: UCA Editores, 2000.

———. "Historia de la salvación y salvación en la historia." In vol. 1 of *Escritos Teológicos*. San Salvador: UCA Editores, 2000.

———. "Historicidad de la salvación cristiana." In vol. 1 of *Escritos Teológicos*. San Salvador: UCA Editores, 2000.

———. "The Historicity of Christian Salvation." In *Mysterium Liberationis: Fundamental Concepts of Liberation Theology*, edited by Ignacio Ellacuría and Jon Sobrino, 251–89. Maryknoll, N.Y.: Orbis Books, 1993.

———. "Human Rights in a Divided Society." In *Human Rights in the Americas: The Struggle for Consensus*, edited by Alfred T. Hennelly and John Langan. Washington: Georgetown University Press, 1982.

———. "La nueva obra de Zubiri: 'Inteligencia Sentiente.'" *Razón y Fe* 995 (1981): 135.

———. "El objeto de la filosofía." Quoted in Antonio González, "Assessing the Philosophical Achievement of Ignacio Ellacuría," in *Love That Produces Hope: The Thought of Ignacio Ellacuría*, ed. Kevin F. Burke and Robert Lassalle-Klein (Collegeville, Minn.: Liturgical Press, 2006), 80.

———. "Salvation History and Salvation in History." In *Freedom Made Flesh: The Mission of Christ and His Church*, 3–19. Maryknoll, N.Y.: Orbis Books, 1975.

———. "La superación del reduccionismo idealista en Zubiri." *ECA* 477 (1988): 633–50.

———. "La superación del reduccionismo idealista en Zubiri," *ECA* 477 (1988): 648. Quoted in Robert Lassalle-Klein, "Ignacio Ellacuría's Debt to Xavier Zubiri: Critical Principles for a Latin American Philosophy and Theology of Liberation," in *Love that Produces Hope: The Thought of Ignacio Ellacuría*, ed. Kevin F. Burke and Robert Lassalle-Klein (Collegeville, Minn.: Liturgical Press, 2006), 103.

———. "La Teología como Momento Ideológico de la Praxis Eclesial." *Estudios Eclesiásticos* 207 (1978): 457–76. Quoted in Jon Sobrino, "Theology in a Suffering World," in *The Principle of Mercy: Taking the Crucified People from the Cross* (Maryknoll, N.Y.: Orbis Books, 1994), 38.

———. "Teología de la liberación y Marxism." *Revista Latinoamericana de Teología* 20 (1990).

———. "Utopia and Prophecy in Latin America." In *Mysterium Liberationis: Fundamental Concepts of Liberation Theology*, ed. Ignacio Ellacuría and Jon Sobrino, 289–328. Maryknoll, N.Y.: Orbis Books, 1993.

———. "Violence and Non-Violence in the Struggle for Peace and Liberation." *Concilium* 215 (1988): 69–97. Quoted in Jon Sobrino, *Jesus the Liberator: A Historical-Theological Reading of Jesus of Nazareth* (Maryknoll, N.Y.: Orbis Books, 1993), 218.

Enright, Robert D. Suzanne Freedman, and Julio Rique. *Exploring Forgiveness.* Madison: University of Wisconsin Press, 1998.

Ericson, Maria. "Reconciliation and the Search for a Shared Moral Landscape: Insights and Challenges from Northern Ireland and South Africa." *Journal of Theology for Southern Africa* 115 (March 2003): 19–41.

Fagan, Eileen M. *An Interpretation of Evangelization: Jon Sobrino's Christology and Ecclesiology in Dialogue.* Bethesda, Md.: Catholic Scholars Press, 1998.

Fitzmyer, Joseph. "The Letter to the Romans." In *The New Jerome Biblical Commentary*, edited by Raymond E. Brown, Joseph A. Fitzmyer, and Roland E. Murphy. Upper Saddle River, N.J.: Prentice Hall, 1990.

———. "Pauline Theology." In *The New Jerome Biblical Commentary*, edited by Raymond E. Brown, Joseph A. Fitzmyer, and Roland E. Murphy. Upper Saddle River, N.J.: Prentice Hall, 1990.

Flannery, Austin, ed. *Gaudium et Spes.* In vol. 1 of *Vatican Council II: The Conciliar and Post Conciliar Documents*, 903–1001. New York: Costello Publishing Company, 1996.

Furnish, Victor Paul. "The Ministry of Reconciliation." *Currents in Theology and Mission* 4, no. 4 (August 4, 1977): 204–18.

Gaborit, Mauricio. "Los círculos de la violencia: sociedad excluyente y pandillas." *ECA* 685–86 (November–December 2005): 1145–54.

Galeano, Eduardo. *Open Veins of Latin America: Five Centuries of the Pillage of a Continent.* New York: Monthly Review Press, (1973), 1997.

Galilea, Segundo. "La liberación como encuentro de la política y de la contemplación." *Concilium* 96 (1974): 313–27.

———. "Liberation Theology and the New Task Facing Christians." In *Frontiers of Theology in Latin America*, edited by Rosino Gibellini. Maryknoll, N.Y.: Orbis Books, 1979.

———. *The Way of Living Faith: A Spirituality of Liberation.* San Francisco: Harper and Row, 1988.

Gallagher, Vincent A. *The True Cost of Low Prices: The Violence of Globalization.* Maryknoll, N.Y.: Orbis Books, 2008.

Gallego, Andres. *El Seguimiento de Jesús en la Cristología de Jon Sobrino.* Lima: Centro de Estudios Y Publicaciones (CEP), 1991.

Galtung, Johan. "After Violence, Reconstruction, Reconciliation, and Resolution: Coping with Visible and Invisible Effects of War and Violence." In *Reconciliation, Justice, and Coexistence: Theory and Practice,* edited by Mohammed Abu-Nimeer, 3–23. Lanham, Md.: Lexington Books, 2001.

García, Ismael. *Justice in Latin American Theology of Liberation.* Atlanta, Ga.: John Knox Press, 1987.

Gaudet, Matthew J., and William R. O'Neill. "Restoring Peace: Toward a Conversation between the Just War and Reconciliation Traditions." *Journal of the Society of Christian Ethics* 31.1 (2011): 37–66.

Goizueta, Robert. "The Christology of Jon Sobrino." In *Hope and Solidarity: Jon Sobrino's Challenge to Christian Theology,* edited by Stephen J. Pope, 90–104. Maryknoll, N.Y.: Orbis, 2008.

González Faus, José Ignacio. "Las víctimas como lugar teológico." *Revista Latinoamericana de Teología* 46 (1999): 89–104.

———. "Sin." In *Mysterium Liberationis: Fundamental Concepts of Liberation Theology,* edited by Ignacio Ellacuría and Jon Sobrino, 532–42. Maryknoll, N.Y.: Orbis Books, 1993.

González, Luis Armando. "Estado, sociedad y economía en El Salvador (1880–1999)." In *El Salvador: la transición y sus Problemas,* edited by Rodolfo Cardenal and Luis Armando González, 30–35. San Salvador: UCA Editores, 2002.

Govier, Trudy. *Taking Wrongs Seriously: Acknowledgement, Reconciliation, and the Politics of Sustainable Peace.* Amherst, N.Y.: Humanity Books, 2006.

Gowan, Donald E. *Theology of the Prophetic Books: the Death & Resurrection of Israel.* Louisville: Westminster John Knox Press, 1998.

Gracia, Diego. "Zubiri, Xavier." In *Dictionary of Fundamental Theology,* edited by René Latourelle and Rino Fisichella, 1166. New York: Crossroad Publishing, 1995. Quoted in Robert Lassalle-Klein, "Ignacio Ellacuría's Debt to Xavier Zubiri: Critical Principles for a Latin American Philosophy and Theology of Liberation," in *Love That Produces Hope: The Thought of Ignacio Ellacuría,* ed. Kevin F. Burke and Robert Lassalle-Klein (Collegeville, Minn.: Liturgical Press, 2006), 122 n. 107.

Grande, Rutilio, S.J. *Homily preached on February 13, 1977.* Quoted in William J. O'Malley, S.J., "El Salvador: Rutilio Grande, S.J.," in *The Voice of Blood: Five Christian Martyrs of Our Time* (Maryknoll, N.Y.: Orbis, 1995), 1–63.

Grieb, A. Katherine. *The Story of Romans: a Narrative Defense of God's Righteousness.* Louisville: Westminster John Knox Press, 2002.

Gutiérrez, Gustavo. *Dios y el Oro de las Indians*, 157. Salamanca, 2nd ed, 1990. Quoted in Jon Sobrino, *Jesus the Liberator: A Historical-Theological Reading of Jesus of Nazareth* (Maryknoll, N.Y.: Orbis Books, 1993), 11.

———. "Liberation Theology for the Twenty-First Century." In *Romero's Legacy: The Call to Peace and Justice*. New York: Rowman & Littlefield Publishers, 2007.

———. "The Meaning and Scope of Medellín." In *The Density of the Present: Selected Writings*. Maryknoll, N.Y.: Orbis Books, 2004.

———. "No One Takes My Life from Me; I Give it Freely." In *Love That Produces Hope: The Thought of Ignacio Ellacuría*, edited by Kevin F. Burke and Robert Lassalle-Klein. Collegeville, Minn.: Liturgical Press, 2006.

———. *On Job: God Talk and the Suffering of the Innocent*. Translated by Matthew J. O'Connell. Maryknoll, N.Y.: Orbis Books, 1999.

———. "Option for the Poor." In *Mysterium Liberationis: Fundamental Concepts of Liberation Theology*, edited by Ignacio Ellacuría and Jon Sobrino, 235–50. Maryknoll, N.Y.: Orbis Books, 1993.

———. *The Power of the Poor in History*. Translated by Robert Barr. Maryknoll, N.Y.: Orbis Books, 1983.

———. *Textos Essenciales: Acordarse de los Pobres*. Lima: Fondo Editorial del Congreso del Perú, 2003.

———. *A Theology of Liberation: History, Politics, and Salvation*, 15th Anniversary Edition. Translated by Caridad Inda, John Eagleson, and Matthew J. O'Connell. Maryknoll, N.Y.: Orbis Books, 1988. In Spanish, *Teología de la liberación, Perspectivas*. Lima: Centro de Estudios y Publicaciones, 1971.

———. *The Truth Shall Make You Free: Confrontations*. Translated by Matthew J. O'Connell. Maryknoll, N.Y.: Orbis Books, 1990.

———. *We Drink from Our Own Wells: The Spiritual Journey of a People*. Maryknoll, N.Y.: Orbis Books, 1984.

Haight, Roger. *Dynamics of Theology*. Maryknoll, N.Y.: Orbis Books, 2001.

Harrington, Daniel. "What Got Jesus Killed." In *Hope and Solidarity: Jon Sobrino's Challenge to Christian Theology*, edited by Stephen J. Pope, 79–89. Maryknoll, N.Y.: Orbis Books, 2008.

———. *Why Do We Suffer: A Scriptural Approach to the Human Condition*. Franklin: Sheed & Ward, 2000.

Hay, Mark, O.M.I. "Ukubiyisana: Reconciliation in South Africa," 158–84. D.Min thesis, Catholic Theological Union, 1997.

Hayner, Priscilla B. *Unspeakable Truths: Facing the Challenge of Truth Commissions*. New York: Routledge, 2002.

Helmick, Raymond G., and Rodney L. Petersen, eds. *Forgiveness and Reconciliation: Religion, Public Policy and Conflict Transformation*. Philadelphia: Templeton Foundation Press, 2002.

Hennelly, Alfred T. "Theological Method: The Southern Exposure." *Theological Studies* 38 (December 1977): 718–25.

Hennelly, Alfred T., ed. *Liberation Theology: A Documentary History.* Maryknoll, N.Y.: Orbis Books, 1997.

Hexham, Irving. "Christianity and apartheid: an introductory bibliography." *Journal of Theology for Southern Africa* 32 (1980): 39–59.

Hinkelammert, Franz. "Globalization as Cover-Up: An Ideology to Disguise and Justify Current Wrongs." In *Globalization and Its Victims,* edited by Jon Sobrino and Felix Wilfred. London: SCM Press, 2001.

Hurley, Michael. *Reconciliation in Religion and Society.* Belfast: Institute of Irish Studies, 1994.

Jeremias, Joachim. *Teología del Nuevo Testamento.* 5th ed., 137. Salamanca: Ediciones Sígueme, 1986. Quoted in Jon Sobrino, *Jesus the Liberator: A Historical-Theological Reading of Jesus of Nazareth* (Maryknoll, N.Y.: Orbis Books, 1993), 79.

John Paul II. "No Peace without Justice. No Justice without Forgiveness." Message for the World Day of Peace, no. 2. (January 1, 2002). http://www .vatican.va/holy_father/john_paul_ii/messages/peace/documents/hf_jp-ii _mes_20011211_xxxv-world-day-for-peace_en.html.

Johnstone, Gerry, and Daniel Van Ness, eds. *Handbook of Restorative Justice.* Portland, Ore.: Willan Publishing, 2007.

Jones, Gregory L. *Embodying Forgiveness: A Theological Analysis.* Grand Rapids, Mich.: Eerdmans, 1995.

"The Kairos Document," Article 3.1, September 1985, http://www.sahistory.org .za/archive/challenge-church-theological-comment-political-crisis-south -africa-kairos-document-1985.

Kärkkänien, Veli-Matti. *Christology a Global Introduction: An Ecumenical, International and Contextual Perspective.* Grand Rapids, Mich.: Baker Academic, 2003.

Kasemänn, Ernst. "Some Thoughts on the Theme 'The Doctrine of Reconciliation in the New Testament.'" In *The Future of Our Religious Past: Essays in Honour of Rudolf Bultmann,* edited by James M. Robinson, translated by Charles E. Carlston and Robert P. Scharlemann. New York: Harper & Row, 1971.

Keenan, James F., S.J. "Radicalizing the Comprehensiveness of Mercy: Christian Identity in Theological Ethics." In *Hope and Solidarity: Jon Sobrino's Challenge to Christian Theology,* edited by Stephen J. Pope, 187–200. Maryknoll, N.Y.: Orbis Books, 2008.

Kelley, Melissa M. *Grief: Contemporary Theory and the Practice of Ministry.* Minneapolis: Fortress Press, 2010.

Keune, Lou. *Sobrevivimos la guerra: la historia de los pobladores de Arcatao y de San José Las Flores.* San Salvador: Adelina Editores, 1996.

Kimbrough, S. T., Jr. "Reconciliation in the Old Testament." *Religion in Life* 41, no. 1 (Spring 1972): 37–45.

Kim, Seyoon. "God Reconciled His Enemy to Himself: The Origin of Paul's Concept of Reconciliation." In *The Road from Damascus: The Impact of Paul's Conversion on His Life, Thought, and Ministry*, edited by Richard L. Longenecker, 102–24. Grand Rapids, Mich.: Eerdmans, 1997.

Lamb, Matthew L. "The Theory-Praxis Relationship in Contemporary Christian Theologies." *CTS Proceedings* 31 (1976): 149–78.

Lam, Sharon. *The Trouble with Blame.* Cambridge, Mass.: Harvard University Press, 1996.

Lassalle-Klein, Robert. "Ignacio Ellacuría's Debt to Xavier Zubiri: Critical Principles for a Latin American Philosophy and Theology of Liberation." In *Love That Produces Hope: The Thought of Ignacio Ellacuría*, edited by Kevin F. Burke and Robert Lassalle-Klein, 88–102. Collegeville, Minn.: Liturgical Press, 2006.

———. "Jesus of Galilee and the Crucified People: The Contextual Christology of Jon Sobrino and Ignacio Ellacuría." *Theological Studies* 70 (2009): 347–76.

Laude, William, J. *Jesus Among Theologians: Contemporary Interpretations of Christ.* Harrisburg: Trinity Press International, 2001.

Lebacqz, Karen. *Six Theories of Justice: Perspectives from Philosophical and Theological Ethics.* Minneapolis: Augsburg, 1986.

Lee, Michael E. *Bearing the Weight of Salvation: the Soteriology of Ignacio Ellacuría.* New York: Crossroad Publishing, 2008.

———. "Liberation Theology's Transcendent Moment: The Work of Xavier Zubiri and Ignacio Ellacuría as Noncontrastive Discourse." *Journal of Religion* 83, no. 2 (April 2003): 226–43.

Lewis, Thomas A. "Actions as the ties that bind: love, praxis, and community in the thought of Gustavo Gutiérrez." *Journal of Religious Ethics*, 33, no. 3 (2005): 539–67.

Libânio, Joâo Batista. "Hope, Utopia, Resurrection." In *Mysterium Liberationis: Fundamental Concepts of Liberation Theology*, edited by Ignacio Ellacuría and Jon Sobrino, 716–28. Maryknoll, N.Y.: Orbis Books, 1993.

Logan, Willis. *The Kairos Covenant.* New York: Friendship Press, 1988.

López Trujillo, Alfonso. "El Cristo Reconciliador." *Vida y espiritualidad* 24, no. 69 (2008): 83–87.

———. *Liberación y reconciliacion: Breve recorrido histórico.* Lima: Editoral Latina, 1990.

Maier, Martin, S.J. "Karl Rahner: The Teacher of Ignacio Ellacuría." In *Love that Produces Hope: The Thought of Ignacio Ellacuría*, edited by Kevin F.

Burke and Robert Lassalle-Klein, 128–43. Collegeville, Minn.: Liturgical Press, 2006.

Marshall, Christopher D. *Beyond Retribution: A New Testament Vision for Justice, Crime, and Punishment*. Grand Rapids, Mich.: Eerdmans, 2001.

Martín-Baró, Ignacio. "Oscar Romero: Voice of the Downtrodden." In Oscar Romero, *Voice of the Voiceless: The Four Pastoral Letters and Other Statements*, translated by Michael J. Walsh, 1–21. Maryknoll, N.Y.: Orbis Books, (1985), 2003.

Martin, Ralph. *Reconciliation: A Study of Paul's Theology*. Atlanta: John Knox Press, 1984.

May, Roy H., Jr. "Reconciliation: A Political Requirement for Latin America." *Annual of the Society of Christian Ethics* 16 (1996): 41–58.

McCarthy, Carmel. "A Response [to Bible and Reconciliation]." In *Reconciliation in Religion and Society: Proceedings of a Conference Organised by the Irish School of Ecumenics and the University of Ulster*, edited by Michael Hurley. Belfast: Institute of Irish Studies, the Queen's University of Belfast in association with the University of Ulster, 1994.

McCullough, Cecil. "Bible and Reconciliation." In *Reconciliation in Religion and Society: Proceedings of a Conference Organised by the Irish School of Ecumenics and the University of Ulster*, edited by Michael Hurley. Belfast: Institute of Irish Studies, the Queen's University of Belfast in association with the University of Ulster, 1994.

McDonald, H. D. *Forgiveness and Atonement*. Grand Rapids, Mich.: Baker Book House, 1984.

McGinn, Bernard. "The Letter and the Spirit: Spirituality as an Academic Discipline." In *Minding the Spirit: The Study of Christian Spirituality*, edited by Elizabeth A. Dreyer and Mark S. Burrows. Baltimore, Md.: Johns Hopkins University Press, 2005.

Meier, John. "The Bible as a Source of Theology." In vol. 3 of *Proceedings of the CTSA* (1988): 1–14.

Metz, Johann Baptist. *Faith in History and Society: Toward a Practical Fundamental Theology*. Translated by Matthew Ashley. New York: The Crossroad Publishing Company, 2007.

Moltmann, Jürgen. *Theology of Hope: On the Ground and the Implications of a Christian Eschatology*. Translated by James Leitch. New York: Harper & Row, 1974.

———. *Theology of Hope*. Quoted in Jon Sobrino, *Christ the Liberator: A View from the Victims*, trans. Paul Burns (Maryknoll, N.Y.: Orbis Books, 2001), 52.

Montes Mozo, Segundo, and Juan José García Vásquez. *Salvadoran Migration to the United States: an Exploratory Study*. Washington: Hemispheric Migration

Project, Center for Immigration Policy and Refugee Assistance, George-town University, 1988.

Montgomery, Tommie Sue. *Revolution in El Salvador: From Civil Strife to Civil Peace.* Boulder, Colo. Westview Press, 1982.

Müller-Fahrenholz, Geiko. *The Art of Forgiveness: Theological Reflections on Healing and Reconciliation.* Geneva: World Council of Churches Publications, 1996.

Murphy-O'Connor, Jerome. "The Second Letter to the Corinthians." In *The New Jerome Biblical Commentary*, edited by Raymond E. Brown, Joseph A. Fitzmyer, and Roland E. Murphy. Upper Saddle River, N.J.: Prentice Hall, 1990.

Murray, Joyce. "Liberation for Communion in the Soteriology of Gustavo Gutiérrez." *Theological Studies* 59 (1998): 51–59.

Oliva, José Armando, and Héctor Samour. *Estudios Sociales y Cívica.* San Salvador: Ediciones Estudios Educativos, 1998.

O'Malley, William J. "El Salvador: Rutilio Grande, S.J." In *The Voice of Blood: Five Christian Martyrs of Our Time.* Maryknoll, N.Y.: Orbis Books, 1995.

Paige, Jeffery M. "Coffee and Power in El Salvador." *Latin American Research Review* 28, no. 3 (1993): 7–40.

Pannenberg, Wolfhart. *Theology and the Kingdom of God.* Philadelphia: Westminster, 1969.

Paris, Roland. "Peacebuilding in Central America: Reproducing the Sources of Conflict?" *International Peacekeeping* 9, no. 4 (Winter 2002): 39–68.

Petersen, Rodney L. "A Theology of Forgiveness: Terminology, Rhetoric & the Dialectic of Interfaith Relationships." In *Forgiveness and Reconciliation: Religion, Public Policy, and Conflict Transformation*, edited by Raymond G. Helmick and Rodney L. Petersen, 3–25. Philadelphia: Templeton Foundation Press, 2002.

Philpott, Daniel. "Beyond Politics as Usual: Is Reconciliation Compatible with Liberalism?" In *The Politics of Past Evil: Religion, Reconciliation, and the Dilemmas of Transitional Justice*, 11–44. Notre Dame, Ind.: University of Notre Dame Press, 2006.

———. *Just and Unjust Peace: An Ethic of Political Reconciliation.* New York: Oxford University Press, 2012.

———. "Peace After Genocide." *First Things*, no. 224 (June–July 2012): 39–46.

———. "Reconciliation: A Catholic Ethic for Peacebuilding in the Political Order." In *Peacebuilding: Catholic Theology, Ethics, and Praxis*, edited by Robert J. Schreiter, R. Scott Appleby, and Gerard Powers, 92–124. Maryknoll, N.Y.: Orbis, 2010.

Pico, Juan Hernandez, S.J. "Revolución, Violencia, Paz." In *Mysterium Liberationis: Conceptos fundamentales de la teología de liberación*, edited by Ignacio
Ellacuría and Jon Sobrino. Madrid: Editorial Trota, 1990.

———. "Una reconciliación frustrada y su superación." *Revista Latinoamericana
de Teología*, 85 (2012): 35–57.

Pope, Stephen J. "The Convergence of Justice and Forgiveness: Lessons from El
Salvador." *Theological Studies* 64 (2003): 812–35.

———. ed. *Hope and Solidarity: Jon Sobrino's Challenge to Christian Theology*.
Maryknoll, NY: Orbis Books, 2008.

———. "Proper and Improper Partiality and the Preferential Option for the
Poor." *Theological Studies* 54 (1993): 242–71.

Prince, Walter. "Christian Spirituality." In *The New Dictionary of Catholic
Spirituality*, edited by M. Downey, 931–38. Collegeville, Minn.: Liturgical
Press, 1993.

Rahner, Karl. *Foundations of Christian Faith: An Introduction to the Idea of
Christianity*. Translated by William V. Dych. New York: Crossroad Publishing, 2000.

———. "History of Salvation and Salvation-History." In vol. 5 of *Theological
Investigations*, 98–114. Baltimore, Md.: Helicon Press, 1966.

———. *Theological Investigations*, vol. 4. Baltimore, Md.: Helicon Press, 1966.

———. *Theological Investigations*, vol. 5. Baltimore, Md.: Helicon Press, 1966

Rettberg, Angelika. "The Private Sector and Peace in El Salvador, Guatemala,
and Colombia." *Journal of Latin American Studies* 39 (2007): 463–94.

Richard, Pablo. *Death of Christendoms, Birth of the Church: Historical Analysis
and Theological Interpretation of the Church in Latin America*.
Maryknoll, N.Y.: Orbis Books, 1987.

Richard, Pablo, Barbara E. Campbell, and Bonnie Shepard. *The idols of death
and the God of life: a theology*. Maryknoll, N.Y.: Orbis Books, 1983.

Ripley, Jason J. "Covenantal Concepts of Justice and Righteousness, and
Catholic-Protestant Reconciliation: Theological Implications and Explorations." *Journal of Ecumenical Studies* 38, no. 1 (Winter 2001): 95–108.

Romero, Oscar. "The Church's Mission amid National Crisis." In *Voice of the
Voiceless: The Four Pastoral Letters and Other Statements*, translated by
Michael J. Walsh, 114–61. Maryknoll, N.Y.: Orbis Books, (1985), 2003.

———. *Voice of the Voiceless: The Four Pastoral Letters and Other Statements*.
Translated by Michael J. Walsh. Maryknoll, N.Y.: Orbis Books, (1985), 2003.

Rovaletti, María Lucrecia. "Man, Experience of God: The problem of God in
Xavier Zubiri." *Xavier Zubiri Review* 2 (1999): 65–78.

Ruggiere, Giuseppe. "Faith and History." In The Reception of Vatican II, edited
by Giuseppe Alberigo, Jean-Pierre Jossua, and Joseph A. Komonchak,
91–114. Washington: Catholic University of America, 1987.

Samayoa, Salvador. *El Salvador: la reforma pactada.* San Salvador: UCA Editores, 2003.

Samour, Héctor. "Filosofía y libertad." In *Ignacio Ellacuría: Aquella libertad esclarecida*, edited by Jon Sobrino and Rolando Alvarado, 103–45. San Salvador: UCA Editores, 1999.

———. *Voluntad de liberación: El pensamiento filosófico de Ignacio Ellacuría.* San Salvador: UCA Editores, 2002.

———. "Zubiri y la filosofía de la liberación." *Realidad* 87 (2002), 371–92.

Sanchez, Ivett S. "Ayuda externa y más pobreza en El Salvador." *Realidad* 47 (1995): 747–94.

Scharding, R. *Exodo en America Latina. El movimiento de poblacion en El Salvador.* San Jose, Costa Rica: Instituto Centroamericano de Derechos Humanos, 1991.

Schirch, Lisa. "Religion and conflict resolution: Christianity and South Africa's Truth and Reconciliation Commission." *Conrad Grebel Review* 29, no. 1 (2011): 101–2.

Schneiders, Sandra M., I.H.M. "Approaches to the Study of Christian Spirituality." In *The Blackwell Companion to Christian Spirituality*, edited by Arthur Holder, 19–29. Malden: Blackwell Publishing, 2005.

———. *The Revelatory Text: Interpreting the New Testament as Sacred Scripture.* Collegeville: The Liturgical Press, 1999.

———. "Spirituality in the Academy." *Theological Studies* 50 (1989): 676–77.

———. "The Study of Christian Spirituality: Contours and Dynamics of a Discipline." In *Minding the Spirit: The Study of Christian Spirituality*, edited by Elizabeth A. Dreyer and Mark S. Burrows. Baltimore, Md.: Johns Hopkins University Press, 2005.

———. "Theology and Spirituality: Strangers, Rivals or Partners?" *Horizons* 13, no. 2 (1986): 253–74.

Schreiter, Robert J. "Future Directions in Catholic Peacebuilding." In *Peacebuilding: Catholic Theology, Ethics, and Praxis*, edited by Robert J. Schreiter, R. Scott Appleby, and Gerard Powers, 421–48. Maryknoll, N.Y.: Orbis Books, 2010.

———. *The Ministry of Reconciliation: Spirituality and Strategies.* Maryknoll, N.Y.: Orbis Books, 2004.

———. "A Practical Theology of Healing, Forgiveness." In *Peacebuilding: Catholic Theology, Ethics, and Praxis*, edited by Robert J. Schreiter, R. Scott Appleby, and Gerard Powers, 366–97. Maryknoll, N.Y.: Orbis Books, 2010.

———. *Reconciliation: Mission & Ministry in a Changing Social Order.* Maryknoll, N.Y.: Orbis Books, 2005.

———. "Religion as Source and Resource for Reconciliation." In *Reconciliation in a World of Conflicts*, edited by Luiz Carlos Susin and María Pilar Aquino. London: SCM Press, 2003.

Schubeck, Thomas L., S.J. *Liberation Ethics: Sources, Models, and Norms.* Minneapolis: Fortress Press, 1993.

Schwöbel, Christoph. "Reconciliation: From Biblical Observations to Dogmatic Reconstruction." In *The Theology of Reconciliation*. Edited by Colin E. Gunton. London: T & T Clark, 2003.

Second General Conference of Latin American Bishops. *The Church in the Present-Day Transformation of Latin America in the Light of the Council.* Vol. 2. Washington: U.S. Catholic Conference, 1973.

———. "Document on Peace, 14." Quoted in Alfred T. Hennelly, ed., *Liberation Theology: A Documentary History* (Maryknoll, N.Y.: Orbis Books, 1997), 109.

Segovia, Alexander. "Integración real y grupos centroamericanos de poder economic." *ECA* 691–92 (2006): 517–82. http://library.fes.de/pdf-files/bueros/fesamcentral/07598.pdf.

Segundo, Juan Luis. "The Future of Christianity in Latin America." In *Liberation Theology: A Documentary History*, edited by Alfred T. Hennelly, 29–47. Maryknoll, N.Y.: Orbis Books, 1997.

———. *Our Idea of God.* Maryknoll, N.Y.: Orbis Books, 1974.

Shriver, Donald W. *An Ethic for Enemies: Forgiveness in Politics.* New York: Oxford University Press, 1995.

———. "Forgiveness: A Bridge across Abysses of Revenge." In *Forgiveness and Reconciliation: Religion, Public Policy and Conflict Transformation*, edited by Raymond G. Helmick and Rodney L. Petersen, 151–67. Philadelphia: Templeton Foundation Press, 2002.

Sigmund, Paul. *Liberation Theology at the Crossroads: Democracy or Revolution?* New York: Oxford University Press, 1990.

Smith, Christian. *The Emergence of Liberation Theology: Radical Religion and Social Movement Theory.* Chicago: University of Chicago Press, 1991.

South African Truth and Reconciliation Commission. Final Report, 5:259. http://www.justice.gov.za/trc/report/finalreport/Volume5.pdf.

Stålsett, Sturla. *The Crucified and the Crucified: Study in the Liberation Christology of Jon Sobrino.* Berne: Peter Land, 2003.

Stanton, Graham. "Paul's Gospel." In *The Cambridge Companion to St. Paul*, edited by James D. G. Dunn. Cambridge: Cambridge University Press, 2003.

Staub, Ervin. "Reconciliation after Genocide, Mass Killing, or Intractable Conflict: Understanding the Roots of Violence, Psychological Recovery, and Steps toward a General Theory." *Political Psychology* 27 (2006): 867–93.

Staub, Ervin, and Laurie Anne Pearlman. "Healing, Reconciliation, and Forgiving after Genocide and Other Collective Violence." In *Forgiveness and Reconciliation: Religion, Public Policy and Reconciliation*, edited by Raymond G. Helmick and Rodney L. Petersen, 205–27. Philadelphia: Templeton Foundation Press, 2002.

Strauss, Scott. *The Order of Genocide: Race, Power, and War in Rwanda*. Ithaca, N.Y.: Cornell University Press, 2006.

Suchocki, Majorie Hewitt. *The Fall to Violence: Original Sin in Relational Theology*. New York: Continuum, 1994.

Susin, Luiz Carlos, and María Pilar Aquino, eds. *Reconciliation in a World of Conflicts. Concilium* 2003/5. London: SCM Press, 2003.

Taylor, Charles. "The Politics of Recognition." In *Multiculturalism: Examining the Politics of Recognition*, edited by Amy Gutmann, 25–73. Princeton: Princeton University Press, 1994.

Third General Conference of the Latin American Episcopate, Final Document. Puebla de Los Angeles Mexico no. 1147. In *Puebla and Beyond: Documentation and Commentary*, edited by John Eagleson and Philip Scharper, translated by John Drury, 265–66. Maryknoll, N.Y.: Orbis Books, 1980.

Thistlethwaite, Susan Brooks. "Suffering: Different Faces and Reactions. Response to Jon Sobrino." In *Pluralism and Oppression: Theology in World Perspective*, edited by Paul F. Knitter. The Annual Publication of the College Theological Society 34 (1988): 179–87. New York: University Press of America, 1991.

Thompson, J. Arthur. "Covenant." In vol. 1 of *The International Standard Biblical Encyclopedia*, edited by Geoffrey W. Bromiley, 791. Grand Rapids, Mich.: Eerdmans, 1979.

Tracy, David. *Christian Theology and the Culture of Pluralism*. New York: Crossroad Publishing, 1981.

Turner, Denys. "Marxism, Liberation Theology and the Way of Negation." In *The Cambridge Companion to Liberation Theology*, edited by Christopher Rowland, 229–47. New York: Cambridge University Press, 2007.

Tutu, Desmond. *No Future Without Forgiveness*. New York: Doubleday, 2000.

United Nations. *From Madness to Hope: The 12-Year War in El Salvador*. Report of the Commission on the Truth for El Salvador. Appendix to UN Doc. S/25500, April 1, 1993. New York: United Nations Publications, 1993.

United Nations Development Program. *Human Development Report 2003*. New York: United Nations Publications, 2003.

———. *Human Development Report 2010*. San Salvador: United Nations Development Program, 2010. http://hdr.undp.org/es/informes/nacional/americalatinacaribe/elsalvador/INDH_El_Salvador_2010.pdf.

The United Nations Economic Commission for Latin American and the
    Caribbean (ELCLAC). "Inequalities and Asymmetries in the Global Order."
    In *Globalization and Development*, 75. New York: United Nations Publica-
    tions, 2002.

Valiente, O. Ernesto. "From Conflict to Reconciliation: Discipleship in the
    Theology of Jon Sobrino," *Theological Studies* 74 (2013): 655–82.

———. "From Utopia to Eu-topia: The Mediation of Christian Hope in
    History," in *Hope: Promise, Possibility, and Fulfillment*. New York: Paulist
    Press, 2013. 213–27.

———. "The Reception of Vatican II in Latin America." *Theological Studies* 73
    (2012): 795–823.

Vallecillos, Italo López. "Fuerzas sociales y cambio social en El Salvador." *ECA*
    369–70 (1979): 558. Quoted in Jeffery M. Paige, "Coffee and Power in El
    Salvador," *Latin American Research Review* 28, no. 3 (1993): 7–40.

Vatican Congregation for the Doctrine of the Faith. "Instruction on Certain
    Aspects of the Theology of Liberation." *Origins* 14, no. 13 (September 1984).

———. "Notification on the Works of Father Jon Sobrino, S.J.: Jesucristo
    liberador. Lectura histórico-teológica de Jesús de Nazaret (Madrid, 199) and
    La fe en Jeucristo. Ensayo desde las Víctimas (San Salvador, 1999)."
    November 26, 2006. http://www.vatican.va/roman_curia/congregations/
    cfaith/documents/rc_con_cfaith_doc_20061126_notification-sobrino_en
    .html.

Villa-Vicencio, Charles. "Telling One Another Stories: Towards a Theology of
    Reconciliation." In *The Reconciliation of Peoples, Challenge to the Churches*,
    edited by G. Baum and H. Wells, 30–42. Maryknoll, N.Y.: Orbis Books,
    1997.

Volf, Miroslav. *The End of Memory: Remembering Rightly in a Violent World.*
    Grand Rapids, Mich.: Eerdmans, 2006.

———. *Exclusion and Embrace: A Theological Exploration of Identity, Otherness,
    and Reconciliation*. Nashville: Abingdon Press, 1996.

———. "Forgiveness, Reconciliation and Justice: A Christian Contribution to a
    More Peaceful Social Environment." In *Forgiveness and Reconciliation:
    Religion, Public Policy and Conflict Transformation*, edited by Raymond G.
    Helmick and Rodney L. Petersen, 27–49. Philadelphia: Templeton Founda-
    tion Press, 2002.

———. *Free of Charge: Giving and Forgiving in a Culture Stripped of Grace.* Grand
    Rapids: Zondervan, 2005.

———. "Living with the 'Other.'" *Journal of Ecumenical Studies* 39, no. 1–2
    (Winter–Spring, 2002): 3–25.

———. "The Social Meaning of Reconciliation." *Interpretation* 54, no. 2 (April
    2000): 158–72.

Vorster, J. M. "Truth, Reconciliation, Transformation and Human Rights." *The Ecumenical Review* 56, no. 4 (2004): 480–502.

Wade, Christine. "El Salvador: contradictions of neoliberalism and building sustainable peace." *International Journal of Peace Studies* 13, no. 2 (2008): 15–32.

Waltermire, Donald. E. *The Liberation Christologies of Leonardo Boff and Jon Sobrino: Latin American Contributions to Contemporary Christology.* Lanham, Md.: University Press of America, 1994.

Weaver, Denny J. "Forgiveness and (Non) Violence: The Atonement Connections." *Mennonite Quarterly Review* 83, no. 2 (2009): 319–47.

Westerholm, Stephen. "Torah." In vol. 4 of *The International Standard Biblical Encyclopedia*, edited by Geoffrey W. Bromiley, 878. Grand Rapids, Mich.: Eerdmans, 1979.

Whitfield, Teresa. *Paying the Price: Ignacio Ellacuría and the Murdered Jesuits of El Salvador.* Philadelphia: Temple University Press, 1994.

Wiesenthal, Simon. *The Sunflower: On the Possibilities and Limits of Forgiveness.* New York: Schocken Books, 1980.

Wolf, Sonja. "Subverting Democracy: Elite Rule and the Limits to Political Participation in Post-War El Salvador." *Journal of Latin American Studies* 41 (2009): 429–65.

Wolff, Hans Walter. "Prophecy from the Eighth through the Fifth Century." In *Interpreting the Prophets*, edited by James Luther Mays and Paul J. Achtemeier. Philadelphia: Fortress Press, 1987.

Worthington, Everett L. "Unforgiveness, Forgiveness, and Reconciliation and Their Implications for Social Interventions." In *Forgivness and Reconciliation: Religion, Public Policy and Reconciliation*, edited by Raymond G. Helmick and Rodney L. Petersen, 171–92. Philadelphia: Templeton Foundation Press, 2002.

Wright, N. T. *Paul: In Fresh Perspective.* Minneapolis: Fortress Press, 2005.

———. *The New Testament and the People of God.* Minneapolis: Fortress Press, 1992.

Zehr, Howard. *The Little Book of Restorative Justice.* Intercourse, Pa.: Good Books, 2002.

Zubiri, Xavier. *Inteligencia sentiente: inteligencia sentiente*, 23. Quoted in Robert Lassalle-Klein, "Ignacio Ellacuría's Debt to Xavier Zubiri: Critical Principles for a Latin American Philosophy and Theology of Liberation," in *Love That Produces Hope: The Thought of Ignacio Ellacuría*, ed. Kevin F. Burke and Robert Lassalle-Klein (Collegeville, Minn.: Liturgical Press, 2006), 88–102.

———. *Inteligencia sentiente: inteligencia y realidad*, 10. Quoted in Kevin F. Burke, ed., *The Ground Beneath the Cross: The Theology of Ignacio Ellacuría* (Washington: Georgetown University Press, 2000).

———. *Nature, History, God*. Translated by Thomas B. Fowler, Jr. Washington: University Press of America, 1981.

———. "El problema teologal del hombre." In *Teología y mundo contemporáneo: Homenaje a Karl Rahner*. Madrid: Ediciones Cristianidad, 1975. http://www .zubiri.org/works/spanishworks/problemateologal.htm.

———. *Sobre el sentimiento y la volición*. Madrid: Alianza Editorial/Fundación Xavier Zubiri, 1992.

Index

44–48, 171–73; Jesus's path of radical conversion, 131–32; in Sobrino's theologal-idolatric structure of reality, 133, 156, 157–58. *See also* perpetrators

option for the poor: the following of Jesus and, 101; the Holy Spirit and, 100; Latin American liberation theology and, 28–30, 100; in Sobrino's liberation theology, 104–6, 228n72

Orientación, 66

orthopraxis, 110

parables, 236–37n67

pardon, 47

Paris, Roland, 55

Paul, St.: Sobrino's "honesty with the real" and, 94, 95; theological understanding of reconciliation, 15–17

perpetrators: concept of "universal noninnocence" and, 22; forgiving, 44–48; God's kingdom and, 186; issues in defining or categorizing, 21–22; the memory of having been forgiven in communities of solidarity, 167; in the process of reconciliation, 20–21; reconciling task for, 22–23; repentance and, 48. *See also* oppressors

personal/narrative truth, 33

Pharisees, 133–34

Philpott, Daniel, 39

Pico, Juan Hernández, 26, 55

the poor: categories in the New Testament, 124; divine preference and, 28–30; in El Salvador and, 52–57, 214n23; God's kingdom and, 186; God's partiality toward, 123–25; hope and, 176; and human rights and justice, 43–44; irruption of as the sign of the times, 60, 61–66, 106–9, 114–15; in Latin America, birth of liberation theology and, 61–63; letting the grace of reality carry theology and, 114–16; the Medellín conference and, 63–64; as the place for the theological task, 105–6, 228n72; Sobrino on, 125, 234–35n31, 235n33;

Sobrino's transforming encounter with, 57, 60–63. *See also* option for the poor

post-resurrection appearance narratives, 144–45

post-totalitarian societies, 23–24

power of the real, 74, 75

praxis: impact of spirituality on, 88–90; importance to liberation theology, 31–32; Jesus's prophetic praxis, 132–35; of living the cross and resurrection, 148–49; meanings of, 30–31; and theory in Sobrino's liberation theology, 110

praxis of reconciliation: forgiveness, 44–48; overview of the critical aspects of, 32; pursuit of justice, 37–44; Sobrino's spirituality and, 48–49; truth-seeking, 32–37

Principe, Walter, 224–25n8

Puebla Conference (1979), 65, 115, 155, 165–66

purity: Jesus on, 133–34

pursuit of wealth, 160

Rahner, Karl: on a deeply interrelated world, 22; on God's self-communication, 222n111; influence on Sobrino's theological development, 58–60, 84; notion of supernatural existence, 76–77; on reality expressing itself, 155

realist philosophy: approach to justice, 39–40, 41; notion of sentient intelligence, 71–73

"reality animal," 223n125

reality/historical reality: concept of sentient intelligence and, 71–73; conflicted nature of, 154–55 (*see also* conflicted reality); Ignacio Ellacuría's notion of, 77–80; faithfulness to, Jesus's mission and, 125–37; "fidelity to the real," 93–94, 96–97, 99; forgiving sinful reality, 168–71; God's communication through, 155; "honesty with the real," 93–96, 99 (*see also* "honesty with the real"); the human person and the theologal dimension of, 73–77; knowing and accepting the promise of, 149–50; "letting

in reconciliation, 33–34; universal noninnocence and, 22

Wade, Christine, 53
wealth: civilization of, 163–64; consequences of the pursuit of, 160
Wiesenthal, Simon, 45
Wolff, Hans Walter, 13
Worthington, Everett L., 45

Zubiri, Xavier: on the human person as a "relative absolute," 73–74; influence on Ignacio Ellacuría, 70–77; notion of religation, 74–76; notion of sentient intelligence, 71–73, 219n86, 220n90; on the power of the real and the fundament of reality, 74; the "reality animal" and, 223n125